The Eyes
of the
Sun

Other Titles From New Falcon Publications

The Eyes of the Sun

Astrology in Light of Psychology

by

Peter Malsin

NEW FALCON PUBLICATIONS
TEMPE, ARIZONA, U.S.A.

International Standard Book Number: 1-56184-099-8
Library of Congress Catalog Card Number: 97-65813

First Edition 1997

Cover art by Denise Cuttitta

The paper used in this publication meets the minimum require-ments of the American National Standard for Permanence of Paper for Printed Library Materials Z39.48-1984

Address all inquiries to:
NEW FALCON PUBLICATIONS
1739 East Broadway Road Suite 1-277
Tempe, Arizona 85282 U.S.A.
(or)
320 East Charleston Blvd. • Suite 204-286
Las Vegas, NV 89104 U.S.A.
email: info@newfalcon.com
website: http://www.newfalcon.com

In memory of my father, Ray
and my sister, Susan

What would become of your heart if
there were no Sun in the universe?
— Paracelsus

ACKNOWLEDGMENTS

Aries, Taurus and Gemini are the alpha, beta and gamma of the astrological alphabet, and it is to a sun-sign character of each that I owe my first three thanks. Maria Bergstad was an absolute Aries angel in turning this book toward fruition, and to her I am deeply grateful. My Taurean wife Gail was my absolute lifeline to Planet Earth through all the years it took me to bring this work in from outer space. Steve Eardley slashed and burned two or three brambly chapters, and put my feet to the fire in time to save me from myself.

Heartfelt thanks to Nick Tharcher and Dr. Christopher Hyatt at New Falcon Publications, who recognized that a different kind of book could develop its own kind of market.

I am grateful to many others who have helped me on my long journey to complete this project. Dr. Daniel Noel at Goddard gently reintroduced me to academia. At Lafayette College, Dr. Howard Gallup helped to energize my interest in psychology for a lifetime, and years later steered me right on a couple of critical accounts. Dr. Robert Chase and Dr. James Vitelli at Lafayette were also real guides as I careened into my adult life.

In the editing process, I was well aided by Rosemary Mills, Becky Langrall and the whole Ditzel family. Thanks, and thank you too to Sonja Hakala; to Jeff Overton for his research; to all the characters in our study groups who taught me in areas where I was weak. And to Jared and Mikaela, who I hope are already looking forward to my next book, *Astrology Is Bunk.*

Among astrologers, the work of Robert Hand and Liz Greene has been inspirational, and I appreciate the people at Samuel Weiser for permission to liberally quote Ms. Greene.

TABLE OF CONTENTS

Part III

Part IV

Appendices

INTRODUCTION

I turned twenty-two on the 17th of August 1971, and on the morning of the 17th I left Berkeley to explore northern California. Having just graduated from college in the East, I was bound that summer to explore my dream of the Golden West. Reaching Highway 101 at the northern edge of the Bay Area, I saw two friendly-looking hitchhikers, and I picked them up. As we traveled north into the hot, dry inland, my eyes occasionally wandered to the rearview mirror to the woman sitting in back. But it was in relation to the man sitting in front that God, or Universal Headquarters, had the more significant encounter in mind. Larry Underhill and I reached an immediate, hearty and striking rapport, so much so that I remember getting red in the face with enthusiasm. Soon I told him it was my birthday.

"Put her there, brother," said Larry, thrusting out his hand in the palm-clasping handshake of the times, "It's mine too."

"All right!" I rejoined, "That's amazing. What year were you born?"

When he told me he was born in 1949—the year of my birth—I felt thunderstruck. Here we were, two people born on the very same day of all time, meeting on our birthday. What made the encounter all the more memorable was that I totally identified with my "cosmic twin." I felt as if I could read his thoughts, and he mine. On that August birthday, moreover, Larry was leaving the Bay area to take an exploratory trip northward— and the same was true for me.

That fall I moved to Eugene, Oregon. One night in November, a friend from college, Gary Sawyer, unexpectedly appeared at my door. Gary, who I had last seen months before and thousands of miles away, soon turned over a little paperback book to me. It was an introductory book of astrology. That evening, as we read the descriptions of the "sun-sign" personality types pertaining to Gary, my housemates and myself, I marveled at the way our respective characters were captured. Staying up deep into the night reading Joseph Goodavage's *Write Your Own Horoscope*, I felt jubilant in seeing aspects of myself somehow "written in the stars." But I was also troubled by what I read.

In this and most of the other astrological books I would read over the next several years, I found that apparently accurate descriptions went hand-in-hand with bizarre predictions ("your home may be washed away by flood"), disturbing characterizations ("you are a chronic worrier"), and fuzzy generalities. Worst of all were the negative and deterministic attitudes: As traditional astrology seemed to portray it, the universal design into which we're born is like a cosmic slot machine, wherein any combination of the "wrong" planets and signs could mean trouble—for the rest of your life.

As I plowed into the study of astrology, however, I already was in trouble—and not because of "the stars." For me, the 1970s were years of strife, emotional difficulty and physical debility. Failing to deal with my problems in productive ways, nothing in my life seemed to improve. But eventually, on a brilliant New England morning in March of 1978, I reached a turning point. After decades of repressing it, I finally came to awareness of the import of the central experience of my early life: My mother had left by the time I was one year old, and I still hurt deeply from it.

From the moment I realized that there were underlying psychological causes to my difficulties, I sought to heal myself. I turned inwards, into my emotions, into the difficult aspects of my experience, into my past. I came to understand connections between old, long-forgotten realities and present patterns of experience. Most importantly, I learned to articulate the truth of my experience, and thereby to release repressed emotions of fear, anger and grief from my system.

In orienting myself toward healing, I returned in a deeply personal way to what had been my best subject in college: psychology. Having gone to graduate school in counseling for a year, I now involved myself with a new understanding of psychology: this time, from the inside out. Yet since it was the aura of psychology that drew me to astrology, I also realized that I wanted to develop my understanding of astrology as a psychological discipline. Toward that end I enrolled in the Goddard

College graduate program, where I was permitted to choose astrology as the focus of my master's thesis.

The Goddard program was structured so that students presented their work to the group of graduate students that began the program at the same time, no matter what subject each pursued. Hence through the nine months of my tenure at Goddard, I cast around in earnest attempt to find ways to explain the psychological meaning of astrology to an odd lot of New England citizens.

To my chagrin, however, instead of succeeding in explicating the psychological meaning of astrology, I triumphed mainly in dramatizing to myself the existence of a tremendous communications gap. I realized that the symbolic language I spoke—full of Uranuses and Sagittariuses and Geminis and Neptunes—was simply alien to people in the Goddard program. For all that the people in my student group seemed to understand, I might as well have been from Pluto.

I left Goddard in frustration, but I learned valuable lessons. I learned that astrology is part of the same world that policemen and engineers and teachers inhabit, and that if I want to talk to them about astrology, I darn well better use words "normal" people comprehend. I realized that common attitudes of cynicism, skepticism and judgment must be respected simply because they are real. Most of all, though, I learned that I had tackled a project much bigger and more complicated than I could do any sort of justice to in a short time.

Using my Goddard experience as compost, I began to grow *The Eyes of the Sun*. In the years spent cultivating this book, I've discovered more than I ever dreamed I might about how astrology relates to "normal" 20th century psychology—both academic and pop psychology—to "normal" 20th century science, and to normal 20th century English. Since 1979, meanwhile, astrology has enjoyed perhaps the greatest growth spurt in its entire history, and the subject now shows greater promise than ever of becoming just what academic psychology has renounced claims to being: a study of the psyche.

If I am biased in this assessment, it is no doubt because I see with the eyes of the sun.

The Upper Connecticut River Valley of
New Hampshire-Vermont, September, 1997

PART I

Chapter I

Astrology, the Psyche and Science

The Inscription on the gate of the temple of science...is:
Ye must have faith.
— Max Planck, as quoted by James Murphy in
Where is Science Going?

Collapsing under the weight of its own largely bogus success at the beginning of the scientific revolution, astrology nonetheless survived into the 20th century, where it has flourished in concert with mushrooming interest in alternative paradigms of growth, healing and self-awareness. Some of these alternative paradigms are new and ancient at the same time.

"Astrology represents the summation of all the psychological knowledge of antiquity,"[1] said Carl Jung, and as Jung recognized, the central significance of astrology is psychological. Around the world, from India to Indiana, millions of people, millions of experiencing "I's", see through astrology something of themselves that is comprehensible in no other way: the nature of the individual psyche. It is no accident that the resurgence of astrology has followed on the emergence of psychology, for astrology is at center a study of psychological nature. Astrology has in effect waited these many centuries for its underlying intelligence to be clearly articulated. As it absorbs the language, principles and perspectives of 20th century psychology, astrology is becoming profoundly contemporary.

To understand astrology in terms of psychology means transforming a very old, and very basic, perspective. From even a brief look at contemporary natal* astrology, it is plain to see that

---

* "Natal" astrology, the most popular area of astrological study, refers to the imprinting of astrological forces at birth.

the sun, the moon, the planets and the signs of the zodiac implicitly refer to all that is *within* ourselves. In striking contrast to
popular myths about our fates being controlled by "the stars," the
symbols of astrology are at bottom a means of perceiving the
phenomena of our inborn natures: predispositions, instincts,
powers and motivations that are inherent to our beings. With this
foundational perspective, astrology changes from a matter of
believing in forces outside ourselves to one of apprehending
psychological forces within.

Turning our celestial world outside in, translating the solar
system and the zodiac into forces of inner nature, astrology offers
rich, complex and detailed answers to the question, "What makes
me the unique individual I know myself to be?" Astrology's
increasingly sophisticated address to this question, combined
with analyses of celestial influences active throughout life, have
sustained the growth of a subculture that now involves a substantial flow of books and publications, research studies, confer-
ences, thousands of professional practices and ten times as many
lifelong students. Few within this lively field would deny that
astrology is a psychological discipline; and a large number
would claim it to be scientific as well.

Psychology and science too? What a sharp contrast to the
routine dismissals of astrology by mainstream detractors: "occult
hogwash," "pseudo-science" and the like. Could this be the same
psychological discipline that never comes close to even being
mentioned in Psychology 101? Are advocates of astrology
collectively deluded? What about its critics?

Astrology is still so far removed from mainstream intellectual
debate that the most important questions about the subject are
rarely even asked in a thoughtful way, much less answered.
Vocal critics of astrology have generally displayed such a blend
of ignorance and prejudice that they have not been the source of
much meaningful dialogue. For their part, proponents of the
subject have typically been too immersed in their own subculture
to cogently address the issues that sustain its ostracism from
mainstream circles.

Not that such issues are in any way simple. Take the dominant
criticism of astrology: that it fails to prove itself as a science.
Beyond the mythology of this judgment, the truth is far from
plain. Strangely, the idea that astrology has been disproven by

science dates back to a time when there was no scientific testing whatsoever in the field.

As a matter of modern record, there is surprising evidence in support of astrology. Many of the most ambitious and rigorous experiments ever undertaken confirm astrological influences as factors in human life, and the sum total of 20th century research supplies at least as much ammunition for proponents of astrology as for opponents. In the diversity of experiments so far conducted, there is absolutely no consensus on methodology, and research issues particular to the subject are only beginning to be defined. Hence it remains totally unclear how a legitimate verdict will ever be achieved within the confines of experimental science. (Chapter 6) What is clear is that battles will be fought in fields of statistics for decades to come.

Statistics form however only the most superficial layer of the issues being contested. Beneath the veneer of astrology as known to both scientists and the general public, astrology reaches the heart of questions of the most fundamental kinds—questions that remain unanswered to this day. These questions include: How do we explain individual differences? What are the origins of personality? What are the roots of individual consciousness? How can we understand the wonders of what we actually *experience* ourselves, and others, to be? What makes us who we are? To what dimensions does being human extend?

Until recently, conventional wisdom had progressively bolstered the notion that such ultimate questions would eventually—and definitively—be answered by science. But while scientists continue to issue promises of Big Answers to these questions, such promises have begun to ring a bit hollow. As with the religious priesthoods of yore, the prevailing attitudes and belief systems projected by the scientific community have, in certain respects, coagulated—unable, ironically, to keep pace with the revolutionary implications of scientific discovery itself.

Chief among the findings of 20th century science is Einstein's equation of matter and energy: $E = mc^2$. This breakthrough was long associated rather simply with the theoretical underpinnings of nuclear energy and the atom bomb. But Einstein's equation represents far more. Combined with developments in quantum physics, it amounts to a stunning revelation that transforms our entire conception of the "material world." The discovery that matter is effectively interchangeable with energy means that we must deal at every turn with the *energetic dimensions of reality.* As if to ignore this message, most scientists continue to proceed on the old Newtonian model that reality can be reduced to its material bases alone. In reducing existence to such material bases, however, they have promoted a world view that tends to leave human beings isolated, alienated and in local charge of a meaningless universe. Meanwhile, scientists bemoan their failure to appeal to the collective imagination, and blame everything but the possible limitations of their own analyses. Claiming the high ground of objectivity, they are likewise loath to admit holding any preconceptions about the nature of reality. Yet it seems increasingly apparent that their reductionist paradigm is itself a massive preconception.

Nowhere are the shortcomings of material reductionism more clear than in psychology. Having long ago shunted aside the immaterial *psyche* in favor of the more quantifiable realm of *behavior,* the science of psychology has become by definition a study of quantities to the exclusion of qualities, of matter to the exclusion of spirit—or, as the case may be, of energy. Consider in this regard the research on near-death experience (NDE). This research deals with common experiences of many near-death phenomena, including continuation of consciousness after clinical death, experiences of moving through a tunnel toward white light, of "spirit guides," reunion with previously deceased loved ones, and consideration of reasons to return to one's body and complete one's life. Addressing the documented facts of these experienced phenomena, intellectual honesty might suggest that scientists at least entertain a *theory* to the effect that consciousness transcends the physical body. But instead of allowing any such notion, most scientists either ignore this research or else insist on explaining the phenomena in question as stemming exclusively from within the confines of the material body.* The

---

* I originally learned of NDE research from an interview on National Public Radio in which a scientist who conducted studies on NDE confirmed the occurrences outlined above. He was quick to add, though, "Of course, none of these findings have anything whatsoever to do with life after death."

Yet as is evident in the three major journals that publish near-death research *(The Journal of Near-Death Studies, Omega* and *Anabiosis),* some few researchers are of the opinion that the findings do indeed indicate the

only thing proven here is that experimental data will serve as evidence for the kind of theory with which the scientific community is already comfortable.

On the face of it, research on near-death experience is evidence of a spiritual/energetic realm, and could be heralded in some sense in support of religion. But housed in old orthodoxies as they are, traditional Western religions seem unable to reform their belief systems so as to embrace spiritual/energetic dimensions on any terms except those dictated in ancient, institutionalized and unchanging forms. In result, the dominant voices of religion either ignore or rationalize the findings of science—while dominant voices in science still seek to extinguish religious cosmologies altogether.

Embedded in this conflict between science and religion is a kind of historical battle of the sexes: a polarization between masculine and feminine perspectives. As if from different worlds—Mars and Venus perhaps—the hard-heads of Mars pay attention mainly to the objectified world, while the soft-heads of Venus pay attention mainly to subjective experience. But as with men and women, object-orientation and subject-orientation attract each other like the two poles of a magnet. Thus the most vital action in this polarity is the integrative *relationship* between the two, while the disintegrative dynamic lies in the isolating insistence that one pole or the other is somehow "right."

Einstein understood the vital necessity of interaction between objective and subjective viewpoints. When asked if everything could be expressed scientifically, he replied, "Yes, it would be possible, but it would make no sense. It would be a description without meaning—as if you describe a Beethoven symphony as a variation of wave pressure."[2] Here Einstein captures the situation precisely: *The quest for objectification must be reconciled with subjective experience and perception,* just as the converse holds

---

existence of an "element of personality that transcends death." Many seem agnostic, while other voices are, like the individual noted above, certain that near-death phenomena are entirely functions of brain physiology. So far, it is the reductionist spin that effectively prevails, for the research has as yet made virtually no impact in the larger field of psychology.

true. The goal of science cannot simply be to objectify subjective experience; to do so literally denies what it means to be human.

Astrology provides particular intrigue with regards to the polarization between objective and subjective viewpoints, because it is uniquely a *feminine science* in both method and subject matter. In method, it combines the feminine approach of qualitative description with masculine approaches of empirical observation and systematization. In subject matter, it points to the objective realities of the sun, moon and planets, while asking its students to listen, as it were, to the music of the spheres.

As the natal astrologer might describe it, the music of the spheres is composed for every individual at birth; yet there is much room for individual interpretation in how the complex harmonies and dissonances are "played." The "notes" and "chords" that comprise the units of this music, moreover, appear in three different but symmetrically correlating kinds: the spheres of the solar system, the signs of the zodiac and the twelve terrestrial directions labeled as the "houses" of the natal chart. (Chapter 8) Hence it is difficult to pick out a single expression and say with absolute certainty: This is the sound of a planet. Or a zodiacal sign. Or a natal house.

In the same music, however, astrologers find ever-unfolding fractal webs of *correlation* between cosmic and human realms. Astrologers find these patterns of correlation to be so compelling that they engage in endless observation, prediction and interpretation. As correlation, prediction and observation also happen to be principles of science a paradoxical loop between astrology and science appears to be completed.

Through an evolving array of approaches, *modern astrology can be posited as a qualitative empirical science.* In its qualitative dimensions, this subject calls on intuitive perception to appreciate values of individual expression in terms of underlying patterns and principles. In its empirical dimensions, astrology is a discipline of observation that demands intellectual integrity, detachment and freedom from preconception. Accordingly, as astrology finally comes of age in the modern world, the realization is spreading that the process of developing astrological knowledge is a function of finding good marriages between (feminine) interpretation and (masculine) careful, systematic observation.

The qualitative and empirical dimensions of the subject are fused most succinctly in the proposition that *each astrological influence contains multiple possibilities of manifestation,* wherein each manifestation holds qualitative relationship to the whole set of manifest possibilities. ("From the one, many.") This proposition translates into the observation not so much of what a given influence causes, but rather *how individuals develop and express that influence.* This is an absolutely crucial distinction.

Throughout history, astrologers have been wont to rationalize particular manifestations they observe as if they resulted from cause-effect relationships. Such implications of determinism have done the subject incalculable harm through the ages, and still appear today in a hundred different guises. For example, the restrictive equation of one influence with a single type of manifestation lies at the core of the habitual assigning of one-dimensional stereotypes, and the associating of simplistic "good" and "bad" attributes with influences of choice. This type of mentality is not only simplistic but itself reductionist, and bound to fail as a translated into quantified science.

Standing at the threshold to its future, astrology carries heavy baggage from its past. Much of the material of astrological interpretation is ambiguous or self-contradictory. The more popular forms of astrology—newspaper and magazine horoscopes, sun-sign blurbs and such—draw attention away from the growing core of brilliant work in the field. Altogether, claims made in the name of astrology range from random thoughts about human life spongily applied to astronomical data to rigorous analyses of good research studies. In between, the great bulk of astrology falls in a gray area that can be confusing even to its students. Even material presented as "serious" is liable to be weakly developed, imbued with solipsistic subjectivity, or excessively reliant on faulty traditions.

The irony in this state of affairs is that so much of the subject matter of astrology is implicitly psychological. The literature of astrology addresses behavior. It deals with experience. It considers influences of motivation and predisposition. It brings into account factors of consciousness, development and the environment. God knows it deals with personality and individual differences. All told, the intrinsically psychological nature of astrology has led many to a striking conclusion: Astrology *is* psychology.

It is such an amazing form of astrology, the astrophile enthuses, that you get a detailed map of your individual nature, and a map for anyone else you're interested in, too. If astrology is psychology, however, it leaves little room for what other people know as psychology. To articulate a sentiment common in the field, "Who needs their psychology; we've already got ours." Well, yes and no. With the major exception of Jungian astrology, the subject remains a highly isolated form of psychology. And clearly it suffers from this isolation.

The literature of astrological interpretation, steeped as most of it is in appeal to popular consumption, prediction, vivid imagery and bold characterization, is rich in psychological suggestion; but it also plays fast and loose with our perceptions. Assessed topic by topic, astrological interpretation yields some pretty impressive hodgepodges of meaning. (Take any five introductory books of astrology, and compare their respective descriptions of the influence of the sun, or the moon, or any of the planets. Try it, and you are liable to be awash in cross-currents of idiom.) Although virtually all astrologers today are conscious of at least some of the psychological implications they weave into their interpretations, they have yet to collectively recognize that *virtually every statement made in the field carries psychological assumptions that need to be articulated.*

Looking at astrology through lenses of psychology brings up all kinds of interesting questions. Just what, psychologically speaking, is a planet? Or a zodiac sign? If astrological influences are inborn and internal, how do they interact with circumstances of childhood and the environment? Are they subject to processes of change, growth and development? If so, how is expression of these influences affected by such processes? How do these influences affect consciousness? Do they play into such intrapsychic dynamics as repression, projection and sublimation? Are popular characterizations of these influences in terms of personality and behavior accurate? Are all Scorpios secretive? Can we validate this correlation? If so, how? Beyond personality, what different sorts of psychological manifestation might Scorpio and other astrological influences generate?

To these and related questions, we find a growing collection of answers. Some of these answers are bad, some are good, and some great; but rarely are they either clear or obvious. Instead, they are implied somewhere amidst the kaleidoscopic interpretations of astrology's symbols.

Called the "algebra of the life" by Dane Rudhyar, astrological symbolism is foundational to the subject's psychological intelligence. Astrology's symbolic language works to integrate many dimensions of psychological meaning, as for example it speaks as much to internal experience as to external behavior. This language is eternally open to new articulation, and translates into infinite permutations of manifestation. Sometimes it is exasperating in its elasticity. Nonetheless it is a psychological language preeminently suited to illuminating the deeper mysteries of the human heart, and to defining the complex nature of the individual psyche.

Inasmuch as symbolism is key to astrology, it is little wonder that Carl Jung inspired a great wave of psychological development in the subject via his brilliant work on the psychology of symbolism. Jung left a virtual blueprint for interpreting astrology, and astrologers steeped in Jungian psychology have used this blueprint to make terrific contributions to the field. In result, Jungian astrology is the best articulated, the most coherent and the most fully realized form of psychological astrology now in existence. But taken by itself, the Jungian template leaves many questions unanswered, and comprises only one among numerous psychological perspectives that can be fruitfully applied.

Translating astrology in terms of different genres of psychology creates many benefits. It brings into focus different psychological forms of meaning that underlie astrological interpretation. It serves to articulate an array of astrology's features that are not otherwise easily recognized. It encourages us to further develop viable new conceptions of astrological influences such as *instinct, predisposition* and *motivation*. It invites us to treat astrological factors as psychological factors that interact with *other* psychological factors, including those of growth, development, consciousness, learning and the environment. It incites us to find out more about what astrology's symbols mean, what the symbols do for us, what astrologers do with them, and what we *can* do with them. It helps us to explore astrology's relationship to (other forms of) science.

If we are to integrate astrology with psychology, we must deal every step of the way with the outstanding fact of 20th century psychology: the schism between academics and pop psychologists, between scientists and philosophers, between hard-headed objectivists who look without and intuitive subjectivists who look within: the Martians versus the Venusians all over again. While clinicians who actually *deal with people* form a broad middle ground in the field, the subject of psychology as studied academically has become highly polarized toward the hard-heads.

By comparison, astrology appears to play to the Venusian soft-heads of the world, and in this regard it bears considerable resemblance to pop psychology. Like pop psychology, its subject matter is geared to appeal to a wide audience. Like pop psychology, it depends largely on subjective modes of response. Like pop psychology, it is ignored by academic psychologists. And like pop psychology, it works on the basis of collectively shared perceptions of phenomena that are difficult to translate into experimental methodologies.

Take for example the perception of the "inner child." Achieving broad currency in the burgeoning recovery/self-help movement, the inner child is as of now one of the most commonly employed concepts in all of psychology, scientific or otherwise. Yet that is what the inner child is: a concept, a construct that depends for its existence on the perceptual faculties and experience of the observer. Because it has not been quantified, the inner child holds no scientific meaning, and as of this writing plays no part in the academic study of psychology. Good science? Possibly.* Good psychology? Yours to answer.

Astrology is full of psychological characters who could be called relatives of the inner child. Translating astrology's symbolic language, in fact, we will bring the inner child into the astrological family and give it a new name: the moon. The inner moon. (Chapter 11) Honoring the clear implications of natal

---

* Possibly not: Even as a perceptual construct, the concept of the inner child can lend itself to experimental study.

astrology, similarly, we could interpret the influences of the sun and each planet as constituting inner psychological dimensions of being; and we could personify all these dimensions according to the catchy metaphors of pop psychology. We could say for example that Mars is the inner warrior; that Saturn is the inner father; that the sun is the inner star; and that Uranus is the inner light bulb(!)

In that the metaphors of pop psychology are both evocative and instructive, they belong in the field as much as any of the more sophisticated work that has appeared in recent years. But however much astrology partakes of the metaphorical approaches of pop psychology, it turns them to its own purposes, and in these purposes it veers away from pop psychology. Astrology eschews the single-metaphor approach of inner-child psychology, describing each planet in terms of a complex set of interrelated potentials. It likewise abandons the one-size-fits-all approach of pop psychology, applying itself instead to the contours, intricacies and idiosyncrasies of individual nature. And astrology forsakes pop psychology altogether by using metaphorical techniques to describe objectified forces of nature, correlating inner dimensions of being human to the perceived influences of the sun, the moon, the planets and the zodiac.

For whatever resemblances that astrology holds to pop psychology, then, it exhibits something far different: the certain trappings of a natural science. Which brings us to a most intriguing intersection. Assuming—just for the moment—the validity of astrology, and assuming the legitimacy of astrology's use of metaphorical techniques of description, the radical idea emerges that *astrological influences are of qualitative nature.* Thus for example the influence of Jupiter is not merely a matter of observing external behaviors caused by an objectifiable imperative, but of recognizing a qualitative realm of being, and likewise of defining a psychological principle centrally in terms of qualitative parameters.

As supported by the sum total of literature in the field, astrological symbols represent, as Dane Rudhyar put it, *qualities which pertain to wholes.* As mediated by these symbols, similarly, the influences perceived in astrology pertain to whole "spheres" of life, spheres that integrate external dimensions of personality and behavior with internal dimensions of consciousness and experience. These spheres in turn constitute *higher organizing principles* that can be articulated at the macro level of human evolution as much as at the micro level of individual psychology. At the macro level, these principles can be delineated in connection with anthropology, biology, ethology and philosophy, while at the micro level they can legitimately be approached from spiritual, imagic, intuitive and mythic as well as empirical perspectives.

At the crux of astrology's "war" with hard science, astrology conveys the message that such human phenomena as individual differences, personality, motivation, subjective experience, not to mention consciousness itself, are all qualitative functions of energetic influences, and so cannot in any wholly meaningful way be measured or explained quantitatively. It conveys the message to academic psychology that the methods of hard science are in certain respects unsuited to the study of those same phenomena, and calls academic psychology to re-embrace classic traditions of qualitative and philosophical approach. It grounds the *psyche* and human nature in planetary dimensions that explode previous parameters of psychological science. It generates organizing principles of such encompassing dimension that the only thing sophisticated enough to measure or comprehend them is human perception.

If we are to objectify the influences, the symbols and the principles presented in astrology, therefore, we must do so at least in part by honoring the qualitative dimensions of the subject. If astrology is in truth a qualitative empirical science, for that matter, it should be appreciable by substantially integrating qualitative and empirical approaches: by carefully applying qualitative analysis to empirical observation, and by developing qualitative description on the basis of careful empirical observation. By way of pursuing such integration, we will outline an emerging science of astrology that is perhaps different than many within the field might imagine it; and certainly different than scientists expect it.

As we will present it, astrology is a natural science of the psyche in which astrological influences, consciousness, internal experience, soul, and so to a large extent human nature itself, derive from energetic dimensions of reality. We will describe a science in which energetic dimensions of human nature do not conflict with but rather reflect, at higher levels, the biological, physical and other material bases of our beings. We will seek to translate astrological principles into psychological principles, and through these principles to show how, as Einstein put it with respect to physics, "sublime order emerges from what appears to be chaos ... in the world of perception."

CHAPTER 2

THE NATURE OF THE BEAST

I can vividly recall how Freud said to me: "My dear Jung, promise me never to abandon the sexual theory. This is the most essential thing of all. You see, we must make a dogma of it, an unshakable bulwark." In some astonishment I asked him, "A bulwark—against what?" To which he replied, "Against the black tide of mud ... of occultism." First of all, it was the words "bulwark" and "dogma" that alarmed me; a dogma ... no longer has anything to do with scientific judgment... To me, the sexual theory was just as occult, that is to say just as unproven an hypothesis, as many other speculative views.

— C.G. Jung, *Memories, Dreams, Reflections*

In a magazine cartoon of the 1950s, a mildly disheveled teenage boy stands before his father in the family living room. As if to address the issue of why he has not lived up to his father's best expectations, the teenager asks, "Which is it, Dad, heredity or environment?" (Either way, Dad is implicated.)

In its offhand manner, this cartoon outlines one of the most profound psychological questions of all time. It also sketches a frame of reference in which the whole subject of psychology may be understood. To rephrase the teenager's question: Am I shaped by influences that are inborn, or rather by the conditions of the environment in which I live and grow? Traditionally cast in terms of the "nature-nurture controversy" and "heredity versus environment," this "contest" certainly has no clear winner. Neither innate influences nor environmental conditions alone are responsible for the individual human condition. Instead, psychologists have come to realize that "nature" actually *interacts* with "nurture" all the time.

32

But what is inborn in human nature in the first place? This question, which has tantalized humanity for ages, continues to be incredibly difficult to answer. Psychologists earlier in this century thought they were close to resolving the matter as they flocked to the work of Charles Darwin. To psychological theorists, Darwin's *The Origin of Species* (1859) was, as Carl Jung put it, as "the great news of the day,"[3] in that it offered a complete—biological—explanation of inborn nature. Mesmerized by Darwin's evolutionary theory, psychologists came to see any and every aspect of human behavior as a function of the biological heritage of our species.

Most famous of the psychologists inspired by Darwin was Sigmund Freud. Freud originally postulated that those two main protagonists of our psyches, the ego and the libido, are rooted in biological sources: in instincts.* He saw the ego—sometimes called the "ego instincts"—in terms of the underlying instinct for self-preservation, and the libido in terms of the underlying instinct for sex. Later, he went on to postulate the existence of a "death instinct" (*Thanatos*), in connection with instinctive drives for aggression and (self-)destruction. It was however the former class of instincts that underpinned the centerpiece of his theory, the Oedipus Complex. Deriving from the sexual instincts, in short, Freud believed that all males develop sexual fixation on the mother.

Although Freud turned the Oedipus Complex into dogma, he changed his thinking about the nature of instincts considerably through the course of his career, and never gained lasting satisfaction on this account. Well on in his life—in 1925—he all but confessed to being ignorant about human instincts:

> There is no more urgent need in psychology than for a securely founded theory of the instincts on which it might then be possible to build further. Nothing of the sort exists, however...[4]

Still, Freud pursued his "sexual theory" with a single-mindedness that today seems entirely subjective. Yet even as this theory was exploding on the public scene, Freud was unable to

---

* Freud used the term *Trieb,* which may be best translated as "instinctual drive." "Instinct" is, however, the most common translation.

keep either his colleagues or his disciples uniformly convinced that biosexual imperatives are supreme. And while his revelation of the existence of the unconscious opened a whole new world for exploration, subsequent history has borne out relatively little of the sexual theory itself. Nevertheless, the popular appeal of Freud's vision of sexual imperatives was phenomenal.

In retrospect, it is apparent that the banner message of Freud's instinct theory lay in the basic assertion that sexual influences are integral to human nature, development and the etiology of neurosis. Freud's instinct psychology galvanized a society long oppressed by Victorian mores, and served as a focal point for the great sexual revolution of the twentieth century not because it revealed any particular scientific truth, but because it brought to public consciousness a long suppressed fact of human nature: we are inherently sexual beings. For all the abuse eventually heaped on him, Freud succeeded in getting everybody talking about sex as part of human nature—a temporary triumph for Western Civilization.

Nearly a century after Freud's heyday, psychologists have returned to biology in search of maps to psychology's territory of the mind. Some are proclaiming breakthroughs on the order of what Freud believed he was making. But even the most remarkable of discoveries regarding biological influences do not promise the kind of answers that psychologists have so long desired. As the renowned psychologist Jerome Kagan put it, "Psychology has not had its Newton or Darwin. Hence there is not a set of principles that explain a large number of psychological phenomena."[5] Researchers have found no DNA of the psyche, no synapses of the spirit, no hormones of the soul. The sum total of what has been discovered—still—justifies no more and no less than an agnostic attitude about what makes up the lion's share of the inborn realm of human nature.

When we look at current findings in the science of Psychology (Chapter 5), we will anticipate the vision of that hypothetical Newton or Darwin of psychology. As research has shown us fascinating glimpses of our genetic inheritance, in short, we will entertain the vision that our genes carry the mother lode of inborn influences. However, it remains a very good bet that when all the reports are finally in, blood will only tell so much: until or unless fundamentally new and different evidence regarding genetic influence is developed, the whole idea that biological influences make us what we inherently are—both as individuals and as a species—is to a large extent a myth. Indeed as it was in Freud's time, so it is again: biology is the source of the most popular non-religious myths about human nature.

History has unfolded five overarching ways of explaining and describing our inherent natures. Along with biology, these explanations come labeled as: mythology, religion, astrology and philosophy. Of these five, both philosophy and classic mythology are not concerned with sources: philosophy and mythology mainly describe *what* the archetypal motivations within us might be, and do not much deal with where they originate. Which leaves us with religion (or religious myth), astrology and biology. These paradigms tell us that our inherent natures derive from (1) God's creation/our immortal souls; (2) the sun, moon and planets, the zodiac, and related forces of our near cosmic environment; and (3) genetic makeup. Of these three, interestingly, only astrology identifies its influences in detailed connection with descriptions of what makes up the unique nature of each individual, and simultaneously identifies the generic motivations that are common to us collectively. Astrology is in fact the only one of these subjects to comprehensively address *either one* of these tasks.

How might astrology do these things? In part through mythology. As Joseph Campbell wrote, the imageries of mythology "are telling us in picture language of powers of the psyche to be recognized and integrated in our lives, powers that have been common to the human spirit forever."[6] With the planets named for the great gods and goddesses of antiquity, and the zodiacal signs associated with a great many other classic myths of Western civilization, mythology is integral to astrology. Astrological mythology, along with the other symbolism and imagery contained in the subject, make it a singularly elaborate and powerful "picture language" of the psyche.

Astrology describes our inherent nature in part through philosophy: a central astrological *modus operandi* is to interpret the subject's system of symbols in coded philosophical terms. Astrology's system of symbols actually presents twelve fundamental philosophical principles, principles that can be seen to underlie *all other* philosophical principles. Foundational to astrology, these qualitative principles are not subject to analysis by methods of hard science.

Astrology describes our inherent nature in part through biology; or at least through the implication of quasi-biological dimensions. Such dimensions are indicated by the signs of the zodiac, which effectively symbolize a universe of human instincts. Composed mainly of symbols of animals, the zodiacal signs signify human analogs of biological powers and predispositions. For example, inasmuch as the scorpion instinctively fights its own kind, the sign of Scorpio symbolizes (among many other things) the human instinct to fight.

Yet astrology elevates its animals into the stars, and in doing so evokes what amounts to a spiritual dimension. Celestial influences speak of a higher, transcendent nature. Pointing to the heavens, astrology turns us to subtler considerations of the spirit and soul, and to the highest potentials it might be ours to know.

Could this be the same astrology that gets caricatured in cartoons of cocktail parties?

Hostage to a public image reinforced by the horoscopes on the comics page of the newspaper, astrology is a gigantic subject that gets boiled down for daily public consumption to advice on whether or not this is a good day for shopping. Making possible such distilled vintage of astrological wisdom is—what is known in the field as—*sun sign* astrology. This is the popular version of astrology in which each person "has" just one sign—your sun sign.

If zodiac signs could talk, one of their first statements might be reminiscent of a Groucho Marx aphorism: We would never want to be part of a club that would have creatures like us as members. In this case, however, the zodiac signs are already members of the club: the sun-sign club.

A sun sign is simply the zodiacal sign in which the sun was positioned at the time of your birth. The sun is in Aries from about March 20th to April 20th every year, in Taurus from about April 20th to about May 19th, and so forth. Sun-sign astrology refers to the casting of personality descriptions on the basis of this one factor. Most people know their sun signs coupled with snippets of corresponding personality descriptions, and little more.

For all its limitations, sun-sign astrology has captured the attention of large numbers of educated people, and despite authoritarian proclamations attacking it, its personality descriptions have proven to be remarkably resilient. To most of those who explore the subject with an open mind, astrology's thumbnail characterizations actually *seem to work.* Cancerians are sweet, shy, domestic, food-oriented and/or crabby and moody. Librans are pleasant as the day is long, wanting to please everyone. Leos want to be the center of attention; they are hams, proud too. Taureans are earthy, stubborn, persistent, pleasure-loving, productive.

Educated, informed people who otherwise have neither investment nor interest in astrology routinely use these sorts of descriptions in affirming an astrological basis of character. In so doing, they casually support astrological explanations of two psychological phenomena that are the subject of millions of work-hours every year in academic institutions: *individual differences* and *personality.* Hence, seen in a certain light, sun-sign astrology could be taken as the first movement in what would become a new wave of psychological astrology.

Leaving aside for the time being the matter of individual differences, let us look at sun-sign astrology with respect to personality—and with respect to the sun. The sun in astrology symbolizes one of the most fundamental motivations in all of human life: personal will and the spirit of self. The sun represents the central, radiant light of one's being, the vital source and center of self, the creative will to express oneself. In a word, the sun signifies the *star* in each one of us. The idea of the "inner sun" as the brilliant, radiating center-of-self creates a personality concept that is at once marvelous and radical, and gives instant meaning to a host of personality-related capacities that are simply glossed over in "normal" (not to mention abnormal) psychology. To take a couple of obvious examples, it is as natural as rain to think of a person with a happy, cheerful—*sunny*—disposition, or a *bright, brilliant, radiant* individual—in terms of a "solar nature," a metaphysical sun shining within.

But alas, the sun is typically eclipsed in the popular brand of sun-sign astrology. What is left is the signs, each accompanied by a set of bold-faced identifying characteristics, along with the misconceived belief that each person is to be identified in terms of only one sign. As far as students of real astrology are concerned, this is a fate almost worse than ignominy. Serious astrologers tend to regard sun-sign astrology like a loud-mouthed relative who they would more or less like to disown.

Sun-sign astrology is poorly regarded within the field on at least three counts. First, it is universally recognized within the field that sun signs constitute only one among many other astrological influences, so that to translate sun signs into personality profiles is both narrow and arbitrary. Second, sun-sign descriptions tend to be not only simplistic but slipshod. Third and perhaps most important, sun-sign astrology reduces personality mainly to adjectives: stubborn, generous, critical, wishy-washy. While suggestions of individual differences contained in such adjectives would be truly significant in and of themselves to the extent that they are valid, they nonetheless fail to convey the existence of whole other dimensions of meaning.

Here let us return to look at the four symbolic functions of the zodiac suggested earlier. First, on the philosophical level, the signs of the zodiac indicate groupings, or "constellations,"* of inherent behavioral powers. These constellated groupings translate in turn into conceptions of underlying principles and *fundamental motivations* in human life. Second, on the mythological level, the signs of the zodiac indicate *archetypes,* or quasi-universal *patterns of experience.* Third, on the biological level, the zodiac comprises a means of identifying inborn sets of predispositions—instincts—that we will describe in connection with contemporary ethological and biological theory. Finally, on an evolutionary level, the signs indicate sets of higher and more subtle *potentials* toward which we, as individuals and as a species are, hopefully, growing.

All these avenues of interpretation belong in contemporary astrology, and we will be exploring them all. In doing so, we

---

* The word "constellation" is used here as a metaphor. The zodiacal signs in Western astrology no longer conform to the original division of the heavens. See Chapters 7-8.

must cut through myths and beliefs to which the public, academic authorities, and often proponents of astrology themselves, succumb. We noted one such myth above: that your sun sign is your only sign. In dispensing with this myth, let us think for the moment of zodiac signs in terms of instincts. Then, let us affirm that the instincts represented by every one of the signs are universal. Hence, *every* sign of the zodiac indicates a constellation of instinctive powers that are inherent in us all. We all have, for example, Scorpio instincts; we all have instinctive powers symbolized by Scorpio. We also all have Leo instincts, Aquarian instincts, and so on. Astrologers turn themselves to study relatively subtle differences in the extent and ways in which these instincts are configured in individual nature.

Yet while sun-sign astrology blots out recognition of all other influences, sun-sign influences do form important elements in the astrological study of individual differences, and few astrologers would deny that the study of sun signs is both consistently intriguing and richly rewarding. In fact as far as descriptions of personality and behavior are concerned, there is no clear dividing line between sun-sign astrology and "real" astrology. By the same token, some of the problems that plague sun-sign astrology are the same as what plague the rest of the field.

One of these problems regards the appearance of unclear, contradictory and ambiguous interpretation. Sun-sign descriptions differ significantly from source to source, and there is no obvious way to reconcile such differences. Comparing interpretations from different sources brings to light not only differences but inconsistencies. Take sun-sign Scorpios. They are described as reserved. They love and hate with a passion. They are highly secretive. They are direct. They are generous and compassionate. They are sarcastic and intense. They make friends easily.

As this collection of traits is purposely drawn from different introductory texts (some superior to others) in order to highlight contradictions, it seemingly illustrates how haphazard the technique behind sun-sign astrology can be. Yet it is difficult even to assert that such contradictions are necessary indications of shoddy interpretation. While some contradictions might well be the result of poor method, others might be not only confirmed but reconciled through more sophisticated methods. In the eyes of many astrologers, divergent characterizations of a given sun sign make up threads in larger patterns of expression.

To illustrate such patterns, let us look again at some of the traits most commonly ascribed to sun-sign Scorpios: deep, controlling, secretive, passionate, intense, reserved and mysterious. My own observations point to a pattern in which these characterizations are visible but not stand-alone. If I had to generalize with single-trait characterizations, I would describe sun-sign Scorpios—many of them, anyway—as being engaging, convivial, enterprising, assertive, competitive and feisty. Illustrating several of these traits are two women born with the sun in Scorpio who are currently in the highest of public profiles: Roseanne Barr and Hillary Clinton.* These characters are nothing if not assertive, feisty *and* convivial. Katherine Hepburn is another famous female Scorpio fitting this pinky-nail description.

In that Scorpio is the only zodiacal sign represented in three different ways—by the scorpion, the eagle and the phoenix—it has been suggested that there are more "types" of Scorpio characters than for any other sign. Rather than saying that there are different types of *people*, however, it may be more appropriate to say that there are different—but overlapping and intersecting—*genres of expression* of the sun-sign Scorpio influence. Along with the genres of expression outlined above, another genre can be characterized in terms of the inclination to sarcasm, to being controlling, and to carry a "sting" either offensively or in retaliation. An overlapping genre is characteristically *self*-controlling and reserved. A different genre is marked by physicality, aggressiveness and/or competitiveness. Yet another genre is engaging and sexy. And a final genre (mostly women) can be defined by the *need to develop* the assertive, feisty and aggressive powers that characterize many other Scorpios.

Now consider two statements by the astrologer Alan Oken: "A Scorpio does not like to have his private life penetrated by anyone but those few to whom he chooses to reveal himself... He will always try to maintain a mask of command over his life situation."[7] Note that while these remarks serve to reinforce the

---

* Subsequent to this analysis, Ms. Clinton became embroiled in controversies where she was, as the *Washington Post* put it, "fending of criticism that she has been secretive..." [Jan. 11, 1996]

"secretive" and "mysterious" labels, they can equally be applied to Scorpios who are competitive, assertive, sexy and/or convivial.

Weaving some further threads, it is meaningful to describe Scorpios as *passionately engaged* with their affairs; and as inclined to be *deeply involved in the business of emotional, physical, economic, and/or social exchange.*

The preceding sketch of sun-sign Scorpios honors a diverse array of observations, and affirms the fact that Scorpios are not all the same. It suggests complex relationships among "Scorpio traits," and evokes the idea that different permutations of traits may develop in different individuals. It begins to convey the sense that such traits are not isolated behaviors, but are rather powers of behavior and personality that are, more or less, fluidly interconnected with one another.

Although this quick treatment of Scorpio begins to deal with some of the complexities inherent in sun-sign astrology, it still suffers other limitations of sun-sign astrology. For instance it ignores the fact that astrological terms like Scorpio refer to *underlying influences* that cannot be packaged exclusively under the labels of either behavior or personality. It only begins to convey the reality that "the Scorpio personality" pertains to far more than any simple set of observable traits.

To illustrate connections between personality and other concepts we have applied to the zodiac, we have only to look at two of the most prominent features of Scorpio symbolism: the scorpion and Scorpio's "rulership" of the sex organs. Between these two symbols are indicated, ironically, the two faces of instinct that Freud saw as primary: self-preservation and sex. Indeed as noted in Principle 8 of Chapter 9, Scorpio symbolizes essentially the same instincts that Freud described, including the inherent predilections to such phenomena as self-destruction, the Oedipal Complex and aggression.

Instead of pursuing the type of narrowly deterministic and limiting conception of instincts such as Freud described, however, we will delineate the "Scorpio instincts" in terms of a broad constellation of inherent powers that are all generally open to development; and we will note that only at base level is this constellation grounded in self-preservation and sex. In this matter of sex and self-preservation, moreover, we will identify Scorpio in terms of *survival instincts,* a concept which bears full relation to the diverse personality traits noted above. All the descriptions of sun-sign Scorpios, in other words, can be interpreted in terms of different aspects of survival instincts as expressed on physical, sexual, emotional, social and financial levels.

That's for starters. Once we get Scorpio straightened out, we might go on to incorporate the *sun's* influence in the sun-in-Scorpio capsule, and so actually begin to paint a complete, viable and coherent picture of the sun-sign "Scorpio personality." We could hope that such a picture would be finely honed by the most careful and systematic observation; that it would do justice to the full dimensions of psychological meaning that astrology conveys; and that it would integrate all the factors—both astrological and psychological— that affect development and expression of the sun-in-Scorpio influence. But this is a vast field we are crossing, and as we cross it we will see that astrological influences escape even the most elaborate attempts to contain them in finite formulations.

The Big Sky covers all. Under it, the astrological beast has been stalked for centuries, and neither scientists, nor pop astrologers, nor anyone else should mistake: This beast is hard to capture alive.

CHAPTER 3

THE JUNGIAN BLUEPRINT

> Archetypes, she declared, are *biological entities.* They are
> present, in related forms, throughout the animal kingdom.
> Like all biological entities they have a natural history:
> they are subject to the laws of evolution. In other words,
> *archetypes evolved through natural selection.*
>   This was a tremendous statement. And it seemed to me
> that in making it Irene [Champernowne] had struck the
> bedrock of psychology as a biological science...
>   My discussion with Irene sent me back to Jung's
> *Collected Works...*
>
> — Dr. Anthony Stevens,
> *Archetypes: A Natural History of the Self*

The star who showed the way for astrology to be translated into
psychology—at least into his own psychology—was Carl Jung.
Jung was quite intrigued by astrology, and published a mono-
graph[8] based on an experiment he conducted involving astrological factors. But his work with astrology *per se* is a matter of
secondary consequence. The service Jung did for astrology grew
instead from his groundbreaking study of symbolism.

Like Freud, Jung regarded instincts as central to psychology;
but Jung's conception of instincts was entirely different from
Freud's. Citing the tremendous diversity of human behavior and
experience, Jung felt that instinctive influences in human beings
must themselves be diverse. Expanding Freud's conception of
the unconscious exponentially, he posited that humans are heir to
a broad spectrum of instinctive influences. Yet he also recognized that it is "very difficult to prove the existence of distinct
types [of instinct] empirically."[9] To be sure, this difficulty has
proved to be one of the most intractable problems in the whole of

43

psychology, as researchers have been unable to either prove or disprove the existence of the general types of biological influence that have been traditionally called instincts.*

Jung however made a crucial contribution to this debate by realizing that whatever their exact nature might be, *internal/biological influences must interact with consciousness.* Decades before academic psychologists began to study cognition, Jung recognized that consciousness must be central to the processes by which internal influences become expressed in behavior. His premise was that in order to understand the nature of instincts in human beings, we must assume that instincts can only be expressed through the prism of consciousness:

> For the organ with which we might apprehend [instincts] —consciousness—is not only itself a transformation of the original instinctual image but also its transformer.[10]

Jung theorized that consciousness intervenes and effectively mediates between instincts and behavior. He saw that beyond infancy, cognitive processes intrude into virtually all human behavior, making it all but impossible to witness human instincts independent of such processes. Hence he thought it counterproductive to concentrate on observed behavior alone.**

Jung proposed that we can learn about instinctive influences in human beings from the content of consciousness itself. Taking a key from Freud's *The Interpretation of Dreams,* he hypothesized that the process through which instinctive influences interact with consciousness is essentially symbolic: that *symbols are the means by which instinctive influences emerge into conscious awareness.* Instincts, in other words, are translated into symbolic imagery in consciousness. This assumption is central not only to Jung's theory of instincts, but also to his theory of archetypes.

---

* Although the terms have changed, an "instinct by any other name" is still the subject of great scientific controversy. Referring to the possibility of a biological predisposition to altruism, for example, the biologist Lewis Thomas asserted, "there is no way of proving or disproving the genetic basis for it." (*Harper's Magazine.* Vol. 269, No. 1610; July, 1984. p. 26.)

** One notable exception to this rule regards infants and small children, who exhibit certain universal behaviors. (Cf. Chapter 11.)

Jung's perception of instincts led him to describe the meaning of archetypes in two separate ways, each of which accords to a different aspect of his conception of instincts. First, Jung defined archetypes as referring explicitly to human instincts—or rather to the human analog of animal instincts:

> It is ... very natural to suppose that [archetypes] are connected with instincts and [are] ... in the end identical with instinctual patterns, namely with the patterns of behavior.[11]

Jung referred to archetypes as "patterns of instinctive behavior." But while he explicitly equated archetypes with instincts, he also claimed that instinctive influences in human beings can best be seen—and perhaps can *only* be seen— in terms of the symbolic images that are appear in consciousness: "Instincts [in human beings] manifest themselves ... and often reveal their presence only by symbolic images. These manifestations are what I call the archetypes."[12]

Hence Jung also defined archetypes in terms of the symbols and imagery that occur in the dreams, literature, mythology and religion of all cultures. As far as Jung was concerned, instinctive influences are the driving forces underlying the generation of this imagery.

Jung felt that the "patterns of instinctive behavior"—archetypal patterns—are manifest in the *themes and motifs* that different kinds of symbolism share. For example, Jung wrote of an eight-year-old girl whose dreams included an image wherein "a drunken woman falls into a river and comes out renewed and sober."[13] To Jung, the imagery of this dream signified the theme of renewal. He in turn identified this motif of renewal with the whole Christian myth of rebirth and redemption. Transcending particular images and myth, Jung proposed that it is the experienced *theme* or *pattern* of renewal and rebirth that is universal.

With the idea of themes or patterns of experience as the unifying constant, archetypes in Jungian psychology refer alternately to instinctive influences themselves and to the symbolic images that presumably derive from those influences. Symbolic images are seen as the primary *representations* as well as the most direct *manifestations* of instinctive influences.

Jung's use of the term "archetype" in these two intertwined ways gives rise to some real confusion. But because he ascribed two essentially different meanings to the concept, we can more easily assess the validity of his archetypal theory on two separate accounts: in terms of a hypothesis concerning the existence of underlying instincts, and in terms of a *process* for coming to awareness of inner psychological forces.

As is the case with many instinct theories, Jung's hypothesis that biological instincts translate into symbolic images/archetypes is provocative but flawed. His evidence for the idea that instincts are universal underlying influences consists of a combination of clinical anecdote and amateur cultural anthropology. While the arguments he made regarding the imagery that spontaneously occurs in dreams and the imagery of world literature, religion and mythology suggest *something* of universal nature, something of "archetypal" nature, and possibly something of biological nature, his assertion that symbolic images, myths and motifs amount to the key manifestations of biologically rooted influences is simply not well supported.[*]

In line with instinct theories of his time, Jung specifically referred to instincts as patterns of behavior. Yet he actually talked very little about behavior itself. Instead he was far more concerned with perceived motifs of *experience*. With regard to the young girl's dream mentioned above, for example, Jung did not bother himself with what instinctive "pattern of behavior" might be at work behind the scenes. We can certainly entertain the experience of rebirth/renewal as a universal theme or pattern. But we cannot conceive of a literal *behavior* of rebirth/renewal, at least not in the biological context of a single lifetime. According to archetypal theory, there would presumably be an instinctive pattern of behavior underlying the ritual of baptismal rebirth in fundamentalist Christianity—bathing for instance?—but Jung left this type of theoretical connection undeveloped. It was the

---

[*] A fascinating argument for the biological basis of Jungian theory appears in Dr. Anthony Stevens' *Archetypes; A Natural History of the Self* (Quill, 1982). Stevens is however a psychiatrist, and ultimately reverts to arguing his case on the grounds of depth psychology. He remarks for instance, "Ultimately, you cannot define an archetype, any more than you can define meaning. You can only experience it." (p. 67)

perception and experience of archetypal *meaning* that fascinated Jung.

More clearly substantial in Jung's archetype theory is his vision of the process by which symbolic images are produced, and how we deal with such imagery in consciousness. Everyone dreams; everyone generates symbols and imagery. The idea that such symbols and images emerge from the interaction of consciousness with deeper interior dimensions of influence is widely supported as indicated by the fact that dream imagery is now central to several different models of clinical practice. One of the principles of this work is that our dreams represent hidden internal influences, and that by giving attention to the symbolism of our dreams we are able to come to consciousness of aspects of ourselves and our experience of which we had been hitherto unaware.*

Jung's work points to symbolism as being key to the relationship between *psyche* and *soma,* between mind and the bodily temple of the inner nature. But while Jung's great work has shown us that the symbolism and imagery of dreams are doorways to our inner natures, we still don't know what those inner natures are made of: Instincts? Archetypes? Symbols?

Astrology rejoins this discussion in two ways. First, astrology lays claim to being the source of the influences that Jung identified as being biological. Second, whether inborn sources of influence are biological, astrological or both, the symbols of astrology are extraordinarily well suited to exposition in terms of Jung's archetypal psychology.

The signs of the zodiac lend themselves to interpretation in archetypal terms in several ways. To begin with, the zodiac signs, like archetypes, are composed of symbols and symbolic images. Like archetypes, the zodiacal symbols implicitly represent inborn, underlying influences. And like archetypes, the nature of these symbols invites articulation according to themes

---

* The symbolic process of coming to realize inner powers of self through dreams is vividly portrayed in the movie *The Wizard of Oz.* Contrary to the implication of the movie's ending, however, Dorothy's insight is not so much about home as it is about her own powers of righteous strength and self-assertion. In killing the witch and confronting the Wizard, she discovers inner strength and bravery, just as her friends discover the inner sources of courage, and intelligence, and heart.

and motifs from classical mythology. Indeed the symbolism of astrology leads us to much of the same mythology that Jungian psychology itself addresses.

Unlike "normal" Jungian archetypes, however, the signs of the zodiac serve to represent specific *powers of behavior.* On this account, ironically, the signs of the zodiac work to indicate underlying instincts, as instincts are more usually understood, much better than do Jungian conceptions of archetypal symbols. The signs of the zodiac lend themselves to interpretation in terms of a wide array of behaviors that we think of as instinctive, including cooperation, aggression, play—and bathing for that matter. As we have noted, Jungian archetypes typically are not translated in such ways.

Inasmuch as astrology's symbols give themselves over to interpretation in terms of both instincts and archetypes, we might expect that Jung related his theory of archetypes to astrology. But Jung apparently did not much consider this connection. His work with astrology focused primarily on the issue of synchronicity, and he did not entertain the astrological symbols themselves to any great extent. He was actually somewhat skeptical about the practice of astrology, writing that "the psychological interpretation of horoscopes is still a very uncertain matter."[14]

Jung did, however, come to appreciate how astrology symbolically portrays the inner realm of the psyche. In the midst of a lengthy essay written late in his life entitled "The Spirit of Psychology" (*Der Geist der Psycholgie,* 1947), Jung invoked the work of the astrologer/metaphysician Paracelsus, who:

> ... beholds the darksome psyche as a star-strewn night sky, whose planets and fixed constellations represent the archetypes in all their luminosity and numinosity... In this vision of astrology and alchemy, the two classical functionaries of the psychology of the collective unconscious join hands.[15]

While Jung was ambivalent about astrology, astrologers have not been ambivalent about Jung. Astrologers such as Dane Rudhyar recognized the significance of Jung's work early on, and by the time that Jung had fully developed his "Analytical Psychology" in the 1930s, Rudhyar was already disseminating his ideas to the field of astrology. Beginning with Rudhyar's *The*

Astrology of Personality (1936), students of astrology learned to see in Jungian psychology whole new ways to approach the meaning of their subject, and likewise found profound alternatives for interpreting astrology's symbols. Assimilating more and more of Jung's work through the years, Jungian astrologers now routinely interpret astrological influences in the context of a whole array of Jungian conceptions pertaining to such phenomena as "projection," the "shadow self," and "confrontation with the archetypes." The clinical effects of cross-fertilizing astrology with Jungian psychology have proven to be powerful.

Jungian approaches to astrology invite us to participate subjectively in recreating the meaning of our experience. Turning the symbols of astrology into experiential motifs, Jungian interpretation serves to generate mythic, *imagic* worlds in which we become the protagonists. For example, it is popular among Jungian astrologers to identify the symbols of both Saturn and Capricorn with the motif of the "Old King." This archetypal motif portrays the experience of being confronted with the presence of an old, worn out or oppressive father/authority figure. It dramatizes the challenge to overthrow the Old King and the effete authority he represents. And it imagines the need to establish a spiritually revitalized basis for exerting authority. In short the Old King must either find renewed integrity if he is to continue to wield power and authority, or he must be usurped. And you are the usurper—as long as you can find the spiritual basis for assuming authority within yourself!

By charging astrological symbols with mythic meaning, Jungian interpretation encourages us to turn our experience into richly contoured dramas. To see yourself in the context of an Old King motif, where someone like your boss or your father is cast in mythic terms as the King who must symbolically die, and where you become the protagonist who is challenged to assume your own individual authority, is a kind of story that draws us into its aura of drama and meaning. It is certainly far more vivid and engaging a way of perceiving the Capricorn or Saturn influence in our lives than fitting ourselves into formulaic personality descriptions.

Drawing on the stories of mythology, Jungian astrologers cultivate meanings that are not only uncommonly evocative, but deep and complex as well. To illustrate, consider Liz Greene, the queen of Jungian astrology, who treats the sign of Cancer in connection with Achilles:

> ... Thetis [Achilles' mother] took an active part in pre-
> venting Achilles from joining the warriors going to Troy,
> as we have seen; and it does seem that Cancer experiences
> the personal mother as holding him back from life. But
> Achilles was discovered hiding among the women by
> Odysseus, who fetched him to the war. Throughout the
> battles we see him being constantly interfered with by his
> goddess-mother, who rushes to his tent bringing new
> armour, proper clothes, clean linen and so on. One is
> surprised Homer does not mention chicken soup ... this
> part of it is painfully funny. The only thing which has the
> power to draw the sulking Achilles from his tent to fight
> is the death of his dearest friend and lover Patroclus. Only
> then is his true courage and mettle revealed. This too
> seems to be a facet of Cancer: that nothing will goad the
> sign into open confrontation with life save deep emotional
> loss.[16]

Greene's interpretation intersects with more well-known astrological formulations of Cancer's influence. For instance the Achilles character, in being so closely tied to his mother, echoes a common characterization of Cancerian individuals. Yes, Achilles is portrayed as something of a mama's boy. Yet for Greene, such aspects of the "Cancerian personality" are second-ary to the deeper experience that the Cancerian character attracts.

Jungian astrology turns the focus of attention from personality and behavior to the inner realm of experience. In doing so, it gives classic forms of meaning to the drama of individual expe-rience, and cultivates the whole ethos of personal life.

Of course, this does not mean that every Jungian-style inter-pretation is profound, wonderful or even the least bit helpful. Many so-called Jungian interpretations seem to do little more than spin mythic imagery into artificially manufactured percep-tions of what people *might* experience, or *ought* to experience. Likewise, the use of mythic imagery can serve merely as a convenient brush by which to paint revisionist psychological slogans or old intellectualized constructs. Equally, the Jungian approach cannot substitute for the empirical process of repeat-edly observing the influences "in action," as they are played out from person to person and from situation to situation; and from assessing these observations independent of preconceived notions. As much as astrology is an empirical discipline, even the most classic archetypal meanings that are applied to given symbols need to be empirically tested. As with other schools of interpretation, Jungian astrologers do good work as much as they build on empirical bases.

CHAPTER 4

THE EVOLUTION OF BASIC INSTINCTS

> The principle that science should be indifferent to values must not lead to the belief that evolution, that most wonderful of all chains of naturally explicable processes, is not capable of creating new values. That the origin of a higher form of life from a simpler ancestor means an increase in values is a reality as undeniable as that of our own existence. — Konrad Lorenz, *On Aggression*

Instincts: You feel 'em, we got 'em.

The idea of instincts in human beings is so common and so generally accepted amidst the public at large that we might as well say that we use the word "instinct" instinctively. Academic psychologists, on the other hand, once decided that we actually do not have instincts.

How could there emerge such a chasm between conventional wisdom and scientific pronouncements on the matter of human instincts? What do instincts have to do with astrology? And what does *instinct* mean in the first place?

To answer these questions, let us consider how people typically conceive of instincts. Specifically, let us consider symbols of animals, which have been used to represent instinctive human powers in the religion, mythology, cosmology, art, folklore and literature of cultures around the world. From the Biblical representation of the snake as sexual desire to the Native American practice of drawing human names from the animal world (Sitting Bull, Crazy Horse), the usage of animal images to symbolize instincts in human life is timeless and universal. In contemporary culture, this symbolization is embedded in language itself. Consider, for example, the power of imitating, or mimicking: in

English, no less than three different animals are used to represent this innate capacity:

> He just *parrots* whatever the boss says.
> *Monkey* see—monkey do!
> *Ape* (n.) ... a person who imitates; mimic.
> — *Webster's New World Dictionary*

In these usages, the names of animals are essentially synonymous with single forms of human behavior. As with other forms of animal symbolization, these word-symbols suggest the existence of biological influences. Yet in the act of identifying human behavior with animals, this kind of symbolism has pejorative connotations, implying that the behavior in question is primitive, unthinking, animalistic. Even when this sort of behavior is not specifically identified with animals, it is still considered undesirable. For instance in his autobiographical account, *A Childhood*, Harry Crews notes:

> Some natural mimic in me picks up whatever verbal ticks or mannerisms it gets close to. That mimic in myself has never particularly pleased me, has in fact bothered me more than a little.[17]

Crews' remark turns us to a critical question regarding the nature of instincts: Do instinctive influences exert direct control over specific behaviors, or are they subject to affect by consciousness and learning? Historically, the concept of instinct has been used in both ways. Charlotte Bronte, in *Jane Eyre* (published more than a decade before *The Origin of Species*), narrates: "I instinctively started with a cry of alarm." In this sentence, the concept of instinct refers to an essentially reflexive physiological reaction, an unlearned behavior having very little to do with consciousness or learning. Later on, however, Bronte employs the same word in a different way: "I felt an instinctive certainty that she would not long endure me under the same roof with her."[18] Here instinct refers not to behavior itself, but rather to an internal influence that is mediated by consciousness.

In contemporary and conventional usage, the concept of instinct applies more frequently to the second meaning than to the first. Instincts commonly refer to influences that are responsive to factors of both consciousness and learning, rather than to fixed and unalterable patterns of biological response.

Let us look at another contemporary usage. Describing the behavior of a woman who had discovered corruption in the highest office of the state government for which she worked, journalist Peter Maas writes, "Marie's first instinct was loyalty."[19] Marie's instinctive loyalty, however, was not fixed and unchangeable. Acting even while afraid for her life, this woman triggered an investigation that resulted in a governor being forcibly removed from office for the first time in U.S. history.* Instinct here does not imply a specific form of unlearned behavior, but instead a predisposition subject to interaction with a complex of other factors.

Drawing from more sophisticated popular usages of the term, it would be fair to define human instincts as *types of inherent powers or predispositions in human behavior whose development and expression are functions of learning, consciousness and the environment.* As we will soon see, such a commonsense understanding of human instincts has much to recommend it empirically. But as with much else in psychology, empirically derived truth is not the same as experimentally derived truth. Looking through their own specially prescribed lenses, mainstream academics long ago judged instincts to be figments of the imagination, and maintained this stance for decades despite the growth of considerable evidence to the contrary.

The origins of this contradiction go back to the time of Freud, when instinct theories proliferated. In one of the most popular conceptions, instincts were seen as fixed and specific patterns of behavior universal to a species. In other conceptions, instincts were understood as being more highly developed in humans than in animals. The great psychologist William James thought that human beings have more instincts than do any other creature.

None of these conceptions were to last. Around 1920, academicians started to issue broadside criticisms of all instinct theories. They argued with increasing vehemence, for example, that remarkably few forms of human behavior are either fixed, specific or universal. But instead of using such criticisms to develop a more valid concept, self-proclaimed "hard-minded"

---

* Gov. Ray Blanton of Tennessee.

scientists ridiculed the whole idea of instincts. One researcher (Ayers) belittled his peers by postulating the human instinct of "belief-in-instincts."

By 1930, the concept of instincts was dismissed outright from scientific circles: "The only obvious and immediate effect of the Great Instinct Controversy," wrote Robert Bolles with reference to the 1920s, "was that the word *instinct* was banished."[20] The exiling of instincts signaled larger changes. Academicians had in fact become disenchanted with the whole biological realm of psychology. Abandoning belief in biological determinism, they became instead enthralled with the notion of *environmental* determinism. The Era of Behaviorism was at hand.

It was also in the 1920s, however, that the less glamorous discipline of ethology, the study of *naturally occurring* behavior, first appeared. From this discipline—a field long ignored by mainstream psychology—eventually emerged the very development that psychologists should have been seeking in the first place: an evolved understanding of instincts.

With pioneering studies by Konrad Lorenz of Austria and Niko Tinbergen of the Netherlands, ethologists documented a growing number of parallels between animal and human behavior. In collaboration with cultural anthropologists, ethologists found that behaviors including attachment, aggression, facial expressions, family units and cooperation appear to be innately organized in human beings much as they are in some animals. Some documented forms of human behavior, such as the communication of emotion through facial expressions, were found to be specific and universal. Many other behaviors were recognized as being normative in cultures throughout the world. Drawing on research on a wide range of animals, ethologists discovered that most instinctive behavior—even in animals—is neither irrevocably fixed, nor truly specific, nor solely a function of inborn factors. Based on such parallels between human and animal behavior, ethologists developed a reformed conception of instincts. According to this conception:

(1) Instinctive behavior results from the *interaction* between environmental factors and innate factors.

(2) In the absence of opportunities for learning from elders, many different versions of instinctive behavior may develop.

(3) The higher that an animal is on the evolutionary ladder, the greater its ability, freedom and flexibility to develop different ways and forms of expressing instinctive influences.

Even among the lowest animals, ethologists have discovered some flexibility of behavioral response. As the great British psychologist John Bowlby put it:

> Even ants, which put other ants into two categories, friend and foe, and treat them very differently, have to learn which is friend and which foe. If by experiment they are brought up in a colony of another species, they treat these others as friends and members of their own species as foes. Instinctive behavior is not inherited: What is inherited is a potential to develop certain ... behavioral systems, both the nature and the forms of which differ in some measure according to the particular environment in which development takes place.[21]

In the ethological conception, instinctive behavior is seen as part of a continuum in which higher levels of evolution correspond to genetic encoding of increasing breadth and flexibility of behavioral capacity. According to this conception, human behavior is a function of the most flexible of innate programming, and this flexibility allows our species to develop by far the greatest diversity and multiplicity of behavioral possibilities.

Altogether, the evidence of ethology and cultural anthropology suggests the existence of a whole spectrum of innate influences in and underlying human behavior. The presence of such a spectrum of underlying influences is likewise recognized by personality theorists, who have long sought a viable taxonomy, or codification, of underlying factors pertaining to personality traits.

Although never known as a study of "naturally occurring behavior," astrology has always been concerned with (oddly enough) just that. As does ethology, astrology addresses the relationship between behavior and influences underlying behavior. As with ethology, some of the influences studied in astrology—those represented in the zodiac—can be identified in terms of instincts. And as with the influences studied in ethology, those studied in astrology can—and should—be studied in connection with factors of development, learning, consciousness and the environment.

As a symbolic vehicle, the zodiac invites a conception of instinctive influences that not only allows for but invites accounting of flexible relation to those psychological factors just listed. When instinctive influences are identified by symbols, it is much easier to assess manifestations of behavior *as functions* not only of underlying influences, but of those other kinds of psychological factors as well. The symbol is the perfect vehicle for indicating the existence of underlying influences that, in connection with other factors, may translate into a whole range of behavioral possibility.

Using the symbols of the zodiac, it is possible to generate a codification of human instincts that might be relevant to ethological and/or anthropological analyses:

ARIES	Pioneering; leadership; individualization
TAURUS	Territorial; agriculture; resource development; storing; ownership; inveterate habit and custom
GEMINI	Imitation, mimicking; kidding and comic antics; repartee; rhyme and word play
CANCER	Home-making; nesting, attachment, bonding; child care; private life; security; personal incentive and personal capital
LEO	Family; play; art and creative self-expression; recreation; acting and drama
VIRGO	Hygiene, health and nutrition; waste management; conservation
LIBRA	Courting; song and dance as social and aesthetic forms; adornment; display

SCORPIO	Mating, self-defense, aggression, fighting, competition and survival; economic exchange; morals and taboos; communal bonding rituals (including initiation, marriage, rites of passage); communal/socialistic sharing of resources
SAGITTARIUS	Migration, tribal, national, clan (team); mores and ethics; theater; symbol and cultural interpretation of such; collaboration of efforts for larger social purposes; systems of ethics, law, philosophy and cosmology
CAPRICORN	"Worker ant" job functions regarding all community operations; construction; mechanical technology; government; elder authority/sanctioned authority; law enforcement
AQUARIUS	Cooperation; communication of news and current events; invention and innovation; altruism.
PISCES	"Schooling instincts": religion and myth; spiritualism; psychic experience; dream interpretation; mind-altering drug usage; healing

While this slant on the zodiac is certainly unusual from the astrologer's point of view, the codification of instinctive behavior according to the zodiac presented here is nonetheless quite consistent with meanings traditionally applied to the zodiacal signs. To place zodiacal symbolism in the context of biology is only to follow, albeit in an unexpected way, the lead of the ancients who first conceived of animals in the stars. As astrology's "circle of animals," the zodiac intrinsically symbolizes a universe of human instincts, and there is every reason to compare "zodiacal instincts" with influences perceived in ethology. By comparing perceived astrological influences with biological influences in terms of apparent similarities as well as differences, we can conceptualize the nature of zodiacal influences in ways that integrate some of the most classic features of modern psychology. Let us mark some of these ways.

First, zodiacal influences, as quasi-instinctive influences, ought to interact with factors of learning, consciousness and the environment, and by these interactions generate a wide variety of different behavioral manifestations. Zodiacal influences should if anything be substantially *more* amenable to interaction with other factors of psychological influence than the genetically "hard-wired" influences explored in biology.

Second, the zodiacal influences perceived in astrology should be integral to processes of *growth and development,* processes that may play out over much of a lifetime.

Third, considering the incredibly variable condition of human beings in terms of such factors as economic survival, moral compass, spiritual integrity and the potential for change in the course of a single lifetime, it would appear that far from having reached some clearly definable evolutionary plateau, the human species is, both individually and collectively, struggling from day to day with dimensions of evolution that intersect with, yet also transcend, biology. While our species faces the same time-less biological and ecological requirements of adaptation faced by other species (and that were faced by our pre-technological *homo sapiens* ancestors), evolution and adaptation are no longer only a matter of biological processes within the human species. (God save us if that were the case.) What makes us more fit to survive *now* is not primarily a matter of genetic change. Instead, arguably the most important evolutionary issues confronting the human animal are those of making economic, social, political, psychological, spiritual and technological breakthroughs. Such breakthroughs are all matters of *developing faculties we already possess.*

Fourth, while zodiacal *symbols* serve to classify more primi-tive behaviors that are clearly of biological origin, astrological *influences* should in contrast be of a wholly more subtle—*and evolved*—nature than biological influences. Responsiveness to astrological influences could define one of the two or three most important constitutional differences between humans and animals. Yet at the same time, it could be that humans vary in their *ability to respond* to the subtle nature of astrological influ-ences, depending for example on how much they are forced to channel their energies into the most basic acts of survival. It might even be appropriate to speak of achieving "triumphs over genetics"—transcending a lower order of imperatives in favor of a higher order of potentials.

Such considerations begin to put a whole new face on astrology, whose students are liable, ironically, to treat zodiacal influences as if they worked according to older deterministic conceptions of biological instincts. It is often assumed, for example, that the traits an individual manifests with respect to a given sign are effectively "fixed and unalterable." Jack the Aries or Jacqueline the Taurus are who they are, and they are going to be that way for life.

How much richer and more complex astrology becomes when we consider such psychological variables as the environment, consciousness, learning and development. Let us integrate some of these variables in a quick study of sun-sign Cancerians. Some of the higher, more refined qualities of the "Cancerian nature" include those of being sweet, gentle, caring, and sensitive. Yet do all people born with strong Cancerian influences exhibit these qualities? Obviously not. What may be valid to say, however, is that Cancerians are *challenged to develop* such values of behavior. Equally, it may be that Cancer indicates a *predisposition* to develop these behavioral traits, but that development may flexibly unfold in a wide variety of other manifestations.

Now consider three black men who have achieved notoriety between 1989 and 1994 by dint of being accused of alternately harassing, raping, abusing and killing women. Clarence Thomas, Mike Tyson and O.J. Simpson were all born with the sun in Cancer. It can well be said that central life themes for these men is the *learning,* at different levels of individual evolution, of the inherent powers of unconditional caring and sensitivity. But it is also clear that the *processes* of learning, growth and development in the lives of these men were affected by crucial environmental factors: absence of the father in all three cases, and constant "interaction" with mean urban streets in the cases of Tyson and Simpson.

If we look at the experiences of these men according to Liz Greene's archetypal interpretation of Cancer as cited in Chapter 3, presumably the actions and the experiences generated by these men, and the legal trials they consequently faced, comprised the *emotional* trials and losses that would push them into deep "confrontation with life." Yet we do not need to apply the archetypal template to see that core challenges to growth and development have confronted these individuals, *however* they came to meet them—or not meet them—"in the absence of opportunities of learning from elders," and specifically in the absence of fathers.

Bill Cosby is another black Cancerian man. In contrast to those characterized above, Cosby seems to have carried an *instinctive* wry sweetness, caring, and sensitivity into adulthood. Yet these instinctive powers were also likely learned, in part, from *his* elders. (Sadly, none of these qualities saved him from experiencing, through the murder of his son, his own deep emotional loss.)

Transcending the most common idioms of astrological interpretation, we have begun to entertain conceptions of astrological influence in terms that include instincts, predispositions, learning, evolution, interaction with the environment, and growth and development. Identifying zodiacal influences in terms of instincts, we can define these influences much as we did "normal" instincts: as *predispositions to develop powers of behavior*—and *powers of experience—in interaction with factors of learning, consciousness and the environment.* In making experience integral to our definition, here we implicitly emphasize the role of consciousness. Indeed let us now acknowledge that the development of inherent powers—especially astrological powers—is not merely affected by factors of consciousness, but is rather a central, ongoing *function of consciousness.* Conversely, consciousness is not simply a "factor" in development; it is a key *vehicle of development* throughout life. Emphasizing the role of consciousness brings our definition of zodiacal instincts more into line with Jungian psychology, which is centrally concerned with processes of consciousness as such processes are capable of changing our experiences of life and self. This emphasis likewise serves to bring into focus the more subjective psychological dimensions of being that are downplayed in academic psychology for lack of means of quantification.

In creating our conception of zodiacal instincts, finally, let us reaffirm that astrological influences, by their celestial, subtle and psychic nature, should be far more congenial to the generation of higher evolutionary values than biological influences; at least as much as we *respond* to them. (But do we listen?) "That the origin of a higher form of life ... means an increase in values is a reality as undeniable as that of our own existence."

Why do psychologists, who have emerged as major players in the game of defining human nature, have such a hard time recognizing that a new paradigm is needed to do justice to a being that transcends biology? Because, of course, they don't think that human nature does transcend the parameters of biology, the brain and learning in the first place. Nor by the same token do they even begin to consider that human nature might transcend the parameters of this third planet from the sun.

CHAPTER 5

ON THE FRINGES OF SCIENCE

Prophesying the death of theology, [Edward O.] Wilson argues that biology can 'explain' religion: 'sociobiology can account for the very origin of mythology by the principle of natural selection acting on the genetically evolving material structure of the human brain.' He goes on: 'If this interpretation is correct, the final decisive edge enjoyed by scientific materialism will come from its capacity to explain traditional religion, its chief competitor, as a wholly material phenomenon.' But ... Wilson admits, 'the spiritual weakness of scientific materialism' is that 'it can claim no 'primal source of power.'

— Dr. Anthony Stevens
Archetypes: A Natural History of the Self

As the values and methodologies of science gained ascendance in psychology through the first few decades of this century, virtually everything that could not be experimentally verified was progressively disregarded. Just as the whole concept of human instincts was being rejected by scientists for lack of hard experimental evidence, so were concepts of such classic psychological entities as the *unconscious*, the *spirit*, the *soul* and even the *psyche* itself cast on the ash heap of scientific history.

By 1930, *behavior* replaced the *psyche* as the defining focus of psychology, and since then the dominant approach to knowledge in the field has been tightly governed by the criteria of the experimental method. By this method scientists have made enormous strides in learning about what we might call the *mechanics* of human behavior: interactions between the brain and nervous system, learning, cognition, perception, physiology, factors of the environment and so forth. When confronted by questions

pertaining to *inborn sources* of behavior, however, scientists
have had the devil of a time. What is the inborn source of
aesthetics? Of art? Of love? Of philanthropy? Of spirituality? On
the individual level, what innate factors make me who I am, and
you who you are?

Although academic psychology lent scant attention to such
questions between 1920 and 1970, the underlying assumption
always was, and still is, that if answers were ever going to come,
they would come from biology. Since 1970, to be sure, certain
biologically-oriented answers have come forth. The first of these
was *sociobiology*. Sociobiology posits the idea that predispositions to behaviors are encoded in the genetic makeup of the
human species, and that these predispositions are entirely a
function of the mechanism of natural selection. Genetically
determined behavior, in other words, derives from how well such
behavior has served the purpose of survival.

Prominent figures in the world of sociobiology included
Edward O. Wilson (a founding father of the subject) and Lionel
Tiger, who devoted a whole book (*The Biology of Hope*) to the
idea that optimism is genetically based. How are such specific
forms of behavior encoded in our bodies? Said Wilson,

> More complex forms of human behavior are almost cer-
> tainly under the control of polygenes (genes scattered on
> many chromosome loci), which in turn create their effects
> through alternating a wide array of mediating devices,
> from elementary neuronal wiring to muscular coordina-
> tion and 'mental set' induced by hormone levels.[22]

Some sociobiologists, seeking to keep matters in perspective,
were careful to minimize claims about genetic determination:
"Sociobiology does not require genetic determinism of behavior," wrote David Barash, "only a genetic influence greater than
zero."[23] Such cautions not withstanding, however, other sociobiologists did in fact make wholesale claims, and placed more and
more of the human condition under their purview. Thus the name
of sociobiology came to be identified with an ideology of sweeping genetic determinism, and controversies erupted that severely
damaged the reputation of the discipline.

Sociobiology faded from public view for a while, only to
resurface around 1990 under a new name: evolutionary psychol-

ogy. Like sociobiologists of old, evolutionary psychologists seek to apply the theory of natural selection to the analysis of human behavior, and like sociobiologists they have come up with some interesting syntheses. Like sociobiologists too, unfortunately, evolutionary psychologists are wont to believe in a genetic determinism hardly less sweeping or absolute than marked the most rabid of previous sociobiological ideology. For example, while Robert Wright begins his book, *The Moral Animal* (Pantheon, 1994), with a study of patterns of human sexual behavior in the context of natural selection—a reasonable proposition—he winds up by suggesting that such behaviors as suicide, infanticide and religious belief all evolve from the "genetic interest" of the human species. Proceeding from the same theoretical viewpoint, he suggests that the motivations of great religious leaders such as Jesus and Buddha derive from nothing more noble than "evolutionarily engrained interest" in social status.[24]

Because evolutionary psychology continues to stress theory at the expense of hard scientific study, it continues to inhabit the fringes of academia. But if sociobiology/evolutionary psychology is not amenable to experimental research, other emerging areas of biological psychology are. The newest of these areas focuses on the study of gene variants; another area deals with twins and adoptees. (Research on the latter is centered in Minnesota, home of the Minnesota Twins). Series of studies in both areas suggest that genes are significant predisposing factors in matters ranging from large-scale dysfunctions—schizophrenia, criminal behavior, depression, suicide and alcoholism—to idiosyncrasies as personal as the use of contraceptives, consumption of coffee and insomnia. Some research has suggested genetic factors in homosexuality.

As with sociobiology, genetic research has spawned hot political controversies on issues including criminality, race and IQ. In contrast to sociobiology and its reliance on theory, however, research in genetic psychology has won broad endorsement. As it appears to be finally developing a real scientific base, indeed, many see genetic psychology on a roll, destined to become the star attraction of 21st century psychology. Strangely though, *research has revealed virtually no evidence of genetics in "normal" aspects of personality.*

This situation appeared to change early in 1996, when researchers tentatively linked a gene to a trait described as "novelty-seeking," which was then considered to be the first time genetic influences were demonstrated to be involved in a normal personality trait.[25] (Presumably normal, anyway: criminals tend to score high in ratings of novelty-seeking behavior.) But then, in a major subsequent study, researchers were unable to verify any trace of the earlier correlation. Interviewed about this later research, a certain Dr. Anil K. Malhotra of the NIMH remained unfazed—and wildly enthusiastic. Malhotra flatly predicted of genetic research: "It's the future." And he claimed categorically: "Our DNA is us."[26]

Such attitudes are oddly reminiscent of those of an earlier generation when, based largely on "rat psychology" experiments on rats—the future was Behaviorism.

As continuing research reveals more hard-wired components of influence, there is little doubt that biological psychology will finally come into its own. But it remains a blind leap of faith to imagine that genetics will one day miraculously explain the marvelous nuances of individual personality. Even if we liberally extrapolate from present research, the kinds of influences that such research reveals do not begin to describe the subtle, unique and complex characteristics of the individual. Nor have current findings begun to explain how it is that, as Winifred Gallagher puts it in summing up *other* kinds of research, "the personalities of siblings are hardly more similar than those of unrelated children."[27]

The fact is that biological research has only begun to identify and explain a few isolated pieces of behavior, and even these behaviors are of the nature of what we can most *expect* to be hard-wired. Lending weight to the skeptics among us who doubt that biology can explain the whole of what makes us who we are, biologists who study the endless intricacies of DNA codes come to the sobering conclusion that "humans and chimpanzees are closer to one another than [are] chimpanzees and gorillas."[28] How human genes, so close to chimpanzee genes, could at the same time be so evolved as to determine the far more subtle and unique natures of individual human personality would be quite a trick. Perhaps researchers will one day discover a Michael Jackson gene.

More likely though, genetic research will continue to give rise to exaggerated claims and faulty assumptions. As in the past, those who blithely assume that "our genes are who we are" will continue to assume it no matter what, exactly, the research reveals. Unfortunately, it is also likely that as such beliefs take on the hard sheen of science, the effect will be more to dehumanize than to humanize psychology. (Current magazine article title: "Do Genetics Determine Our Happiness?") Instead of illuminating the subtle and profound wonders of the human species, psychologists will continue to ignore that which they cannot explain.

And the fundamental questions will remain: Who am I? What makes me the crazy odd interesting person I am? Why do I experience the things that I do? Why am I so completely unlike my brothers and sisters that there may as well have been a mistake at the hospital? How is it that everyone can be so completely *different* in all the curious and colorful ways that they are?

Academic psychologists did not always avoid dealing with such wonders. Thirty years ago, ironically, belief in genetics was integral to the thinking of the academic father of humanistic psychology, Abraham Maslow. When Maslow formulated his manifesto, *Toward a Psychology of Being* (1962), he was clearly assuming that transcendent, illuminating discoveries in genetics would soon be forthcoming:

> There is now emerging over the horizon a new conception of human sickness and of human health, a psychology that I find so thrilling and so full of wonderful possibilities that I yield to the temptation to present it publicly even before it can be called reliable scientific knowledge.
>
> The basic assumptions of this point of view are:
>
> • We have, each of us, an essential *biologically based* inner nature, which is to some degree 'natural', intrinsic, given and, in a certain limited sense, unchangeable, or, at least, unchanging.
>
> • Each person's inner nature is in part unique to himself and in part species-wide.
>
> • It is possible to study this inner nature scientifically and to discover what it is like—(not *invent—discover*)... (p. 3)

To most people, it probably doesn't matter whether researchers come up with the kind of discoveries Maslow was anticipating. Science or no science, people believe deeply in the genetic inheritance of personality. (From my own sampling, the typical American is convinced that genetics determine as much as 80% of who we are. Such assessments of course do not leave much room for all other categories of influence combined.)

To many others, however, attitudes toward the "psychology of being" are entirely different. If Maslow was the father of humanistic psychology, then his children have gone far afield in search of knowledge of inner nature—beyond biology, beyond science and beyond psychology. In search of self, the children of the 60s made it acceptable to explore such diverse realms as Eastern religion and reincarnation, meditation, psychedelic drugs, spirit quests and Native American cosmology, Gestalt therapy, feminism, transpersonal psychology—and astrology.

As much as they have turned to astrology in search of the inner self, it is only fair to ask the same questions that we ask with respect to the issue of genetic influence: How much science is there in it? What kind of research has been conducted? How far beyond science do adherents go in making their claims? To these questions there are two directions of pursuit: those in the direction of hard (quantitative) science and those in the direction of soft (qualitative) science. Regarding hard science, there are two directions still: to natural science, for theoretical explanation, and to experimental science, mainly for validation. Over the following chapters, we will pursue answers in all three directions. In each direction, what we find may be seen as inhabiting either the fringes or the frontiers of science.

Although astrology is weak on traditions of both theoretical and experimental science, it does have a long, if also erratic, tradition of development as a qualitative science. Qualitative science is of course nothing new to academia: sociology, economics and education are prime examples. In academic psychology, however, qualitative areas of study have been rejected. Accordingly, the subject matter of astrology picks up more or less exactly where the science of psychology leaves off, seeking to describe and explain realms of motivation, personality and experience that fall outside the bounds of academic consideration. The descriptions of these realms are about exactly as subtle and qualitative as we might expect them to be with respect to the kinds of the natural forces that might produce them. Such natural forces would have to be forces of physics. Consider in this regard the following tenets:

(1) Astrology is based on the perceived influences firstly of the sun, moon and planets, and secondly of the cosmic directions identified in terms of the zodiacal signs.

(2) The sun, moon and planets are all *forces* in the classic definition of physics: $F = ma$. All are masses accelerating through the curvatures of their orbits. (In the case of the sun, it is the Earth's orbit that provides acceleration.)

(3) The Western zodiac is a function of the Earth-sun relationship. Accordingly, the zodiacal signs exert influence as *functions of directions in space: vectors.*

(4) The forces of the sun, moon and planets and the vectors of the zodiac are translated into electromagnetic forces. Einstein's Unified Field Theory predicts such translation with regard to gravitational forces.

(5) Astrological influences affect humans in terms of electromagnetic forces. As electromagnetic forces, astrological influences are *field phenomena* that interact with the holographic brain/electromagnetic brain field, most critically at birth but also throughout life.

We will outline a somewhat more detailed version of a theoretical physics of astrology at the end of Chapter 6. For now though, let us follow through on some of the implications of astrological influences as a matter of subtle forces of electromagnetism and field phenomena. If astrological influences, as they affect us on Earth, effect electromagnetic changes in the brain and the "brain field," the nature of these influences would be unlike anything that academic psychologists are accustomed to dealing with. Indeed, to postulate astrological influences along these lines is to conceptualize an almost literally *meta-physical* dimension of psychology, a dimension that gives new form to the classic concept of the *psyche* so long perceived by thoughtful observers.

Until or unless astrology is validated by the kind of spectacular proof that no one could rationalize, such talk of the metaphysical psyche will likely remain beyond the fringe of academic circles. But whether it is definitively validated or not, it is such subtle dimensions of psychology that astrologers (not to mention depth psychologists and many other clinical psychologists) observe and perceive. Here let me tell a bit of my own story. When I turned professional as a consulting and counseling astrologer in 1985, I had studied astrology for almost fifteen years. In that time I had developed what I thought to be a decent (if also somewhat evangelical) repertoire centered on psychological interpretation of the core astrological influences, the signs and the planets. I had attended graduate school in counseling, and had gained some clinical experience in counseling in other ways .

As I discovered, however, neither my education nor my study nor my training had sufficiently prepared me to respond to the reality of alternately needy, confused, sharp and skeptical individuals, many of whom had an agenda that they did not want to reveal.* Faced with the responsibility of offering useful information, perspective and advice for one or two hours at a time, I progressively realized that I needed a lot more in my "black bag" than I was currently carrying.

Although I had dozens of astrology books at my disposal, I found most of them useless. Much of the material struck me as either unsupported assertion made in the name of tradition, as fabrication or intellectualization. To be fair, I should also acknowledge that I was then unaware of several very good books that were available, and that since the time of which I speak, the number of valuable books in the field has increased exponentially.

At any rate, I responded to my situation by generating my own source material. In this regard I went about researching the influence of *aspects,* which refer to the angular relations made between planets at birth. (See Appendix 3.) I studied the influences of these angular connections by systematically recording every major aspect in play at the birth of clients, friends, family,

---

* "Modern persons have become accustomed to consider psychoanalysis or psychiatric healing a long and costly process; but they still expect astrological consultants to bring them solace, hope and faith in themselves in an hour or two. The consultants are under pressure to immediately discover magical factors which will free the mind from anxiety and cause everything to turn out well *very soon.*" Dane Rudhyar, *Astrology and the Modern Psyche.*

acquaintances, famous people, people in the news and the like. Aside from the availability of birth data, my main criterion for recording such data was having some significant knowledge of the person's life. So far, I have collated information on aspects for upwards of 2000 people, and I continue to record data in my (literal) black books of aspect research, these encompassing roughly 400 different aspects. In researching aspects, I look for modalities in populations born with a particular aspect: similar trends, underlying themes, patterns of development, patterns of experience, common issues and common features.

My research has been tremendously rewarding. Studying the influences of aspects has provided me with a vital set of keys to natal astrology. In researching aspects I see a myriad of ways by which the different basic "parts" of ourselves, represented by the planets, interplay with one another within the individual. Considering such interplay, aspects speak to me of the most fundamental dynamics of individual personality.

In pursuing my research, I think of myself as having few preconceptions as to what observation will reveal. Hence for instance I was surprised in what I found in researching the aspect known as the "Mars T-Square." This phrase refers to the configuration in which Mars is positioned at the apex of a right triangle with respect to two other planets which are opposite to one another.

As my list of people born with the Mars T-Square grew, the more I was impressed at how the characters—colorful characters!—fell into three or four relatively distinct but intersecting categories. Limiting ourselves for present purposes to famous people, I found writers and entertainers given to drink, drugs and adventure: Ernest Hemingway, Jack Kerouac, John Steinbeck, Jerry Lee Lewis, Lenny Bruce. I found characters who found themselves at the focal points of juicy political, moral or social intrigues and controversies: Henry VIII, Mata Hari, Mo Berg (Red Sox catcher/OSS spy), Clarence Thomas, Woody Allen. I found characters who rose to positions of power and used it with unflinching iron resolve: William Randolph Hearst, Indira Gandhi, Strom Thurmond, General George Patton (and again Henry VIII). And I found characters who were unafraid to fight for political and moral causes: Harriet Tubman, Dan Berrigan, Andrei Sakharov, George McGovern.

Altogether, the aforementioned individuals comprise 18 of the 42 famous people in my "Mars apex T-Square" file. Combined with a roughly equal number of people born with this influence who I have known personally either through my clinical work or otherwise, I consider that I have a reasonably good sample popu-lation* from which not only to recognize the types of manifesta-tions to which Mars-apex-T-Square influence correlate, but also to gain insight into the *underlying dynamics* that conspire to produce such manifestations. As with many other aspects, I have had very good success in applying my research to the "clinical" context of my practice.

As a psychological astrologer, it strikes me as being utterly besides the point to try to quantify my research. It strikes me as more or less ridiculous, for example, to try to quantify what percentage of people born with Mars at the apex of a T-Square grow to be "unafraid to fight for moral and political causes." As I translate and interpret it, my data does not lead to hard-and-fast conclusions, but rather to a complex set of perceptions as to how an astrological influence may be developed and expressed in individual human subjects. Taking into account the observation of diverse elements and patterns of manifestation, these percep-tions are geared to articulation in terms of whole constellations of meaning, such as are evident in Chapter 16. To try to isolate parts and pieces from such constellations for experimental pur-poses impresses me the way that using the electricity from nuclear reactors to heat uninsulated homes does: a poor applica-tion of a particular form of energy for not much gain.

My methods of studying the influences of aspects, which I have only illustrated in the barest form here, can be criticized on several accounts. Yet these methods are arguably *appropriate* to the subject matter: human subjects. And while the knowledge that I have generated through such methods is more of the nature of insight than fact, it is nonetheless in line with the whole of modern psychological astrology. And factual or not, this kind of knowledge can be of real clinical value.

Although not experimental, moreover, the process by which I have developed such knowledge is *empirical*. It centers on direct,

---

* On the order of 3-4% of the general population was born with Mars at the apex of a T-Square.

first-person observation and experience. As such it tends in the direction of science. It accords to broader principles of science. Being essentially qualitative, it is a kind of empirical knowledge that does not easily lend itself to being measured, proven—or disproved—except by similar methods of approach.

Mexicans have a saying about their country: *Oh Mexico; so far from God, so close to the United States.*

Astrologers and many psychologists could have a similar saying about academic psychology: *Oh Psychology; so far from the psyche, so close to the experimental method.*

On to the experimental method.

CHAPTER 6

EXPERIMENTAL RESEARCH: THE WILD FRONTIER

Dr. Norman Geschwind, a neurologist at the Harvard Medical School, said Mirabile's work confirms previous studies on the effect of the solar cycle on behavior, but that "what is particularly interesting ... is the suggestion there's also a lunar cycle." Little research has been done on that subject, Geschwind said.

Because variations in illness have been linked by Mirabile to the new moon, which sheds no light, they may be due in part to the gravitational effects of the moon, which are responsible for the rising and falling tides.

"Perhaps during the course of evolution, the brain organized its development around these geophysical cues," Mirabile said.   — *Associated Press*, April 18, 1984

Reports of astrology's demise as a science, to paraphrase Mark Twain, are greatly exaggerated. As the 20th century reaches its close, in fact, a moderately large and totally inconclusive array of experimental results pertaining to astrology has been generated. Considerable research data emanating from many different sources tends to confirm astrological influences as significant factors in behavior, while other data points generally in the opposite direction. Contradictory findings, however, are nothing new to science, and given the vastness of the field, what is most evident is that more research is needed; much more research. Yet astrology is an orphan science if there ever was one. Its mother, traditional astrology, responds with extreme ambivalence whenever results do not conform to the traditional canon. Its father, academic psychology, wants nothing to do with it in the first place—at least not when its mother is publicly identified!

Within the scientific community, just a few brave individuals have intentionally set out to conduct research on astrological factors *per se*. (Research purposely conducted on astrological factors usually involves correlation between celestial phenomena and human behavior as a function of the time of birth.) Many academicians, however, have studied astrological influences when such influences were not associated with astrology. Most of this latter research pertains to the direct and immediate effects of the sun and the moon.

Positive research on influences of the sun and moon is well-represented by the ambitious study quoted at the beginning of this chapter. In research conducted on 4000 mental patients in Connecticut, Dr. Charles Mirabile concluded that, "at the time of the full moon, and especially during the full moons of the summer and fall, psychotic mental patients display their most inappropriate appearance and strongest irrational fears."[29] Reminiscent of the ancient belief that the moon exacerbates or catalyzes mental illness, the findings of this study are consistent with astrological perceptions of the moon's influence. (See Principle 4, Chapter 9.)

Does it take a "lunatic" to think that these results are significant to astrology? Removing the rhetoric from this question, let us ask instead: How good a case has been made with respect to the moon's influence on irrational behavior, or on any other form of behavior? Well, it depends on who you talk to—and what studies they might cite to support their points of view. Mirabile's work adds to a growing collection of studies of lunar influences on mental patients.* The results of these studies have come down both for and against the hypothesis that the moon affects irrational behavior. Similarly mixed results have arisen from studies on the moon's effects on homicide and other crimes.

Because of academic prejudices against astrology, most of the research conducted with intentional reference to the subject has been carried on outside the halls of academia. Such work is exemplified by a study carried out by Steven Forrest who, in the early 1970s, was employed by the National Institute of Mental

---

* For a sampling of past research on the psychological effects of the moon's phases, see "The Moon and Madness: A Comprehensive Perspective", *Journal of Clinical Psychology,* October 1980; Vol. 36, No. 4.

Health in an agency involved in sociological research. In-depth interviews were conducted with a random sample of residents of central North Carolina; their answers to a series of questions were analyzed statistically. Mr. Forrest, now a well-known astrologer, took some of this data and analyzed it in terms of astrological variables. Using the same methodology as the NIMH-funded study, he showed that the most basic astrological variable—the sun sign—was a significant factor affecting the subjects' answers to a variety of questions. For example, in an attempt to measure influences on introversion and extroversion, 551 people were asked, "When you walk into a room of people in which some are strangers and some are people you know well, do you most enjoy joining in the talk of the group or talking separately with the people you know well?" The responses to this question revealed dramatic differences when broken down according to sun sign:

	"Joining in talk of group"		"Talk with known friends"	
	%	# of respondents		
ARIES	62.7%	32	37.3%	19
TAURUS	51.1%	23	48.9%	22
GEMINI	52.6%	20	47.4%	18
CANCER	33.3&	12	66.7%	24
LEO	42.5%	17	57.5%	23
VIRGO	60.3%	41	39.7%	27
LIBRA	69.5%	41	30.5%	18
SCORPIO	46.2%	18	53.8%	21
SAGITTARIUS	57.4%	27	42.6%	20
CAPRICORN	34.1%	14	65.9%	27
AQUARIUS	54.1%	20	45.9%	17
PISCES	60.0%	30	40.0%	20
TOTAL		295		256
AVG. %	53.5%		46.5%	

SIGNIFICANCE = 0.0085

TABLE I

The "significance" factor of 0.0085 means that the chances of these results occurring by chance are about 118 to 1.[30]

As with much other good research on astrology, this study supports *some* traditional astrological associations, but seems to confound others. Sun-sign Leos, for instance, would be expected by astrologers to want to be the center of attention, and yet a solid majority of the Leos responding said they would rather congregate with close friends. Hence, while this finding challenges a common astrological belief, it supports the larger notion that sun signs play *some* significant role in personality.

As with other research reflecting favorably on astrology, the scientific community has never taken notice of Forrest's work. One remarkable individual, however, made it his business to scale the heights of academia's ivory towers: Frenchman Michel Gauquelin. With the help of his wife, Françoise, Mr. Gauquelin generated an impressive body of research spanning almost four decades. Presenting his work in books such as *Cosmic Influences on Human Behavior* (1973) and *Birthtimes* (1983), Gauquelin's research includes a great many studies that consistently confirm certain kinds of astrological correlations, yet fail to confirm other kinds. Because Gauquelin's methods of procedure were in painstaking conformity with the standards of experimental investigation, *and because of the magnitude of his experiments,* his findings constitute the strongest experimental case yet made for astrology.

The best known of Gauquelin's work correlates outstanding achievement in specific professions to planetary positions at birth. In scores of studies involving thousands of subjects—several studies producing results at the level of 100,000 to 1 against chance—Gauquelin proved that diurnal positions of the moon and several of the planets at birth have demonstrable connection to later success in particular professions. The Gauquelins found, for instance, that if the planet Jupiter had recently risen over the eastern horizon, or was just past its zenith at birth, a child born at those times would have a significantly better chance of becoming a highly successful actor, playwright, politician, executive, or journalist than would a child born with Jupiter at any other place in the heavens.

Gauquelin's volume of research could in and of itself form the basis of a full and healthy debate regarding the scientific validity of astrology. Seeing himself as "no longer swaddled in comfortable illusions either for or against astrology,"[31] and imbued with the attitudes of a careful scientist, Gauquelin pioneered research procedures in the field, and likewise identified a number of issues germane to research on the subject.

As far as astrologers are concerned, the most controversial of Gauquelin's studies are those that tested the validity of the most common currency of astrological interpretation: traditional sun-sign descriptions. According to Gauquelin, given sufficient databases and careful procedure in collecting data, it should be possible to prove or disprove the most common descriptions of personality based on the position of the sun at birth.

Gauquelin's research on sun signs involved tests for 50,000 character traits, and a data base of many thousands of people. Using clusters of traits as profiles, Gauquelin found that traditional sun sign descriptions did *not* significantly correlate with sun-sign influences. "The only conclusion," he wrote, "is that the influence of the signs of the zodiac is not confirmed by an objective study of the behaviour of thousands of people—or, to put it crudely, the signs of the zodiac are valueless."[32] This is quite an indictment coming from the man who has done more to put astrology on the scientific map than anyone else in recent history.

If Gauquelin's research on sun signs was extensive, however, it was also narrow. His format was just one of ten or more different experimental methodologies that could be developed in connection with sun signs alone. Even within Gauquelin's chosen methodology, some of his assumptions regarding astrology were flawed. For instance, Gauquelin believed that sun-sign descriptions all closely resemble one another:

> The books on astrology almost all provide the same interpretation of your being an Aries: it means you are 'spontaneous, combative, passionate, given to excitement, enthusiasm, full of initiative, enterprise, delighting in conquest, novelty and adventure'. We have quoted one astrologer. Experience has shown that another will give almost exactly the same account... I cannot accept any claim that this ... cannot be tested scientifically.[33]

As conveyed in Chapter 2, such suppositions are simply not true. With regard to Aries, one has only to consult Myrna

Lofthus' *A Spiritual Approach To Astrology*, for example, Rob Hand's *Horoscope Symbols*, or the delineation of Aries presented in Chapter 9 of this volume, to see articulation of numerous characteristics, capacities and powers aside from the ones noted above. To pick a specific set of characteristics is arbitrary. Furthermore, many astrologers do not accept the simplistic personality-based formulations popularized in sun-sign astrology in the first place. Yet Gauquelin took such formulations to be pivotal.

Gauquelin's research also fails to appreciate the extraordinarily complex issue of personality measurement. Psychological testing for personality traits is widely known to be fraught with problems. Although numerous personality trait inventories have been developed over the years, they have been challenged on a number of accounts. For instance, as Morton Hunt put it in *The Story of Psychology*, "It seems clear that the units we seek in personality and in motivation are relatively complex structures, not molecular. But trait measurement is molecular."[34]

As if to confound the issue further, other research conducted by Françoise Gauquelin (on Michel's request) demonstrated that the same positions of the same planets* that were previously correlated to career success *also* correlate (though less strongly) with personality traits. Most of the correlated traits, moreover, conform not only with traditional perceptions of the influences of the planets in question,[35] but with the zodiacal signs that the planets are said to "rule."**

We will explore the issue of measuring personality traits with respect to sun-sign influences further in Chapter 7. For now, suffice it to say that Gauquelin's research on sun signs raises more questions than it resolves—but at least to good cause. A gadfly to astrologers as much as to scientists, Gauquelin's work will ultimately have a variety of healthy effects on astrology. Beyond his successes in turning experimental science to address astrology, Gauquelin infused the polarized debate about astrology with an iconoclastic spirit that should be refreshing to all.

---

* Correlations to career success as well as personality traits were found with respect to the moon, Venus, Mars, Jupiter and Saturn. The absence of the sun in this set is conspicuous.

** For discussion of rulerships, see Chapter 8 and Appendix 4.

Like a weathervane in a windstorm, Gauquelin's attitudes toward astrology veered this way and that. While he was usually quick to disavow the idea that his work justified traditional astrology, and even quicker to shoot holes through most of the experimental results produced by those biased in favor of the subject, in virtually the next breath he might wonder if maybe his research did not reflect favorably on astrology as a whole after all. In concluding what may have been his most important book, *Birthtimes,* however, he returned to the attitude of a true scientist, hoping that his efforts would serve chiefly to expand the scientific debate about "cosmic influences on human behavior."

Michel Gauquelin died in 1992, never having received anything like the full hearing—or credit—he deserved. In spite of its scientific integrity, his work was either denigrated or ignored by the scientific community during his lifetime. Most compelling about the poor treatment he received is that it was based not on scientific principle but on prejudice. As Gauquelin saw it, a motto for the true scientific attitude is, "Deny nothing *a priori,* assert nothing without proof." Yet the scientific community's reaction to his research was anything but scientific. Summing up "scientific" response to his work only too clearly, Gauquelin wrote, "Our archives are filled with letters from scientists saying, in essence, 'We refuse to examine your work on planetary influences, for planets cannot exert influences.'"[36] This is, of course, an *a priori* rejection: presupposition without investigation.*

In a 1990 article discussing experimental research on astrology,[37] Richard Crowe of the University of Hawaii cited Gauquelin's work as being uniquely credible. Crowe rejoined, however,

---

* Gauquelin's book, *Birthtimes,* opens with the story of a most remarkable instance of arbitrary judgment of astrology. In 1975, *The Humanist* printed an anti-astrology manifesto signed by 192 leading scientists; the project was spearheaded by Bart J. Bok. The manifesto concludes with the assertion that "individuals who continue to have faith in astrology do so in spite of the fact that there is no scientific basis for their beliefs and, indeed, that there is strong evidence to the contrary." Yet in the accompanying article written by Bok, Gauquelin looked "in vain for the proofs announced in the manifesto. Indeed, it appears that Professor Bok has never studied the question: 'At one time,' he admits, 'I thought seriously of becoming personally involved in statistical tests of astrological predictions, but I abandoned the plan as a waste of time…'" *Birthtimes.* pp. 1-4.

with the notion that if the effects observed by Gauquelin are scientifically valid, those effects must then not be astrological! If it's good science, in other words, then it can't be astrology.

In 1981 Gauquelin wrote:

> Could it be that astrology—through some unhappy quirk of fate, through some opportunity overlooked by the researchers ... has missed out on the attention necessary for it to be radically transformed over the years (like physics, astronomy or medicine), in order for it to become ... the science of the influence of the stars on men?[38]

Although Michel and Françoise Gauquelin did far more than anyone else to change this "quirk of fate," the fateful pattern is slow to die. Given the relatively paltry amount of research done on astrology to date—and most of this conducted outside the academic environment—it is still impossible to even begin to assess how the subject squares in relation to experimental methodologies. It is equally impossible to say when or how the attitudes of academicians will attain some semblance of open-mindedness.

The literature of astrology provides suggestions of many thousands of possible psychological correlations, all of which could presumably be tested in some form or other. In the larger scheme of things, astrology is (to wreck an ancient Chinese saying) 10,000 hypotheses waiting to be tested. What a field day for experimental psychologists!

Despite resistance from both opponents and proponents, a Pandora's box of scientific research on astrology has opened. Out of it have flown flurries of studies that are generally troubling to both sides.* A perusal of the 600 fine-print pages of Dean and Mather's *Recent Advances in Natal Astrology: A Critical Review 1900-1976,* shows a field beginning to reckon with the realm of modern experimental science. It shows the crude and questionable procedures, along with the curious, con-

---

* The August 12th edition of *Time* Magazine reports the results of a survey of users of E-mail and/or the Internet. A whopping 18% of users responding were born with the sun in Taurus, while a remarkably puny 7% were born with the sun in Aquarius—the sign that astrologers would most expect to be drawn to these forms of communications.

trasting and contradictory results that one might almost expect of first attempts to transform this occult science into statistical methodologies after 3,500 years.

Among the many issues that Gauquelin raised, perhaps the juiciest has to do with science's demand for articulation of the physical mechanism by which astrology might work. Pointing out that such phenomena as gravity and genetic inheritance were observed anywhere from fifty to several hundred years before the underlying physical mechanisms were understood, Gauquelin rightly asserted that the validity of astrology cannot be judged on the lack of proven basis of physical causation. This lack notwithstanding, however, astrology must develop plausible theoretical explanations of astrological phenomena, explanations that stand a decent chance of eventual confirmation. Hence here follows:

A BRIEF FORAY INTO THE THEORETICAL REALM

Natal astrology centers on the idea that the influences of the sun, moon and planets, plus the influences of the *directions in space* defined by the signs of the zodiac, act on the individual to key effect at the moment of birth. The astro-psychological paradigm asserts that the influences of the planets and zodiacal signs become assimilated into (what then becomes) the inherent nature of each individual at birth. We conjecture that receptivity to the influences of the sun, moon and planets was made possible in part by evolving *diminishment* of genetic influence on behavior, and by expanding receptivity of the evolving brain. ("During the course of evolution, the brain organized its development around ... geophysical cues"—Charles Mirabile.) The big question to ask here is: To exactly what form of influence might the brain/body have become sensitized?

The type of influence that could most clearly affect brain functions is electromagnetism. Yet it initially seems unlikely that astrological influences could reach the Earth in the form of electromagnetism. Aside from the sun and Jupiter, the planets produce relatively small amounts of electromagnetic radiation. Even accepting the vast distances involved, the magnetosphere of the Earth effectively blocks out all but small segments of the spectrum of electromagnetic radiation anyway. Sunlight forms a major part of the electromagnetic energy that does get through the magnetosphere. While a certain amount of radiation from Jupiter also penetrates, there does not appear to be sufficient basis here on which to build a theory of astrological influence.

To focus on the effects of electromagnetic emanations alone, however, is to rely on old forms of physics, whereas Einstein's physics offers far more fertile possibilities. The crucial point to consider in this regard is the relationship between electromagnetism and gravity.

On the Newtonian model, gravity was seen to act independently of other physical forces, and to have no effect on them. According to Einstein, by comparison, gravity is, like electromagnetism, a *wave* phenomenon. Einstein posited that gravity works at the speed of light, as do electromagnetic phenomena, and that gravity *interacts with* electromagnetic forces in what amounts to a *unified field*. Although it has never been proven (and apparently needs theoretical revision*), Einstein's Unified Field theory holds enormous intellectual integrity, and continues to appeal to a wide array of scientists. Recent discoveries in astronomy and physics continue to hold out promise for this theory.

Gravity was long put forth as the primary vehicle of astrological influence. Accordingly, scientific critics of astrology pointed out that the direct gravitational influence of the planets on individuals is so small that the gravitational force of another person in the same room is greater. This is because, along with distance, gravitational forces are not only a function of the mass of the "sender;" they are also a function of the mass of the "receiver." The "gravitational field potential" of individual human beings is minuscule.

But with electromagnetism and the Unified Field as missing links, the mass of the Earth becomes a critical component in a larger equation. The Earth itself, with its huge gravitational field potential, can be seen as the initial "receiver" of the gravitational forces of the sun, moon and planets. Simultaneously, if the

---

* Einstein devoted most of the last thirty years of his life to working out equations pertaining to the unified field. He introduced his revised field theory in 1950, at the age of 71. With the subsequent discovery of other basic universal forces—strong and weak nuclear forces—contemporary researchers now seek a "Grand Unified Theory."

Unified Field theory is valid, the Earth's own electromagnetic field is affected by the gravitational forces of the planets, meaning that the moving gravitational forces of the planets effectively become translated into changes in the Earth's electromagnetic field. Thence the Earth's electromagnetic field, interacting with the electromagnetic fields of individual Earthlings, becomes the final medium by which the gravitational forces of the planets might come to affect humans.

This type of scenario reflects trends in current thinking in which brain research is moving toward integration with astrophysics. Central to these trends is the perception that *the brain creates a field that responds to and interacts with all manner of other field phenomena.* In result, writes Barbara Brennan, "The whole universe appears as a dynamic web of inseparable energy patterns. [It is an] inseparable whole which always includes the observer in an essential way." The brain, Brennan goes on to say, structures information and experience holographically. "This information is distributed throughout the system, so that each fragment can produce information of the whole."[39] Dr. Valerie Hunt, professor emeritus at UCLA, has found that the human electromagnetic field *reflects changes in thought,* which means that our electromagnetic fields interpenetrate with consciousness.[40] Hunt has also shown that each person's electromagnetic field is unique.

The brain's electromagnetic properties are only beginning to be appreciated. Harry Oldfield, a British researcher, has hypothesized that the brain works as an electromagnetic transmitter. The shape of the brain resembles both a dipole transmitter and also, uncannily, the shape of the Earth's magnetic field. Oldfield posits that the brain governs bodily processes in part by wave transmission, that is, by wireless telecommunications.[41] Inasmuch as the brain is a transmitter, moreover, *it may well also be a receiver.* As Elaine Marieb (author of *Essentials of Anatomy and Physiology)* notes, "everything that we have ever experienced has left its imprint" on brain wave patterns. "[E]ach of us has a brain wave pattern that is as unique as our fingerprints."[42]

How closely related are brain wave patterns and the electromagnetic "brain field"? Might the gravitational fields of the solar system, as translated into electromagnetic field phenomena, interact with, and so leave uniquely patterned imprints on the brain, the brain field and the body field, at the moment of birth? And might these gravitational fields continue to interact with our individual electromagnetic fields throughout our lives? Stay tuned.

CHAPTER 7

THE POLITICS OF ASTROLOGICAL EXPERIENCE
FROM PLATO TO PLUTO

> An unfailing experience of mundane events in harmony
> with the changes occurring in the heavens, has instructed
> and compelled my unwilling belief.
> — Johannes Kepler

In May of 1988, the press revealed that President Ronald
Reagan—actually his wife Nancy—had consulted an astrologer
on numerous occasions during Reagan's two terms in office.
Reagan was embarrassed not by an illicit affair or by illegal
activities, but by something entirely more curious. Here one of
the most powerful men on Earth was found to be taking counsel
from a kind of professional ridiculed in mainstream circles.
Sweeping the matter under the rug, the Teflon President made
little attempt to justify or defend his actions, but neither did he
disavow them.

Had Reagan not been indulged as a well-meaning eccentric
(Aquarian that he was), the controversy over the affair might
have been pretty impressive: How can we reconcile the fact that
in the late 20th Century, the President of the United States consulted an astrologer?* As it was, reaction in the media was a
predictably unenlightening mix: titillation, intrigue, scandalized
amusement. Astrologers were interviewed for a wave of packaged newspaper stories, while academic bigwigs used sound
bites to debunk the subject. Some surprisingly significant ex-

---

* Reagan was apparently not the only world leader of the time to consult an
  astrologer: President Francois Mitterand of France was reputedly advised by
  Madame (Germaine) Soleil, a celebrated Parisian astrologer.

changes occurred in a lively *Nightline* debate or two; but overall "Stargate" produced far more pap than anything else.

Too bad. Opportunities for good dialogue about astrology are all too rare. Why? Mainly because astrology is caught in a Catch-22. In order to be entertained in serious debate, it ostensibly must prove its scientific value; but in order to prove such value it must be researched by the very academic authorities who *a priori* give it no credit.

With no forums for real debate, proponents of the subject mostly preach to the converted, and are rarely forced to hone their arguments. Regarding the most crucial issue—whether astrology is a science or not—there is nearly universal agreement within the field: Astrology is a science.* This viewpoint is of course adamantly rejected by university scientists, who see astrology as nothing more than a *pseudo*-science. And they would seem to have a point, as virtually nothing of what astrologers convey in their work derives from hard science—science as it is known in the university setting. Since scientists presumably know what science is, who is going to naysay them on their own territory?

But this argument cuts both ways. Every science develops methodologies that are accepted within the parameters of that discipline, and certain methodologies might well be legitimate in astrology. As it coalesces, one key methodology combines two different—and broadly scientific—approaches to knowledge: the *rationalist* (idea-based), and the *empirical*. On the latter account, *astrology is an empirical science to the extent that it develops, and is confirmed, on the basis of the observation and direct experience of those who study it.*** In this light it is astounding how little direct experience of the subject is conveyed by those who debunk it most readily. One of the most famous quips in the field is, "Sir, I have studied the subject; you have not."

---

* In January of 1993, I gave a talk based on material in this book to a gathering of about 70 people sponsored by an astrological society. I asked the group whether they thought astrology was more like pop psychology or more like science. The unanimous response was that astrology is closer to science. The question was something of a trick: as indicated in Chapter 1, contemporary astrology is a blend of both.

** Empiricism derives from the Greek *empeiria*, "experience."

The truth of this remark came home to me in May of 1996, when I had the opportunity to have a dialogue with the renowned astronomer and astrology-basher Carl Sagan. Sagan, who was lecturing on "Science and Superstition," claimed to have made a "thorough study" of astrology, and characterized the subject in terms of cynical appeals to gullibility. But when (responding to my challenges) it came to detailing his case, Sagan displayed an astonishing ignorance. Proclaiming that astrologers "neglect the precession of the equinoxes," and referring repeatedly to the signs of the zodiac in terms of "constellations," Sagan progressively revealed that he assumed that astrologers still use the stars to define the zodiac—whereas this is only the case in Indian (Vedic) astrology. The Western zodiac has not been defined by the stellar constellations for centuries, and virtually no one in the field even uses the word "constellation" anymore, except for metaphorical purposes. Western astrology calculates the zodiac according to the Earth-sun relationship (see Chapter 8), and thereby ignores the stellar constellations altogether; thus it does in fact proceed by taking exact account of the precession of the equinoxes.

Sagan's failure to learn such basic facts about astrology was matched by—and was in fact largely due to—an equally basic unwillingness to engage in open dialogue on any aspect of the subject. He was completely unwilling to talk about Gauquelin's experimental evidence, and he eventually reverted to a type of argument he had decried elsewhere: that astrology is invalid because there is no apparent means of physical causation. Reminiscent of Bart J. Bok's *Humanist* manifesto, Sagan's approach was consistently a matter of inflated, pompous and aggressive rhetoric, backed by no arguments whatsoever based on genuine scientific investigation.[43]

Sagan has left us, but as we reach the end of the 20th century, the academic community continues to operate on the basis blindly accepting party-line viewpoints about astrology. Most of these viewpoints are based on no real investigation, and yet serve to ridicule the viewpoints of all those who have come to validate the subject through investigating it for themselves. Academic attitudes consist largely of culturally conditioned perceptions, and academicians are liable to invoke the names of Science, Skepticism and Objectivity merely to justify uninformed viewpoints, all the while abrogating basic scientific principles of independent investigation and observation.

THE RELATIVITY OF "SCIENTIFIC" VIEWPOINTS

It was a scientist—Einstein—who effectively punctured the notion of intrinsic scientific objectivity. Einstein cast all knowledge into the realm of relativity by proving that *any observation is a function of the viewpoint of the observer.* Einstein also showed that it is within uniform frames of reference that observations can agree uniformly. A direct corollary to this principle is that it cannot be assumed that a given viewpoint is somehow more correct—objective—than another. Although Einstein was a physicist, his revolutionary conception of a relative universe applies with a terrible irony to any collective entity that claims its frame of reference to be the only or absolute truth.

To those whose experience has revealed other truths, the capacity of scientists to invoke the name of Science to assert the truth of their viewpoints might be laughable if it were not so exasperating. "Scientific" pre-judgments of other truths are now being contested on at least a half dozen different fronts. In medicine for instance, scientific authorities have been increasingly challenged by collectives who engage in such practices as chiropractic, homeopathy, herbal medicine, the therapeutic use of vitamins and minerals, and acupuncture. In each case a similar pattern has emerged. While numerous open-minded doctors and scientists have responded with interest, the more general reaction has been to deny the validity of, and to suppress practice in, these fields, simply because their efficacy has not yet been proven—or even studied—experimentally. What fails to be appreciated is how various practices have developed by empirical observation and clinical experience involving, in some cases, thousands of practitioners over thousands of years.

The generic response of recognizing only what has been proven by experimental investigation is of course even more counterproductive in psychology, where the goal of objectifying the human subject creates the most artificial of dichotomies. Exclusive reliance on experimental methodology ignores the ultimate necessity of embracing knowledge of the objective world—and of human beings—*as experienced, perceived and interpreted by observing subjects.*

In contrast to the experimental bias of academic psychology, astrology affirms a continuum in which observation, perception, experience and subjectivity are not segregated from one another. Placing the observer squarely at the center of the discipline, it entertains the realities of ambiguity and ambivalence. It embraces the idea that perceived meaning cannot be completely separated from observed fact. It assumes that the observer is also the perceiver. It affirms the principle that the middle ground between subjective perception and objective observation is a fertile area for developing both knowledge and meaning. It unites perceptions of subjective experience with observed behavior in the context of a higher order of psychological organization.

This does not mean that credence ought to be given to any subjective perception that comes down the pike. It does mean however that astrology's methodologies need to be reckoned with on their own terms. Instead of merely judging astrological methodologies for what they presumably don't do, it is fair to consider what they do.

In good part, what natal astrology's methodologies do is promote the observation and description of qualitative dimensions of individual differences. In order to apprehend such differences, astrology encourages the observation of subjects in the context of the existential world where individuals spontaneously display themselves. Instead of creating artificial experimental situations, astrology proceeds in vital measure by means of the science of individual ethology: the study of *naturally occurring* individual behavior. Outside the clinical observation of infants and children, ironically, this science is perhaps practiced *only* in the field of natal astrology, where naturally occurring individual differences form the central focus of attention.

And while astrology relies on the observer to collate, correlate and interpret observations, there is nothing to stop all others, both within the field and beyond, from using *their own* faculties of observation to confirm or reject what astrologers claim. Contrary to the beliefs of figures like Sagan and Bok, the subject has grown in the 20th century because intelligent observers have investigated the subject on first-person empirical bases, and have communicated what they have found.

Reflecting the prevailing cultural values of the modern era, many contemporary students of astrology look to their own observations to validate, contradict, call into question, reinterpret and/or revise what they read and learn. Hence it is common for good astrological observers to meet situations in which an influence does not appear to manifest in ways that fall neatly within the observer's existing astrological "file." (Simple form: You don't act like [I've learned that] a Scorpio [normally acts].) Good observers find correlations that fly in the face of conventional wisdom. The relationships they find between observed phenomena and corresponding astrological indicators are sometimes counterintuitive. In other cases, observers do not recognize any significant signs of manifestation at all. In still other instances, observers recognize manifestations of an influence, but find themselves challenged to articulate their perceptions in terms of fresh ideas.

All told, astrological methodology in our times is increasingly becoming a cybernetic system in which independent observation leads to multiple new tracks of development. This represents a radical departure from traditions that have at times devolved into mechanical application of old, questionable techniques and narrow, deterministic interpretations.

ASTROLOGICAL EMPIRICISM THROUGH HISTORY: THE GOOD, THE BAD AND THE UGLY

Since astrology was regarded as something of a science for much of recorded history, astrologers were long free to issue pronouncements with quasi-scientific authority. To the extent that they were not held accountable, they were likewise free to hawk superstition—and they often did. By the same token it is clear that much of astrology's popularity, especially during its boom cycles, has been fueled by the credulity of the public.

But it is also evident that the subject has a sprawling empirical tradition dating back to the time when people first correlated the cycles of the sun with the seasons, and the moon with menses. Astrology has stimulated peoples' minds for thousands of years, and its most influential figures have hardly been charlatans playing to a superstitious public. From the early Chaldeans through the greatest of the Greek philosopher-mathematicians, from Claudius Ptolemy to Johannes Kepler to the hundreds of today's astrologers who are researching correlations of a thousand different kinds, the figures who have driven astrology's intermittent growth have been doing their own independent, and empirical, work.

The era of astrology's emergence spanned a thousand years, and involved cross-fertilization of developments in ancient Mesopotamia with advances in the high cultures of Egypt, Greece and Rome. Between roughly 700 BC and 200 AD, interest in astrology was intertwined with critical developments in astronomy, mathematics, technology—and philosophy. No less a figure than Plato plays a part in this story, in part because it was Plato who first conceived of *essential unity* in the universe—between macrocosm and microcosm, between the celestial sphere and the human. Stoic philosophers translated the perception of such unity into the rudiments of a psychological astrology.* Arising from a wide variety of sources, a rich and sophisticated array of predictive techniques evolved well into the Roman era, in comparison with which much of early modern astrology looks quite crude.

Spreading through the Middle East during the Dark Ages,** astrology enjoyed a great resurgence in the West around the 12th Century. By the time of the Renaissance, according to one expert, "everybody ... believed to some extent in astrology."[44]

---

* For example, we have in the following poem from the 3rd Century BC (author unknown) this perception of astrology's influences as being internalized. Echoes of Plato's *Timaeus* are evident.

 Seven stars turn circling on Olympus' threshold.
 With them Time accomplishes his endless revolution.
 The Moon that shines in the night, lugubrious Saturn,
 the dear Sun, the Paphian [Venus] who prepares the bridal bed,
 impetuous Ares [Mars], swift-winged Hermes [Mercury]
 and Zeus [Jupiter], first author of all birth, whose issue is Nature.
 These same stars have shared out the race of men
 and *in us are* Moon, Zeus, Ares, Paphian, Kronos,
 Sun, and Hermes. [Emphasis added]
       — Jack Lindsay, *Origins of Astrology.*
     London: Frederick Muller; 1971. pp. 120-121.

** "[O]n the highest level, namely in metaphysical and gnostic works, the powerful symbolism of astrology has been integrated perfectly into Islamic esotericism. In these works astrology is revealed to be in this symbolic aspect a means whereby man rediscovers his own cosmic dimension and becomes aware of his own angelic and archetypal reality and the influence of this reality upon his terrestrial existence." S.J. Tester, *A History of Western Astrology.* NY, Ballantine Books; 1987. p. 151.

Reaching a zenith of popularity in the 16th Century, it suffered a precipitous demise in the 17th.

A number of myths have been perpetuated to explain astrology's great decline. One myth holds that the Catholic Church persecuted astrology out of existence. Historical records, however, lend at best partial credence to this notion. It is true that the Church did, at times and to varying degrees, prohibit and/or censor the practice of astrology. But on the other hand, belief in astrology was actually allied with the long-standing cosmology of Catholicism. Deriving from both Ptolemaic and Platonic thought, Catholic cosmology conceived of the universe as designed by God to hold the Earth at the center, surrounded by the concentric spheres, or "Orbs," of the sun, moon and planets. As the Church invoked God to sanction this cosmology, it could do nothing but try to suppress the Copernican theory. By the same token, the Vatican tended to regard astrology as being generally in line with its world view, and censored astrologers more for the *political* nature of their predictions within the realm of Church politics than for any other reason.

A related myth is that the Copernican Revolution made astrology scientifically untenable. As with the myth of persecution, there is an element of truth here, for astrology's reputation did suffer as an indirect result of the Copernican Revolution. The rise of the Copernican theory was central to an overall shift in world views, in relation to which astrology became increasingly seen as archaic superstition. Yet astrology never depended on Ptolemaic astronomy, and the Copernican theory held relatively little direct relevance for astrology. Contrary to what would be expected, in fact, both Galileo and Kepler—the twin towers of latter 16th century astronomy who confirmed the Copernican theory—were also practicing astrologers who found no cause to renounce the subject. Rather, while both men were scathingly critical of the way that astrology was commonly practiced, both contributed to dialogue about the subject with a sophistication born of their astronomical as well as astrological experience.

Closer to the truth concerning astrology's demise is that it fell victim to its own success, and failed to evolve in crucial ways until long after it fell into disrepute.

While the stature of the astrological profession increased through the Renaissance, the actual techniques on which astrologers based their predictions remained largely fossilized. As late as the 17th Century, many astrologers relied on techniques derived from Claudius Ptolemy's *Tetrabiblos,* which was written in the 2nd century AD. Meanwhile, prediction as visible to the public focused in great part on phenomena notoriously dangerous to forecast: the weather. In agrarian cultures whose yearly fates and fortunes still depended in a literal sense on the skies, astrologers compiled almanacs replete with meteorological predictions made months and even years in advance. With the printing press making possible broad dissemination, astrological almanacs became enormously popular in the 16th and 17th centuries; the English astrologer William Lilly sold as many as 30,000 per year as late as 1660.[45] Yet popular distribution meant that wrong predictions would be widely observed as much as accurate ones.

In one of the most famous cases of false prophecy ever made, would-be astrologers flocked to make apocalyptic predictions about a major conjunction of planets in Pisces in 1524. Pisces being a water sign, predictions centered on floods of Biblical proportions. By the time the alignment of planets actually transpired, no less than 124 prophetic tracts had circulated, inspiring widespread panic and fear, especially in Italy. Unfortunately for the astrologers alone, rainfall that year was about average.

Thus in a climate of growing intellectual skepticism, it was the weather as much as anything else that precipitated the culminating crisis for astrology. While not oblivious to the pitfalls of astrological weather-forecasting, however, astrologers (at least in England) were reluctant to give it up. In the effort to save the hoary practice, one astrologer invoked the empirical method in "probably the most determined attempt ever to test the influence of the planets on the weather."[46] John Goad (1616-1689) compiled thirty years worth of careful records of the weather, and tried to correlate these records with day-by-day changes in planetary positions. The irony of Goad's lifetime of work as published in *Astro-Meteorologica* (1686) is that a scientific method was applied so conscientiously, and so early, in an area of astrology that would never again be seen as a viable application for the subject, even by people within the field.

Another way that astrologers brought on their own demise was by turning prediction to political purposes. Just as astrologers had been censored in Imperial Rome for issuing partisan predictions within the Roman orbit, astrologers in the 16th and 17th centuries were censored for issuing politically motivated prophecies affecting both the Church and state. William Lilly, who gained unparalleled success as an astrologer, was widely—and accurately—credited with predicting the downfall of King Charles I of England. But protestations to the contrary notwithstanding, Lilly was deeply committed to seeing the English monarchy fall, and was as fully invested in making partisan predictions as the astrologers who dueled with prophecies for their political clients in ancient Rome. No wonder that Restoration authorities clamped down on astrologers, and no wonder that despite his preeminent reputation, Lilly did not well serve the higher cause of astrology.

Like the public they consulted to, astrologers were unable to put astral influence into perspective. Much as modern-day psychologists have inflated Freud, Behaviorism and genetics into the Answer of Answers, both the astrologers and their public of earlier times believed in the power of astrological influences to unilaterally determine—and predestine—human affairs. In so doing they failed to comprehend the larger truth that, as Cassius put it in *Julius Caesar,* "The fault, dear Brutus, lies not in the stars but in ourselves." Cassius first spoke his lines on stage in the time of Galileo and Kepler, and thereby succinctly summed up the cause of astrology's demise in 17th century Europe as well as in Imperial Rome.

Beyond its practice as a mantic art amidst the public at large, astrology played a complicated role in the intellectual life of the era until the last stages of its decline. The subject was integral to study at many of Europe's great universities as, for example, the chair held by Galileo at the University of Padua governed astrology, mathematics, astronomy and philosophy.* Physicians learned astrology as part and parcel of their education, and many used it in their practices. Some of the most learned figures of the era worked with the subject in connection not only with medicine but mental illness. Girolamo Cardano, considered the greatest

---

* Galileo was a "competent astrologer" who taught the subject. His papers "contain a sizable group of horoscopes, with full calculations." Lynn White Jr., *Medieval Religion and Technology.* Berkeley: University of California Press; 1978. p. 20.

mathematician of his time (1501-1576), published an astrological study of 100 of the greatest figures in history. But perhaps the truly key figure of the time was Johannes Kepler.

Kepler remains one of the most influential figures in the history of science. On the basis of his work on the orbits of the planets, he is credited even more than Galileo with confirming the Copernican theory. He developed "the foundation for all of the advances in our knowledge of the structure and function of the eye:" optics. Yet it was his lot in life to make his living as the astrologer to the Court of Emperor Rudolph II of Prague.

Keenly aware of the tenor of popular astrology, Kepler had nothing but contempt for what he called the "cothurnus" (tragedy) of superstitious belief in astrological prediction. He referred to astrology as the beautiful daughter of the "wise mother" astronomy, but he warned that this daughter was turning into an "ugly slut." Yet through many years of working with astrology, Kepler gained a deep and abiding respect for the subject, and often viewed astrology as he viewed optics and astronomy, as a study of natural law. In this regard he repeatedly took to task the dogma of traditional astrology, suggesting for example that the "simple rules [that] have been laid down ... were deceptive from the start."[47] He stated the need to "select the gems from the slag," and sought to articulate an astrology that "I have recognized to be in accord with nature."[48] Seeing that he swam against the currents of the times, he also anticipated that his "researches" on the subject would "fall into oblivion."

Diverging from astrological orthodoxy, Kepler recognized astrological influences to be subject to interaction with numerous other dimensions of influence. As to the nature of astrological influences themselves, he "advanced two theories, one that concerns the type and archetype which I regard as Platonic..."[49] While his conjectures concerning planetary influence incorporated such exotic considerations as Pythagorean geometry and spiritual metaphysics, Kepler was nonetheless able to transcend the misguided belief in astral determinism that eventually brought ridicule on the subject. He even articulated the nucleus of psychological perspective that could ultimately redeem this errant relative of astronomy: "*It is the nature of man ... that* lends to the planetary radiations their effect on itself."[50] (Emphasis added.)

From his many years of practice, Kepler knew that to study astrology is to encounter a host of complications. He knew the uncertainties of prediction, and indeed he knew the painful embarrassment that comes of being forced into the business of astrological weather-forecasting. For all his travails, however, Kepler sustained a basic experience of astrology's essential truths. Just as he avowed by his own extensive work an empirical validation of astrology's "hidden recesses," moreover, he noted that the truth of astrology was "verified ... by the experience of [other] people that can in no way be regarded as stupid."[51] Kepler was not the only scientifically oriented luminary of the times to validate astrology in the act of seeking to reform it. For example, Sir Francis Bacon (1561-1626) argued for a "sane astrology," remarking, "I would rather have it purified than altogether rejected."[52]

The problem was that, with the possible exception of Kepler, no one knew just what a "sane astrology" would do—or how astrologers would go about doing it.

EMPIRICISM AND EXPERIMENTATION

Astrology's present situation is in major respects the reverse of what it was three or four centuries ago. Whereas during that era educated people increasingly found the subject to be folly in the larger cultural context of long acceptance, it now happens that educated people are validating the subject on the basis of independent investigation—in the cultural context of long-standing ridicule. Whereas much of the practice of astrology in the earlier era consisted of the application of techniques and interpretations derived from some few ancient sources, its modern practice is a function of a plethora of different techniques and sources. And whereas astrology's great demise was brought on in part by dint of false predictions being widely disseminated, its current regeneration is being aided in part by the widespread dissemination of material—predictions included—that tend to be verified on a relatively widespread basis.

No one of Kepler's fame is currently involved with the study of astrology. Nonetheless the field today has its own "stars" who shed light in good part according to empirical methods. Consider for example the astrologer Robert Hand, and his most renowned work, *Planets in Transit* (Para Research, 1976). Widely considered a major achievement in the field, *Planets In Transit* catalogues the effects of each planet as it "transits," or comes across, positions in the zodiac that form major angles (0°, 60°, 90°, 120°, 180°) to the zodiacal position where any given planet was at one's birth. The phenomena of transits form the primary basis of prediction in astrology.

Predictions regarding transits describe occurrences that are seen as likely to happen in individual life. Because the time periods of transiting influences can be clearly demarcated, and because only a relatively small number are typically "in play" at a given time for a given individual, these influences generally lend themselves to observation better than natal influences.

As compared "tall dark stranger" prophecies, the "events" that Hand predicts are almost as much internal (functions of experience) as external (functions of events). Addressing a number of possible eventualities, Hand's predictive analyses focus not only on possible outcome but on experience: what kinds of experiences are we likely to have. Frequently conveying a sophisticated psychological sensibility, Hand details how we may effectively create the realities/outcomes we eventually experience according to the attitudes we adopt. *Planets In Transit* correlates discrete types of attitudes and experiences, as well as possible eventualities, with respect to hundreds of different transiting influences.

To observant students of the subject, much of Hand's work in *Planets In Transit* is transparently empirical. But none of it has been experimentally tested, and it is questionable whether it can ever be tested to universal satisfaction. Even if the extensive resources that would be required to rigorously test even one of the many hundreds of delineations in the book were organized, the development and testing of experimental hypotheses would present staggering issues of methodology.

An obvious test of the correlations presented in *Planets In Transit* would begin with drawing together a group of people who were currently "under the influence" of a particular type of planetary transit. Soon after this period of influence was over, this group would be given three or four descriptions that would supposedly apply to the experience of that transit. One of these descriptions would be drawn from *Planets In Transit,* while the others would be artfully contrived counterfeits. A control group not undergoing the transit would be given the same set of delineations. The question to be measured: Would a significantly high percentage of respondents in the test group pick Hand's delineation?

This type of study would be similar to experiments conducted on natal delineations of character and personality, most notably regarding sun signs. But in resembling such experimental studies, it would be plagued by the very same problems that plague that whole genre of experiment. Central to these problems is the apparent fact that respondents cannot be trusted to recognize what most applies to themselves!

In 1985, Shawn Carlson of the University of San Francisco conducted an experiment he designed in collaboration with astrologers. The object was to see if respondents would choose delineations of their personalities created by professional astrologers over other possibilities. The results showed that astrological delineations were chosen at little higher than at the level of chance. As Carlson astutely noted, however:

> The subjects were *also* unable to select their own CPI [California Personality Inventory] profile at better than a chance level... We believe there exists presently no scientific evidence from which one can conclude that subjects can select an accurate description of themselves at a significant rate.[53] [Emphasis added]

Carlson pointed out that 30% of the academic studies on astrology (typically focusing on sun signs) are of this type.

Addressing the vicissitudes of self-reporting, astrology proceeds on the premise that *well-trained individuals* can make sophisticated observations of behavior, either directly or through questioning of subjects. This premise can be translated into experimental methodologies, and indeed a 1988 study by Angenent and DeMan found a 73% rate of agreement between predictive statements by astrologers and observations made by psychologically trained evaluators.[54] In this study (published, surprisingly, in *Psychological Reports*), the investigators solicited the observations of psychologists who had worked with the subjects individually over time. These observations were compared with characterizations contained in astrological reports individually written for the subjects.

From the astrologer's point of view, the Angenent and DeMan study allows for the psychological observer to engage with the subject over time, and thereby to progressively appreciate the unique features of the subject. Here, as in astrology, observers are affirmed as integral to the process of observation, not only by virtue of what they "factually" observe, but by how they are able to interpret and articulate their observations.

Let us consider how this sort of methodology might apply to the material contained in *Planets In Transit*—and let us revise a bit of this material in the process.

Among the 700-odd interpretive pieces in *Planets In Transit* is a five-paragraph treatment of the influence of Jupiter as it comes into opposition to where Pluto was at a person's birth. Hand interprets this influence as representing, in part,

> ... the culmination of a long drive for success or power. However, it is very important that you proceed with caution, because the forces opposing you are likely to be strong, and you must make an effort to placate them. This can be a time when you get a promotion in your work or gain power... But it can also be a time when all your efforts come to nothing and you find yourself losing out in a perpetual war with people in power.
>
> [You may feel] that you alone are right about some matter... Avoid becoming totally convinced of your own righteousness... Your ideas may in fact be quite good, but your problem comes from the style you would be likely to use...[55]

Inasmuch as this influence is supposed to bring into focus issues of dealing with powerful opposing forces, it may as well be written for politicians, and indeed as this influence came into the lives of world leaders, politicians and others in roles of power at the end of 1996, the need to make a change of attitude in dealing with opposing forces was vividly evident. Bob Dole was subject to this transiting influence just as, bowing to the advice of his handlers, he made the decision to "go negative" late in his 1996 campaign against President Bill Clinton. A couple of months later, this influence was operative when President Alberto Fujimori of Peru, faced with the holding of scores of hostages at the Japanese embassy in Lima, signaled that he would change his hard-line position against negotiating with terrorists; but that he would in no case consider the Tupac Amaru's basic demand that he release imprisoned rebels. Under the same influence, Bill Parcells—not a politician but the powerful head coach of the New England Patriots football team—appeared to simultaneously bow to and defy the powers-that-be when, reacting to rulings by the NFL, he signed as a "consultant" with the rival New York Jets—thus catalyzing dealings that allowed him to become head coach of the Jets immediately. A month or so later "under the influence," Bill Clinton met the opposing force of Boris Yeltsin—and specifically Yeltsin's opposition to NATO expansion—in Helsinki. His knee also met the opposing force of Greg Norman's steps.*

Reflecting in quality (if not kind) the experience of circumstances faced by world leaders, a sampling of individuals subject to this same influence in early 1997 likewise suggested the culmination of dealing with inevitabilities of "opposing forces" that were powerful within the smaller orbits of their personal lives. An artist suffering from Chronic Fatigue Syndrome reached the unfulfilling culmination of efforts to find a doctor/health-practitioner who would be her ally. A man involved in a long-frustrating marital relationship reached the point of entering into counseling with his wife. A smoking architect spontaneously decided to heed the writing on the wall, and made the move to quit smoking.

In all these cases, it is possible to see a signal change of attitude, the taking of a different tack, in confronting powerful, insuperable circumstances. There is the quality of being challenged to cope and reach resolution at a level beyond what one has theretofore achieved, or else fight to the end. There is the element of the irresistible force meeting the immovable object, where something has to give way. There is the sense of height-

---

* Slowing down to a virtual stop, or "stationing," at the end of its yearly retrograde cycle (see Chapter 16), Jupiter will oppose the natal positions of Pluto for both Clinton and Al Gore through the end of September and the whole month of October in 1997. Normally the span of this influence is only about ten days.

ened intensity and tension. All told, there is the implication of being moved to *intensify efforts to meet existing challenges,* possibly by taking a new direction of approach.

Assuming that such dimensions of experience and change are close to the center of what is catalyzed by the influence of Jupiter opposing natal Pluto, we might think of testing for the appearance of these dimensions in the lives of people who have recently been subject to this transiting influence.

In such an experiment, there is again no direct way of ascertaining whether individuals actually experience the Jupiter-opposing-Pluto influence in the ways noted above. We would certainly not ask the test group and the control group some question as, "Have you recently experienced yourself to be confronted by powerful opposing forces, and did you feel yourself compelled to change your fundamental attitude in dealing with such forces?" (Or perhaps: Have you recently been involved in the takeover of a foreign embassy by terrorists?)

Taking the lead of Angenent and DeMan, perhaps a better way to test for such influences would be to engage psychologists or similarly qualified observers, to provide these observers with the kind of information and perspective that we have here generated, to allow these observers to engage in double-blind dialogue with individuals randomly selected from both test and control groups, and to let them come to their own conclusions about each individual.

Because this type of approach depends on the quantification of qualitative observations, many questions would be left unanswered. How much information and perspective such as that supplied above would be sufficient to impart to the observer? What would constitute the circumstances of observation? Would other transiting influences, and pertinent natal influences, be taken into account in screening both the test and control populations? If positive correlations were demonstrated, what exactly would be proven? To whom? How would different people interpret the results, whatever they might be?

As with research on near-death experiences, the answers to the last few of these questions will inevitably depend on who is asked. Subjective dimensions of perception and attitude can never be removed from "science" when it comes to such soft and qualitative issues as are raised in connection with human experience. Nonetheless, instead of abandoning astrology's indigenous methodologies in the effort to achieve quantification, it would seem natural to try to extend those methodologies into the experimental realm. Along with testing hard data such as the timing of suicides, high success in professions, and disturbances in mental hospitals, softer methodologies could use qualitative material as bases for engaging in systematic observation. In such methodologies, the observer becomes focal.

In astrological methodology, the central emphasis is on observers who can spontaneously call into play perceptual, intuitive and intellectual faculties. These faculties are employed both in assimilating complex formulations about underlying influence, motivation, behavior and experience, and in assessing how much and how well such formulations apply to observations of different individuals.

Many of the human faculties on which astrological methodologies depend are combined in the *gestalt* mode of perception. Gestalt refers to the phenomenon by which people make whole patterns out of parts and pieces. As *Webster's New World Dictionary* puts it, "gestalts" are:

> ... any of the integrated structures or patterns that make up all experience and have specific properties which can neither be derived from the elements of the whole nor considered simply as the sum of these elements.[56]

Through gestalt perception, observers can integrate many fragments of data (sensory and otherwise) into perceptual wholes that are more than the simple sum of separate units. Konrad Lorenz stated that "*Gestalt* perception is capable of discovering unsuspected laws which the rational function ... is totally unable to do."[57] So it is with the "laws" contained in astrology.

THE NAKED TRUTH: ASTROLOGY EMBRACES PHILOSOPHY

If astrology requires observers to perceptually integrate an exceptionally large array of informational elements in the process of observing exceptionally subtle and complex forms of manifestation, it is because astrological influences are no less multivalent than the human subjects being observed. Consider that with reference to the delineations in Chapter 9, a single unit of astrological influence can translate into any permutation spun together from among thirty or forty discrete concepts pertaining to powers of behavior and experience. These concepts/powers interrelate with one another in endless ways, and it takes human faculties to both observe and synthesize connections among them. Similarly, observed phenomena in astrology are significant mainly in the extent and ways in which such phenomena relate to *other* observed phenomena, all in the context of larger constellations of meaning. Formulating the interrelationships that make up such constellations is central to astrological knowledge, and proceeds by *philosophical* methodology as much as by any other approach. Consider the definition of philosophy:

1. Philosophy refers literally to "principles underlying conduct." (*Webster's New World Dictionary*)
2. Principles, in turn, refer to "fundamental motivations."
3. Let us equate "conduct" with "behavior."
4. Replacing the terms in statement 1 with their equivalents from statements 2 and 3, we can well define philosophy as the study of *fundamental motivations underlying behavior.*

The influences studied in astrology fit this definition of philosophy precisely. Astrological influences are not microscopic; they are not some cosmic variant of infinitesimal genomes that might be supposed to determine such isolated behaviors as drinking coffee or becoming a religious fundamentalist. Astrological influences are macroscopic, global, planetary, and lend themselves to observation and perception by such means as can comprehend their encompassing dimensions. The influences studied in astrology are nothing if not philosophical: They describe overarching motivations underlying conduct. Astrology brings whole spheres of underlying motivation into focus with symbolic lenses that are geared to relate specific manifestations to broader principles.

Characterizing astrological influences in philosophical terms might be seen as begging off from science, but in fact the philosopher's role of articulating fundamental principles has been integral to scientific inquiry since ancient Greece. Deriving from Platonic philosophy, it is well recognized that one of the main epistemological approaches within the larger realm of science is the rationalist approach, which centers on the perception that knowledge is contained in self-contained "Primary Ideas." By nature these "ideas," or principles, lie beyond the scope of hard empirical proof. The principles of astrology qualify as such primary ideas.

Astrology's twelve principles can be articulated in purely philosophical terms, and without doubt they should be. These principles are of intrinsically philosophical nature, and if proponents of the subject are only vaguely aware of this fact, critics are totally unaware of it. Even if its empirical roots were weaker than they are, astrology could stand as a philosophical system for interpreting meaning and direction, and make claim to science exclusively on this rationalist basis.

As it is, astrology is remarkably much a hybrid of philosophical and empirical approaches, and its marriage of philosophy with empiricism creates its own parameters. One of these parameters mandates that observation be interpreted in terms of principles, and while the dangers of solipsism and self-fulfilling prophecy in this mandate are ever-present, there are also a plethora of potential benefits. Hence inasmuch as experimental scientists demand that astrology's methodologies be forsaken in favor of quantified observations, they demand the impossible: You can't tear out astrology's philosophical heart and still have astrology.

THE FUTURE OF ASTROLOGICAL SCIENCE

How much could astrology's parameters change so as to accommodate experimental approaches? This question may have several answers. Different methodologies may be appropriate in different contexts. There is no reason that experimental research cannot generate important contributions of its own, as it already has. If Gauquelin along with numerous others have been able to establish correlations involving astrological factors, might not thousands of more studies eventually do likewise, to all manner of unsuspected results? It is entirely possible that experimental science will help to revolutionize the field, put out to pasture a herd of tired old clichés, and generate a plethora of major new correlations—all welcome developments.

Still, the name of Science simply cannot destroy the core realm of meaning that is central to the subject. Although astrological meaning should be open to reform in relation to experimentally generated data, the experimental method can never replace either the empirical and philosophical sensibilities, or for that matter the mystical, metaphorical, imagic, intuitive and *gestalt* sensibilities, that are all in different ways integral to generating knowledge in the field. (These remarks, again, would equally apply to psychology, had not that subject already been split in half.)

On the other hand, as the astrological community comes to realize how crucial empiricism is to its ongoing development, it moves toward recreating astrology as a genuine social science. Since thousands of people in the field already engage in empirical observation, it is only a few steps to developing values and standards for such observational processes, and for observers to enter into earnest dialogue with one another. A million discussions regarding divergent observations and interpretations have already happened, and in the millions yet to come, there is all the room in the world for productive outcomes. It is not difficult to imagine the time when the value of developing interpretation on the basis of careful and systematic observation is universally embraced.

Even with a vastly improved empirical base, however, the role of perception and interpretation will hardly diminish; for there always remain the core units of influence—the signs, the planets and the houses of the natal chart—which can only be articulated in terms of complex constellations of meaning. Like Plato's primary ideas, these basic units of influence, these constellations, come to be known, as Plato put it, through "recollection," through perception and through thoughtful consideration. It is therefore the never-ending task of the astrologer to describe and articulate the nature of these ideas/principles/influences. In doing so, the astrologer-as-interpreter is charged with marrying observation with ideation.

In early 1996, I spoke to a group of Dartmouth College students. A young women in attendance offered me this story: At the end of her senior year in high school, she was visiting with many of her friends at a house where the residing mother happened to be interested in astrology. As a casual experiment, the "attending mother" read personality descriptions of various sun signs, but without identifying the sun sign in question. On hearing a given sun-sign description, the young adults gathered would spontaneously call out: "Oh that's Cheryl." Or Jason. Or whoever. And they invariably would be right. The teller of this story was impressed because she and her friends were not conversant with astrology. They barely knew their own sun signs, knew next to nothing about other sun signs, and weren't aware of the sun signs—or in most cases even the birthdays—of others anyway. They were simply responding spontaneously to characterizations of personality in the context of personal knowledge of their friends.

I was intrigued by this story. It reminded me of the first time I read sun-sign descriptions, and how impressed I was at that time. I recalled Shawn Carlson's experiment, and that of Angenent and DeMan too. I thought about how the observers involved in the Dartmouth student's "experiment" were apparently able to develop spontaneous *gestalt* connections between their familiar experiences of "naturally occurring" individuals on the one hand, and personality descriptions drawn according to sun signs on the other. While these observers were obviously not trained, they were at once relatively sophisticated, informed as to their human subjects, and yet also detached.

I wondered if the methodology of this event could be replicated in a formal context. First I thought that it could not; then I thought that, with modifications, it might. And I wondered: Whose sun-sign descriptions was that mother reading anyway?

PART II

CHAPTER 8

THE SYSTEM AND STRUCTURE OF ASTROLOGICAL SYMBOLISM

> The future belongs to those who can deal with reality in symbolic ways.
> — *True Basic Bulletin*

Knowledge in astrology is generated by a unique synthesis of empirical observation and symbolic interpretation. Because every astrological symbol translates into a wide variety of manifest values, and because observation itself is open to interpretation, there can be no definitive or absolute interpretation of astrology's symbols. As psychological symbols, the symbols of astrology must take on a life of their own in the mind of the perceiver. They must themselves be the alpha and the omega of the interpretive process, a process to which intuition, myth, intellect, experimental data and observation are all integral.

The astrological system of symbols is elegantly organized into twelve principles. Each of these principles has three major symbolic and psychological categories.

- The sun, moon and planets represent *fundamental motivations* and motivational *potentials.*
- The twelve zodiac signs represent *instinctive powers* and *predispositions.*
- The twelve houses of the astrological birth chart represent areas and directions of life *experience.*

These categories correlate with one another on a one-to-one-to-one basis. (See Figure 1.) The planet, sign, and house of each principle share common essences of meaning.

Sphere	Sign	House #
Pluto	(1) Aries	1
Earth	(2) Taurus	2
Asteroids	(3) Gemini	3
The moon	(4) Cancer	4
The sun	(5) Leo	5
Mercury	(6) Virgo	6
Venus	(7) Libra	7
Mars	(8) Scorpio	8
Jupiter	(9) Sagittarius	9
Saturn	(10) Capricorn	10
Uranus	(11) Aquarius	11
Neptune	(12) Pisces	12

FIGURE I
SYMBOLIC CORRELATIONS IN
ASTROLOGY'S 12 PRINCIPLES

These planet-sign-house correlations form the central structure of astrological symbolism. Yet students of astrology will immediately recognize that some of the planet-sign correlations presented here diverge from modern tradition. Scorpio for example is usually said to be "ruled" by Pluto, and not, as shown here, by Mars. In another contemporary tradition, Scorpio is ruled by *both* Mars and Pluto.

No single version of planet-sign correlations has been worked out to universal satisfaction. (There is no disagreement regarding correlations between signs and houses.) Although astrology maintained a stable system of correspondences/rulerships for many centuries before the outermost planets were discovered, these discoveries necessitated wholesale reform in the system. But there is as yet no consensus that real reform is needed, and so different practitioners use different systems of correlation.

In the system presented in Figure 1, the correlations between planets and signs follow a pattern that begins with the unquestioned correspondence of the moon and sun with Cancer and Leo respectively. From there on, the signs correlate consecutively with the concentric rings of the planets. Thus Mercury, the closest planet to the sun, correlates with the 6th zodiac sign, Virgo; the next closest planet, Venus, with the 7th zodiac sign, Libra, and so forth. This progression culminates with Neptune corresponding to the 12th sign, Pisces, and then correlates Pluto with the next sign, Aries. Certainly the last two correlations (Earth-Taurus, Asteroids-Gemini) do not conform to this pattern. Still, the symmetry of the system presented here is greater than that of other systems and, as explicated in Chapter 9 and Appendix 4, incorporates a host of natural symbolic connections inhering in the respective pairs of planets and signs.

ZODIACAL SYMBOLISM

The zodiac forms the central frame of reference for the whole astrological system of symbols.

Contrary to popular belief, the zodiac in Western astrology no longer has much to do with the stars. Instead, the Western zodiac is defined by the dynamic relationship between the Earth and the sun—the same system by which the twelve months of the seasonal year are delineated. The sun's passage through the zodiac serves as the means of measuring the seasons, and vice versa.

The 360 degrees of the zodiac's circle are divided into twelve equal parts—signs—of 30° each, and also four equal parts of 90° each. It is the sun's apparent passage through these four larger parts that defines the four seasons. The points in the heavens where the sun appears at the equinoxes and the solstices—the points at which the seasons begin—also mark the major divisions of the zodiac. For instance, the position of the sun at the spring equinox (the first day of spring) simultaneously defines the sun's entrance into the first degree of Aries—the beginning of the zodiac. In the same way, the passage of the sun across the first degree of Cancer—precisely one quarter of the circle of the zodiac beyond the first degree of Aries—coincides with the summer solstice and the beginning of summer.

Inasmuch as the seasonal year coincides with the astrological year, it should be no surprise that the first three signs of the zodiac are called the Spring signs, which are followed by the Summer signs, Fall signs and Winter signs. In connection with the symbolism of the seasons, these four divisions of the zodiac correspond to Carl Jung's conception of the four principal "psychological types":

1. The SPRING signs—Aries, Taurus and Gemini—represent *intuitive* types of innate power. The Spring signs also indicate predispositions to *individual* orientation.

2. The SUMMER signs—Cancer, Leo and Virgo—represent *feeling* types of innate power. The Summer signs also indicate predispositions to *personal* and *familial* orientation.

3. The FALL signs—Libra, Scorpio and Sagittarius—represent *sensational* or *relational* types of innate power. The Fall signs also indicate predispositions to *social* orientation.

4. The WINTER signs—Capricorn, Aquarius and Pisces— represent *thinking* types of innate power. The Winter signs also indicate predispositions to *community* and *collective* orientation.

The zodiac is further divided so as to represent predispositions to three primary *modes* of behavior:

1. The first or CARDINAL signs of each season—Aries, Cancer, Libra and Capricorn—represent powers of behavior that are inherently *initiating* and *generating*.

2. The middle or FIXED signs of each season—Taurus, Leo, Scorpio and Aquarius—represent powers of behavior that are inherently *sustaining* and *integrating*.

3. The last or MUTABLE* signs of each season—Gemini, Virgo, Sagittarius and Pisces—represent powers of behavior that are inherently *adaptive* and *responsive*.

The zodiac is also organized according to the symbolism of the classical elements of fire, earth, air and water so as to represent instinctive powers of *elemental* nature.

1. The FIRE signs—Aries, Leo and Sagittarius—represent instincts of *creative*, *spirited* and *inspiring* nature.

2. The EARTH signs—Taurus, Virgo and Capricorn—represent instincts of *practical, concretizing* and *material plane* nature.

3. The AIR signs—Gemini, Libra and Aquarius—represent instincts of *communicative* and *verbal* nature.

4. The WATER signs—Cancer, Scorpio and Pisces—represent instincts of *emotional* nature.

---

* The Mutable signs are sometimes called the Distributive signs.

The categorization of the zodiac signs according to the classifications outlined above is shown in Figure 2. Each sign of the zodiac refers to a unique combination of season, mode and element. These combinations will be recounted and briefly reinterpreted at the beginning of the delineation of each of the twelve principles in Chapter 9.

1. ARIES is the	CARDINAL	FIRE sign of	SPRING
2. TAURUS is the	FIXED	EARTH sign of	SPRING
3. GEMINI is the	MUTABLE	AIR sign of	SPRING
4. CANCER is the	CARDINAL	WATER sign of	SUMMER
5. LEO is the	FIXED	FIRE sign of	SUMMER
6. VIRGO is the	MUTABLE	EARTH sign of	SUMMER
7. LIBRA is the	CARDINAL	AIR sign of	AUTUMN
8. SCORPIO is the	FIXED	WATER sign of	AUTUMN
9. SAGITTARIUS is the	MUTABLE	FIRE sign of	AUTUMN
10. CAPRICORN is the	CARDINAL	EARTH sign of	WINTER
11. AQUARIUS is the	FIXED	AIR sign of	WINTER
12. PISCES is the	MUTABLE	WATER sign of	WINTER

FIGURE 2
SYMBOLIC CLASSIFICATIONS OF THE ZODIACAL SIGNS

Another structural division of the zodiac is that of masculine and feminine signs. The odd-numbered—masculine—signs are the fire and air signs, and represent generally *creative* and *proactive* powers. The even-numbered—feminine—signs are the earth and water signs, and represent *receptive* and *yielding* powers. According to the terminology of Eastern philosophy, the fire and air signs are *yang* (creative), while the earth and water signs are *yin* (receptive). The masculine signs perceptually relate to *figure,* while the feminine signs relate perceptually to *ground.*

Finally, the signs of the zodiac are said to "rule" bodily parts and organs. The parts of the body so ruled contribute to the meaning of the signs by virtue of the symbolism of their respective physiological functions. For example, Virgo rules the intestines. Physiologically, the intestines act to break down, digest and assimilate the component elements of food. On the physical level, this is a process of *analysis.* Similarly, psychological functions symbolized by Virgo are to *mentally* analyze, "digest" and assimilate.

THE ASTROLOGICAL HOUSES

The twelve houses of the birth chart comprise the third primary set of astrological symbols.* The houses form a set of directions independent of, yet intersecting with, the zodiacal directions of "cosmic" space. (With the exception of Pluto, the orbits of the planets all run on one plane, or disk-like shape, called the ecliptic. Pluto veers by as much as 17 degrees from this plane.) The houses serve to place the planets and zodiacal signs in the *terrestrial* context of the place of one's birth (as a function of the time of birth). The principal directions defined by the astrological houses are up, down, east and west. Likewise the four cardinal points of the circle of the houses of the birth chart refer to the midheaven, the nadir, the eastern horizon and the western horizon. Opposite to normal maps, the left-hand horizontal line in every natal chart represents the eastern horizon at birth, while the right-hand horizontal represents the western horizon.

The wheel of the houses in the natal chart orients the place and time of one's birth to the solar system and the zodiac. As the "frame" or initial structure, the wheel of houses is the one constant of every natal chart. In every chart, that is, the 1st house begins with the left-hand horizontal line (representing the eastern horizon at birth)** and extends 30 degrees downward, whence the 2nd house begins, and so forth. The planets and the zodiac may overlay on this wheel in any one of an infinite number of ways, according to the unique pattern of the solar system as "captured" at the individual moment of birth.

---

* Although the astrological houses are not interpreted extensively in Chapter 9, their influences are arguably almost as great as those of the planets and signs. Explication of the houses is minimal because their meanings correlate so closely with the meanings of the signs.

** In every natal chart, the wheel of the houses works as a 24-hour clock with the sun acting as the hour-hand pointing to the general time of birth. For example, all people born at "true" sunrise (as if the sun were rising over a flat horizon) will find the symbol of the sun, in their natal charts, straddling the left-hand horizontal line. This will be the case no matter what sign the sun was in.

FIGURE 3
THE HOUSES OF THE NATAL CHART

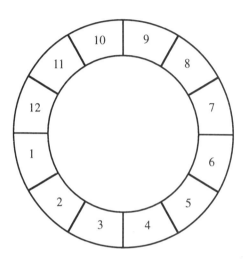

The wheel of astrological houses indicates a set of universal directions in human experience. Akin to the signs, the houses each represent a constellation of closely related capacities of experience. Each house designates one area of the spectrum of life experience. *Planets positioned in a given house at birth signify that the individual will be drawn to experiences designated by that house.* The type of experience indicated by each house corresponds in principle to the meanings indicated by the sign of the same number.

The realm of life experience, of course, is not the exclusive domain of the houses. The planets, and more especially the zodiacal signs, can be interpreted in terms of experience, and it is exceedingly difficult to define clearly how sign influences differ from house influences on this account. (Interestingly, both the signs and the houses refer to *directions in space*; the former to cosmic space, the latter to terrestrial space.) It would be convenient if the influences of the signs translated solely in terms of instinctive predispositions, and the houses solely in terms of the

realm of experience, but this is not so. Sign influences may translate into dimensions of experience, and house influences into
dimensions of behavior and personality. When it comes to differ-
entiating between these different genres of influence, it can often
seem arbitrary to make distinctions between behavior (or personality) and experience, or between instincts and experience.
Nonetheless, these two genres of influence do differ from one
another, albeit in subtle ways, and on the whole it is useful to
think of house influences primarily in terms of experience, and
sign influences, again, primarily in terms of instincts and predispositions.

The influences indicated by houses refer to dimensions of
experience in which consciousness of meaning to oneself is, or
becomes, central. In representing areas of experience which
become consciously meaningful, houses refer to areas of life
experience in which we feel challenged to *fulfill* ourselves.

In contrast, the signs represent inherent powers that are experienced and expressed more intuitively. Whereas house influences serve to generate consciousness of the internal meaning of
experience, zodiacal influences in a sense inform the process of
consciousness itself, "coloring" consciousness according to the
qualities of the inherent powers generated. At the same time, the
inherent powers indicated by sign influences are powers to be
developed. We are *challenged to develop* the instinctive powers
indicated by the signs so as to more effectively manifest and
express ourselves.

Altogether, *the sign placement of a given planet can be seen
in terms of powers to be developed, and as means of fulfilling the
experiential potentials represented by the house placement of
that planet.*

Such distinctions being made, the correspondence between a
given sign and the house of the same number translates into
considerable overlapping of meaning, quality of experience and
observed character of expression. The instinctive powers indicated by a given sign are not only powers of behavior, they are
powers of experience, and cannot be finally separated from experiences indicated by the house of the same number. The meanings of signs and houses are overlays of one another, comprising
different but liberally intersecting dimensions of the same principle. And then of course, the planet associated with each principle

comprises a third fundamental dimension of influence and meaning. Commerce among these dimensions is ubiquitous, meaning that almost any given observed manifestation may be a function of influences of either the sign, the house or the planet of a given principle.

SYMBOLISM AND PHILOSOPHY

The symbols of astrology are imbued with not only psychological but philosophical meaning. In codifying the motivations, powers and capacities inherent in human nature, astrological symbolism delineates a spectrum of philosophical principles and values intrinsic to every action, point of view, argument, attitude and experience there is in life. Astrology's symbolic system serves to organize and juxtapose meaning in terms of principles that apply to collective as much as to individual experience.

FIGURE 4
ELEMENTAL TRIPLICITIES

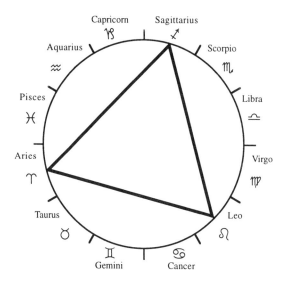

Fire Signs

FIGURE 4 (CON'T)
ELEMENTAL TRIPLICITIES

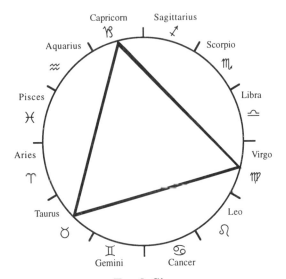

Earth Signs

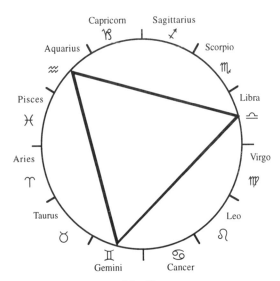

Air Signs

FIGURE 4 (CON'T)
ELEMENTAL TRIPLICITIES

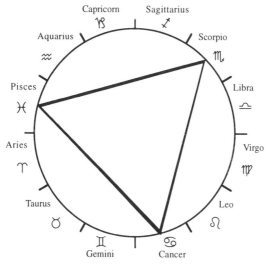

Water Signs

To illustrate how this symbolic system organizes meaning, note that each trio of signs identified in terms of the same element forms an equilateral triangle. (See Figure 4.) These relationships of triangularity are themselves meaningful. Consider for example the controversy over abortion that continues to rage in the United States. The key positions taken by the opponents in this debate devolve to three different astrological principles, those symbolized by the water signs Cancer, Scorpio and Pisces.

Simplifying the positions taken, the pro-choicers base their arguments primarily on the right to *privacy,* which is primarily a Cancerian value. They also argue on behalf of a women's *right to control* her own reproductive choices, which is philosophically a Scorpionic position. On the other side, the pro-life camp bases its arguments primarily on *moral* grounds, which happens also to be a primary value indicated by Scorpio. Yet pro-lifers further appeal to *religious* values regarding the sanctity of human life—centrally a Piscean point of view. The upshot here is that while the pro-choicers lay sole claim to values deriving from Cancer, and pro-lifers lay sole claim to values deriving from Pisces, *both* sides lay claim to the middle ground of Scorpio values. Appropriately enough, it is the moral rights and wrongs symbolized by Scorpio—a sign of competition and contest—that are most hotly contested.

Regarding the triangular relationship of the astrological principles symbolized, the implication is that the antagonists go round and round about abortion, never directly addressing key philosophical positions assumed by the other side. The symbolism of triangular vectors implies that positions adopted by each side (those indicated here by Cancer and Pisces) do not intrinsically confront or oppose one another.

Taking this analysis a step further, it can be said that pro-choicers effectively cede the whole Piscean principle to their opponents. While pro-lifers invoke religion to back up their morality, that is, the pro-choice camp has not attempted to claim any basic religious or spiritual values for its own. Yet this need not be the case. If for instance one believes in a transcendent soul, then the soul must at some time enter the physical body. And if the fetus does not yet "contain" a soul, the act of abortion does not truly amount to the taking of a human life. Thus the pro-choice camp could invoke a spiritually based (and fundamentally Piscean) argument that would give it a third philosophical leg to stand on. (Of course, the adoption of this type of viewpoint would be liable to generate battles on theological grounds, as the Catholic religion holds a one soul-one life position, wherein souls are spun out of thin air at conception, and then go up or down for good after death.)

For an illustration of arguments that are symbolically opposed to one another as represented in the astrological system, consider the classic liberal-conservative argument about the proper role of government. While liberals argue that government should play a strong and substantial role in the affairs of a country—a Capricornian orientation—conservatives promote private and capitalistic interests—a fundamentally Cancerian orientation.* (See

---

* These astrological poles are liable to be politically reversed when other issues are assessed. For example, while liberals believe that government should *protect* and *support* those who are not in a position to help themselves—a

Figure 5.) Looking at this juxtaposition astrologically, it is apparent that neither side of the public-private debate is necessarily right or better. Both positions represent fundamental principles that ought to be honored in their own rights. As with all opposing forces, they should be balanced and dynamically integrated with one another.

FIGURE 5
THE QUADRUPLICITIES

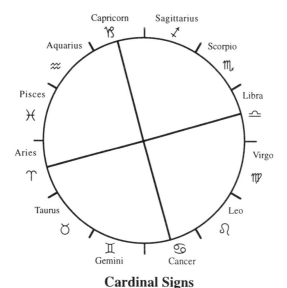

Cardinal Signs

Cancerian position—conservatives argue that every individual must take *responsibility* for bettering his own lot—a Capricorn position.

FIGURE 5 (CON'T)
THE QUADRUPLICITIES

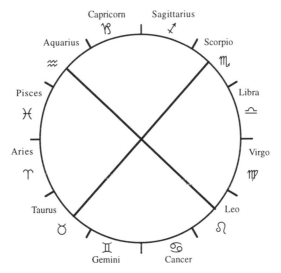

Fixed Signs

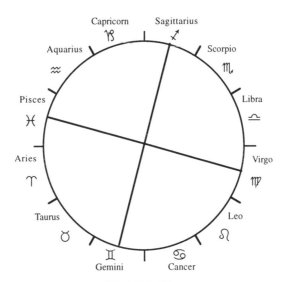

Mutable Signs

CHAPTER 9

THE TWELVE ASTROLOGICAL PRINCIPLES

♈ THE FIRST PRINCIPLE: ARIES / PLUTO

ARIES is the sign of the RAM and rules the HEAD.

Aries is the CARDINAL FIRE sign of SPRING, indicating powers of *creative individual initiative.*

The keywords of Aries are "I AM." The color associated with Aries is RED.

The First Principle

The first principle addresses the *power of one.* Both Aries and Pluto symbolize the power of individual initiative to effect change, to act independently, to create the model, to be the first. This principle emphasizes "self unto self": focus on self as free agent in the world. Accordingly, the first house indicates experiences centering on self-orientation, experiences that generate the perspective of being wholly, purely and unabashedly at the center of one's own universe.

The imagery of fire is central to both Aries and Pluto. Aside from Aries being a fire sign, this imagery is evident in Aries' color (red) and in its glyph, which symbolizes not only the horns of a ram but the upsurging of fiery intuition, the rushing of blood to the head in fiery impulse. Regarding Pluto, the symbolism of fire emerges in connection with atomic energy: the underground fire of nuclear fission. Pluto symbolizes the potential for psychological *transformation* through "purification by fire."

Highlight/Sidelight: Being the first sign of the zodiac, Aries is sometimes considered to indicate the most primitive, the crudest of the lot. And it is perhaps true that Aries characters are capable of being exceptionally crude, primitive and primal. But as is the case with all zodiacal influences, the instincts represented by Aries can be developed and expressed at every evolutionary level.* Hence the lamb is as valid a symbol of Aries as the ram, and along with more crude ram-like instincts such as head-butting, Aries signifies lamb-like capacities for purity of spirit, sweet innocence and supreme self-sacrifice. Jesus has been called the "Lamb of God," and he may as well have been a sun-sign Aries, combining as he apparently did the classic Aries traits of leadership, primal intuition and lamb-like purity. The lamb represents a power of innocent trueness-to-self that is totally impervious to outer conditions. Similarly Aries symbolizes the innocence, purity and clear-headed intuition of the angel.

♈ Aries 🐏

"Ram" refers to "striking force," and the sign of the ram—the first sign of spring—symbolizes the impelling, irresistible impulses that "spring" forth within an individual in the form of new ideas, first impressions, and fresh inspirations. Just as the ram is known for its headstrong, impulsive rushes, Aries represents the power of "ramming" head-first into new projects, projecting self headstrong into whatever seizes interest. Aries symbolizes the ram-like *power of impulse,* and in connection with the symbolism of the number one indicates instincts for *independence* and *self-reliance.*

Aries' rulership of the head complements the symbolism of the ram in indicating powers of independent thought and action. As in the phrase, "using your head," Aries represents the power of thinking for yourself, and as the fire sign of spring it symbolizes the intuitive and creative powers that are fundamental to

---

* In a related tradition, the distance of a planet from the earth is taken as a measure of depth or breadth of psychological potential, Reckoning by this type of thinking, planets such as Mercury, Venus and the moon indicate potentials of (relatively limited) personal and social nature, while the outermost planets indicate potentials of both transpersonal and depth realms.

Curiously, this mode of interpretation results in Pluto—Aries' planet—indicating the deepest and most transcendent of potentials.

leadership. The "head" of a group or organization is its leader, and Aries indicates the predisposition to take your own lead, to "head" out in new directions, to take charge, to pioneer. The "heady" symbolism of Aries likewise indicates the power of unabashed independence in individual perspective, the predisposition to speak from and act on one's point of view with fresh, unreflecting, fiery boldness.

The keywords of Aries, "I Am," symbolize the eternal being and becoming of self, the irrepressible power of being whatever and whoever you are, even in the extreme. Relating to the ram's impetuous, headstrong nature, the "I Am" represents powers of being intuitively *self-directed.* In connection with the first house, Aries refers to experiences and activities of self-directed nature, including yoga, solo dancing, and activities such as river rafting and rock climbing that demand major individual initiative. As the first sign, Aries symbolizes the power of the solo, and indicates a predisposition to solitary activities.

The Arian power of intuitive self-direction naturally translates into the trait of self-absorption, which means that the popular characterization of Aries personalities as self-absorbed can be accurate without being pejorative. Aries indicates the predisposition to become totally absorbed in—or seized by—impulses to thought or activity in which the self and the moment become one. It is only when the power of impulse is channeled into imposing self *on* the moment that self-absorption can become obnoxious.

Aries' color, red, is the first color of the visible spectrum, and represents the beginning of any new cycle. Aries represents the inspiration of the first and the new, the power of *self-projection* and self-propulsion into new activities and new beginnings. Relating to the symbolism of being the cardinal fire sign of spring, Aries indicates the power of the individual to generate *spirit* in *action.*

In Greek mythology, the Arian spirit of action imbues the character of Jason, and actually the whole adventure of Jason and the Golden Fleece is charged with archetypal Aries symbolism. In this myth the ram's fleece represents Jason's spiritual birthright, and Jason's mission to retrieve it begins with the aura of a sacred spiritual quest. But while Jason ultimately succeeds in gaining the fleece, he ironically rejects the spiritual identity that the fleece symbolizes. Making a mockery of his spiritual quest, he makes ruin of many lives, his own included.

Jason's self-destruction is one of the greatest tragedies in the entire Greek lexicon because in betraying his spiritual identity, he also betrays the love of Medea. With her powerful magic, Medea makes possible the success of his quest, and proves herself to be his true love and soul partner. Yet Jason abandons Medea and their two children for a new woman, newfound power and new adventure. Jason's thirst for action, adventure and danger are all classic Aries traits; but these very traits serve to blind Jason from the more profound challenges that confront him. For while he is ever ready to run off to conquer new worlds—and new women—he does not realize the importance of being true to Medea, who represents the deeper callings of his heart. Jason must conquer the split between his heart and his head, between this deeper spiritual and intuitive powers—represented by the ram's fleece—and the insistent impulses of his ego, impulses of the head. In modern life, Aries characters are often challenged to throw off not only impulses of egotistical nature, but of intellectual and/or rationalistic *conditioning* so as to respond to deeper dimensions of spirit and intuition.

The story of Jason is filled with instances of the most vile treachery and betrayal among family members. These episodes culminate in Medea, taking her cue from Jason, wreaking a particularly cruel and self-destructive revenge.* Strangely however, implicit in much of this treachery are basic vital urges of the protagonists to *lead their own lives*. Indeed throughout this myth, there is a motif expressing the urgent need to cut oneself off from family, and to declare independence by whatever means available, simply to become free to be oneself. Yet within this Aries theme of *individuation* are constant reminders of how individualistic urges can degenerate into a completely destructive mentality. So perhaps the ultimate challenge for the Aries character symbolized here is: Lead your own life without betraying or rejecting others—especially those who truly love you.

---

* Using her two sons—both sired by Jason—as accomplices, Medea murders Jason's new bride. Seeing no way to save her boys from retribution, she then kills her sons.

Aries instincts are expressed in the Archetypes of the Leader, the Impressionist, the Figurehead, the Individualist, the Single Voice, the Libertarian, the Rock Climber/Winter Camper/Outward Bounder, the Renegade, the Sparkplug, the Primal, the First, the Zealot, the Upstart, the Fool (jumping off the cliff—Tarot), the Cherub, the Angel, the Solo, the Solo Adventurer, the Independent, the Instigator, the New Project, the Impulse of the Moment, the Breath of Fire.

Famous People born with the sun in Aries include Catherine de Medici, Wernher von Braun, Wilhelm Reich, Vincent Van Gogh, Isak Dinesen *(Out of Africa),* Jane Goodall, Harry Houdini, Marcel Marceau, Charlie Chaplin, Robert Frost, Pat Robertson, Lyndon Larouche, Jerry Brown, Eugene McCarthy, Thomas Jefferson, Cesar Chavez, Sandra Day O'Connor, David Letterman, Howard Cossell, Camille Paglia, Leonard Nimoy, Baba Ram Dass (Harvard professor, LSD pioneer), Kareem Abdul-Jabbar, Pete Rose, Hugh Hefner, Francis Ford Coppola and Elton John.

In Personality, Aries indicates predispositions to being adamant, direct, fresh, butch, primal, impertinent, impetuous, bold, impish, brash, unabashed, single-minded, impatient, insistent, irrepressible, independent, solitary, hard-headed, self-reliant, self-absorbed, inwardly turned and self-directed. On the negative side Aries indicates capacities for being imperious, impervious, egotistical, opaque, combative, oblivious/blind to the obvious, blunt, obnoxious, blatant, rash, abrasive, bumptious, explosive, extremist, self-imposing, arbitrary—and self-absorbed.

♀ Pluto ♀

The smallest and most distant known planet of the solar system, Pluto was named after the god of the underworld, and symbolizes a motivation that emanates from the deepest hidden depths. Yet it also represents a potential of immense power, well symbolized by the form of energy that was beginning to explode in the minds of scientists at the time—1936—the planet was discovered: atomic energy.*

Pluto symbolizes a motivation of the nature of nuclear fission. Metaphorically it symbolizes a tiny nuclear reactor burning away at the deepest level of being that fissions with irrepressible and potentially uncontrollable intensity. Pluto symbolizes a fissioning inner fire that, when uncontained, can turn into the most intense and inexplicable of obsessions, irrational impulses, unquenchable compulsions and violence. In its most negative expression, the Plutonian force represents the potential for blindly chaotic, destructive and self-destructive urges. Pluto indicates the archetype of the burning obsession.

Within the same nuclear metaphor, however, Pluto represents a fissioning fire that, *when contained,* fuels a dynamo of individual power. Like Aries, Pluto's atomic symbolism pertains to the number one: the atom as indivisible entity. Much as the explosion of the atomic bomb signaled the atomization of society—the beginning of an era when, for the first time in human history, no longer did the bonds of family, community, or tradition hold sway over the individual—Pluto symbolizes the potential for the individual to become the autonomous, atomic unit of society. It represents an atomic fire in each of us that impels us to do or to be that which ours and ours alone to do and to be.

Pluto symbolizes the motivation for *depth transformation,* where the molten energy at the core of self can become channeled to powerfully positive individuated purposes. The natural process of creating diamonds, the gem traditionally associated with Aries, is a metaphor for this psychological process: Much as the intense heat and pressure within the Earth work to transform coal into diamonds, Pluto, the god of the Underworld, symbolizes the deep internal tumult, the fiery inner purgatory, through which each of us is progressively *purified* and transformed from a lump of coal—the dross of self—into the diamond crystal of individuated selfhood. The fissioning of Pluto refers to a kind of

---

* The symbolism of two of the three outermost planets of the solar system centers on the temporal connection between the discovery of the planet and the collective coming-to-consciousness of a new form of energy. The other connection ties the discovery of Uranus to the first breakthroughs involving electrical energy. See Principle 11.

self-immolation that occurs at the core of being, wherein intense experiences and extreme conditions both outside and within work both to destroy and create. In this creative-destructive aspect, the symbolism of Pluto relates to the Hindu god Shiva, who is known as Destroyer as well as Creator. Pluto indicates potentials for depth *catharsis,* and for burning away what is old.

Pluto symbolizes the *daimon* (or daemon), a cross between the irrational *demon* spirit and the *diamond* crystal of selfhood. The daimon as represented by Pluto is the divine yet also *irrational spirit* within us. It is a spirit whose irrationality can, as with atomic energy, be channeled as much to creative as to destructive purposes. In positive development, this daimon, this irrational spirit, fuels the individuational process. As the irrational spirit symbolized by Pluto is purified, its diamond fire can become totally creative.

On a more mundane level, Pluto represents a motivation for the high-energy fissioning that develops in any highly concentrated human environment, especially in cities. It represents the potential for urban individualism, the intense, highly charged and in ways highly individualized life that urban environments engender. Another Plutonian/urban potential is the phenomenon of "mass energy." Just as atomic fission depends upon the presence of a critical mass, Pluto represents the potential for generating intense and unpredictable energy in people densely concentrated in cities, crowds and other mass situations. It likewise symbolizes the potential for explosive mass movements, spontaneous mass actions, the wildfire spread of incendiary ideas, riots and anarchy. Pluto indicates the potential to channel mass energy into fanatic and unitary causes according to some sweeping new idea, such as in Nazism or the Cultural Revolution in 1960s China. It signifies the capacity for internal psychological chaos and extremism, for *inner turmoil,* and for deeply disturbed modes of ideation.

As god of the underworld, Pluto represents dimensions of being that are unseen, hidden and deep: esoteric. In connection with the symbolism of the number one, it symbolizes intense individual identification with some entity, archetype, realm or idea. It symbolizes the potential for spontaneously generating fiery internal *ideation,* for intense individual concentration, and for *pioneering* new, esoteric and/or hidden domains. Symbolizing the deepest, innermost psychological core, it indicates the drive to delve into the deepest of psychological realms. Similar to Aries, it represents the motivation for *autonomy,* for unitary and solitary focus; and like Aries it indicates a motivation that can be characterized by positive self-absorption, the zeal for discovery, and by irrepressible spirit.

Plutonian motivations are expressed in the Character or Image of Burning Intense Concentration, Inner Turbulence and Turmoil, the Irrational Spirit, the Esoteric Idea, the Inspiring Spirit, the Extremist, the Fanatic, the Possessed, the Obsessed, the Compulsive, the Creatively Obsessed, the Madman, the Genius, the Innermost Core, the Loner, the Pioneer, the Creative Dynamo, the Powerful Catharsis.

Pluto's placement by house in the natal chart indicates the area of experience where you might undergo deepest inner tumult in a long-term process of purification and transformation; where you bring chaos into your life in order to find your individual *daimon,* your deepest individual essences; where you are most willing to dive into major new experiences; where you seek the deepest sense of autonomy; and where your most profound potentials for individuation lie.

First House

Planets in Aries' first house of the natal chart draw you to experiences of an individual and solitary nature; activities that are individual-centered (e.g., art, music, surfing); to activities that promote inner body awareness (meditation, yoga, dance); to experiences that challenge you to generate an individual point of view and individual outlook on life; strong individual impulses and identifications; promotion and self-promotion; the urgency of the moment. (Planets in Aries and/or Pluto emphasized by aspect in the natal chart may effect similar experiences.)

THE SECOND PRINCIPLE: TAURUS / EARTH

TAURUS, the second sign of the zodiac, is the sign of the BULL. Taurus rules the NECK.

Taurus is the FIXED EARTH sign of SPRING, indicating powers of *intuitive and sustaining practicality.*

The keywords of Taurus are "I HAVE." The color associated with Taurus is RED-ORANGE.

The Second Principle

The bull is an agricultural animal, and symbolizes powers of *earthy, agricultural* and *organic* nature. The second principle addresses all that grows from Mother Earth, all that is *native, indigenous* and *inherent.*

In connection with the productive potentials of the Earth, Taurus indicates *powers of material sustainment.* The bull is a prime *stock* animal, and this principle indicates powers of ownership and sustainment pertaining to the cultivation of different kinds of stock. It indicates the power of owning livestock, stock in trade, stocks of goods for supply, and stock exchanged on the financial markets. Just as a "bull market" signifies the growth of stock value, Taurus indicates the power of growing material value. Similarly this principle refers to the life-sustaining values of genetic stock, the root stock of family lineage and the stock of one's body.

In tandem with the second house, Taurus indicates experiences of *inheritance:* inherited wealth—or poverty—inherited land and resources, inherited traditions, traits, liabilities and strengths.

This principle signifies the *importance of place,* connection to the land, rootedness, growing roots and rooting. (Go native team.) It refers to the roots of one's being, to heritage, ancestry and *origins.* It indicates the principle of life as a process of organic growth and development rooted in the past, a process in which the future and the present as organic functions of the past. Thus it symbolizes the *historical* process. As a sign of agriculture, Taurus represents all organic processes, and casts both collective and individual life in the context of organic unfoldment.

Highlight/Sidelight: Taurus symbolizes steady rhythms of dialectic alternation between complementary phases of organic cycles: summer and winter, waking and sleeping, accumulation and depletion, exertion and rest. Key among the cycles indicated here is that of *growth* and *stabilization*. Much as the spring and summer months are when plant and animal life begin their yearly cycle of growth, followed by hibernation and dormancy through the fall and winter, Taurus represents the instinct for pushing into phases of new growth and development, followed by the pull to stabilize, consolidate and habituate the benefits of the growth achieved. It is when habituation becomes the norm—and the eternal need for new growth lost sight of—that the Taurean character stagnates. Conversely, the vital Taurean possesses an uncanny instinct for intuiting what is needed for new growth.

♉ Taurus

The bull is an archetype of raw organic power, and in its rulership of the neck Taurus symbolizes the power of "yoking" metabolic energies to the industry of life sustainment and the "plowing in" of work and resources to productive yield. Taurus represents instincts for *industry, productivity* and *investment.*

As an agricultural animal, the bull symbolizes powers of *cultivation* and *culturing.* Taurus represents the power to cultivate all *individual resources* of both non-material and material nature. Similarly it indicates the power to grow, through sustained effort, all that is one's own: one's profession, means of making a living, household, farm and, not least, one's children. Related to culturing-as-growing, Taurus indicates the instinct for *enrichment,* for enriching culturally, intellectually and materially.

As a spring sign, Taurus signifies the ability to become intuitively *attuned* to all process of growth and development, and likewise attuned to all organic processes. Taurean processes that can be intuited include the weather, body metabolism, child development, animal development, ball games, long-term projects and gardens. Signifying an instinctive sense of the organic unfolding of life processes, Taurus indicates a wealth and depth of intuition.

As in the image of the contented cow grazing in the fields, Taurus symbolizes the capacity for pure integration into organic processes, for sheer *contentment* with vital rhythms, and for fertility. Symbolizing basic and habitual life processes, it indicates the predisposition to develop ingrained habits and deeply rooted patterns of procedure.

Inasmuch as Taurean instincts for organic development can be frustrated, Taurus symbolizes the capacity for *rage*—the raging bull. As symbolized by another Taurean namesake, the bulldozer, this sign represents the power of bringing tremendous intuitive energy to bear in taking a determined course of action or thought. It signifies a predisposition for entrenched determination that can translate into cussed stubbornness, but also into tremendous *persistence.* Taurus indicates the intuitive and sustaining power of *building.*

The prodigious dimensions of the bull's body symbolize the power for robust development, and Taurus represents the power of producing richness, abundance, profusion, wealth, plenty and ample supply. It indicates the instincts to own, hold and accumulate resources in storekeeping, supplying and shopping. (Hence Taurus represents the proverbial "shopping instincts.") In connection with the fruits of labor and production, Taurus symbolizes capacities for experiencing luxury, material pleasure, *leisure,* and "luxuriating in the goods."

The bull's yoke symbolizes archetypes of bondage and slavery. Taurus indicates the capacity to be yoked or chained to a job, to unyielding circumstances, a life style, a habit, and/or a relationship.

In mythology, the Greek goddess Aphrodite evokes a number of classic Taurean themes. For example, Aphrodite was famous for her natural *endowments,* and Taurus signifies powers born of natural endowment. At the sight of Aphrodite, "the winds flee before her and the storm clouds; sweet flowers embroider the earth; the waves of the sea laugh."[58] As thus described, Aphrodite was a classic *force of nature* and symbolizes the Taurean power of *being* a force of nature. Aphrodite further symbolizes Taurean predispositions for *sensuousness,* for indulging in earthy pleasures, and for *polymorphous perversity.*

Much of the mythology of Aphrodite centers on her marriage to Hephaestus, the lame and ugly god of the forge. Powerful about the neck and shoulders, Hephaestus was himself a Taurean figure, though in ways far different from Aphrodite. Hephaestus became misshapen by being thrown—twice—from Mt. Olympus to the Earth. Yet Hephaestus overcame his disfigurements and difficulties not only to become the indispensable "divine smith," but to win the love of beautiful Aphrodite. The Taurean moral in this story is that it's not what you're given, but the challenge of *how you develop it;* what you do with it, what you *make* of it. The complex relationship between sublime beauty and earthly ugliness conveyed in the mythic marriage of Aphrodite and Hephaestus suggests the challenge to cultivate deep and vital strains of being.

Taurean instincts are expressed in the Archetypes of the Farmer, the Homesteader, the Stoic, the Developer, the Realtor, the Foundation, the Founder, the Producer, the Shopper, Churning It Out, the Storekeeper, the Owner, the Geologist, the Native, the Real McCoy, the Earth Mother, Salt of the Earth, Champion of the Native Land and the Native People, the Force of Nature, the Developmental Psychologist, the Historian, the Originator, the Original, the Crooner.

Famous People born with the sun in Taurus include Sigmund Freud, Dr. Benjamin Spock, T. Berry Brazelton, Karl Marx, Nikolai Lenin, Ho Chi Minh, Golda Meir, Malcolm X, Louis Farrakhan, John Muir, John James Audubon, Farley Mowat, Pete Seeger, Irving Berlin, Johannes Brahms, Peter Ilich Tchaikovsky, George Lucas, Frank Capra, Gary Cooper, Ella Fitzgerald, Bing Crosby, Perry Como, Barbra Streisand, Stevie Wonder, Judy Collins, Willie Nelson, Yogi Berra and Studs Terkel.

In Personality, Taurus indicates predispositions to being steadfast, steady, staunch, stolid, stable, stoic, determined, deliberate, habitual, enduring, persistent, productive, industrious, earth-wise, rooted, deeply intuitive, placid, churning, sensuous and original. On the negative side are indicated capacities for being stubborn, obstinate, bullheaded, intractable, unyielding, relentless, uncouth, bullyish, proprietary, possessive, envious, and for holding grudges.

⊕ The Earth ⊕

While the Earth is not considered to be an influence in astrology (we in effect *are* the Earth), the classic symbolism of the Earth nonetheless corresponds fully to the "fixed earth" sign of Taurus. "Mother Earth," the provider and sustainer of life, indicates potentials of fertility, organic growth and roots.

As with Taurus, the Earth refers to the land and the soil from which life springs, to profusion and abundance yielded by the Earth. It symbolizes the means and the substance we have by which to live and endure, the prolific, prodigious life-supporting natural resources of this third planet from the sun. In connection with Taurus, the Earth represents practical intuition and the motivation to keep your feet solidly on the ground.

Second House

Planets in Taurus' second house draw you to experiences of *finding place* in the world; sinking roots and slow growth; the land and inheritance; developing individual resources and means of making a living; the rhythms, manner and style of life that individual resources allow; deep intuitively based values and intuitive sensibilities; challenges to stand on and develop what is your own. (Planets in Taurus may effect similar experiences.)

♊ THE THIRD PRINCIPLE: GEMINI / THE ASTEROIDS

GEMINI is the sign of the TWINS. Gemini rules the LUNGS, SHOULDERS, ARMS and HANDS.

Gemini is the MUTABLE AIR sign of SPRING, indicating *adaptive* powers of *intuitive communication.*

The keywords of Gemini are "I THINK." Gemini is associated with the color ORANGE.

The Third Principle

While the traditional "ruler" of Gemini is Mercury, the asteroids arguably form a better symbolic companion to this sign. For inasmuch as Gemini evokes the image of the "split personality," the asteroids offer hundreds of possibilities: the makings of a *multiple* personality. Only kidding—partly: the third principle signifies *multiplicity, possibility* and *diversity.*

Gemini indicates the ability to respond to a given stimulus in diverse, random and multiple ways. It represents the power of possibility, the power of reacting to the immediate situation through whatever comes to mind, and the predisposition to *immediate association.* Ruling the hands, Gemini symbolizes the ability to respond to the *situation at hand.* Although the powers symbolized by Gemini can translate into a philosophy of *expedience*—life as moment-to-moment, adaptive responses to the present situation—it is also a Geminian instinct to *vivify* the here-and-now.

The third principle refers to phenomena of *juxtaposition* and *proximity.* The placing of A in close relation to B invites reaction, and the sign of the twins represents the power to react directly to the moment according to the juxtapositions and points of reference in the immediate environment, locality or present circumstance. It symbolizes powers of quick dialogue, repartee, shooting the breeze, small talk, short orders, brief communications and off-hand knowledge. The type of thought symbolized in Gemini's keywords—"I Think"—is that developed by juxtaposing and associating, of placing one thing in immediate relation to another. Although this type of thought can be superficial—Gemini does indicate a proneness to being vacuous and superficial—it can also be brilliant.

The third house and Gemini indicate relationship to the *near environment* through experiences of making *direct contact,* short trips and frequent communications. This principle signifies the capacity to take on the character of the local environment, and indicates potentials for provinciality and local color. It refers to the imprint of youth on the whole of life, and the tendency of early life experiences to color adult experience.

Highlight/Sidelight: Gemini indicates a penchant for reacting to circumstances by assuming one side of a story, switching to the opposite—and then back again. This oscillation between two sides or poles is often described in terms of flighty and mindless changeability, but it also pertains to becoming "of two minds" about core issues and experiences. The Geminian predisposition to identify with first one and then the other side of a given issue can coincide with the experience of both identifications being intense and even profound—for the time being. Thus the only thing that could be characterized as superficial about such bipolar identifications is their temporal nature. While oscillation between opposing poles may happen in a matter of seconds or minutes, moreover, the impulse to switch from one pole to the other can occur over the course of weeks, months, or even years.

♊ Gemini ⚎

The mutable air sign of spring, Gemini indicates the power of intuitively communicating and interacting with any situation. Gemini, like the chameleon, symbolizes the power to reflect or take on the colors of the immediate surroundings, and so to adapt. It represents predispositions to *versatility, quick-wittedness,* quick grasping of concepts, the aptitude for making contact and striking up relationship. It indicates instincts for *mental agility,* for facility in learning specific abilities and language. Signifying the power of acrobatics, Gemini indicates powers of mental gymnastics as well as physical dexterity. It indicates potentials for becoming adept at intellectual dialogue, poetic turns of phrase and sleight-of-hand tricks. Gemini is the sign of the juggler and indicates predispositions for doing different things at the same time; also for developing multiple abilities and diverse interests. It represents powers of communicating in quick rhythms, and for talking with one's hands: gesticulating.

The twins' mirror-imaging of one another is a trick of nature in which two characters are indelibly *identified* with each other, and Gemini symbolizes the power of identification. As the confusing sight of twins suggests, however, Gemini also represents the capacity for making mistakes in identification. Such mistakes are a primary source of *comedy,* and Gemini symbolizes the comic power of all mix-ups, double-takes, tricks, gimmicks, jokes, pranks, funny situations and zany possibilities that result from mistaking one thing for another. A classic expression of the comic possibilities arising from mix-ups in identification is Shakespeare's *The Comedy of Errors,* which plays on the mutual misidentification of two sets of twins.

On the other hand, there are many situations in life where the phenomenon of I-thought-it-was-this-but-it-was-really-that is not at all funny, and Gemini indicates the capacity for the real-life *confusion* that results from mistaking one thing for another. It represents the capacity for confusion about what to do in one's immediate life situation, as well as the maddening predilection for the left hand to forget, overlook or cross up what the right hand just did.

The twins are *reflections* of each other in the sense that images are reflected in a mirror, and Gemini represents "reflective instincts" of *imitating,* mimicking, miming, copying, duplicating, and repeating. It indicates the power to *learn by imitation and example.* With many possible "angles of reflection," further, Gemini represents instincts for responding to tangents, take-offs, distractions and momentary diversions.

Gemini's twins, Castor and Pollux, represent an archetype of all things youthful, and Gemini symbolizes youthful predispositions to *fascination, liveliness,* distraction, short attention span, restlessness, changeability and *curiosity.* It indicates the eminently youthful instinct for *kidding,* and the tendency to identify throughout life with both the environment and experiences of youth—to experience life like a kid. The sign of the twins represents the power to respond to friends as kin to oneself, to imitate the ways of siblings and others, and to look to siblings and such figures as examples.

Archetypally, the juxtaposition of the twins symbolizes the experience of the *alter ego*. In resembling one another so completely, the impetus for twins to *differentiate* themselves from each other is all the more important. Faced with the superficial reflection of oneself, the instinctive inclination of the twin character is to take the opposite tack, to think, "If you are this then I am that, and if you are that then I will be the other." Yet in this act of polarizing, only about half the world can be identified as one's own, and life inevitably leads to confrontation what has been pushed away as not-self. The urge to create *alter ego* experiences applies to all sibling-type relationships.

Two resolutions of the *alter ego* experience are suggested in different versions of the myth of Castor and Pollux. In the most well known version, Castor dies, but Zeus allows each twin to share the other's fate. Hence they both live "Half the time beneath the earth and half/Within the golden homes of heaven."[59] In a second version, the twins also dwell in twin places, heaven and Earth; but they are never in each other's company, for while one is spending his time in heaven, the other is on Earth, and vice versa. In different ways, both versions represent the challenge to be able to walk in the other's shoes, to identify with the other's point of view, to experience the other's experience.

An entirely different Gemini archetype is that of the *nature spirit*. Gemini signifies the urge to get close to nature, and by doing so to become *refreshed*.

Gemini instincts are expressed in the Archetypes of the Juggler, the Poet/Lyricist, the Acrobat, the Comic, the Clown, the Chameleon, the Brother/Sister, the Evil Twin, the Alter Ego, the Kid, the Johnny-on-the-Spot, the Wit, the Speaker/Orator, the Clever Intellectual, the Trickster, the Nemesis, the Mimic, the Nature Spirit/Nature Boy, the Dits.

Famous People born with the sun in Gemini include Paul Gauguin, M.C. Escher, Walt Whitman, Allen Ginsberg, Cole Porter, Benny Goodman, Bob Dylan, Paul McCartney, Marilyn Monroe, Judy Garland, Jacques Cousteau, Rachel Carson, Marian Wright Edelman, Johnny Weissmuller, John Wayne, Clint Eastwood, Arthur Conan-Doyle, Ian Fleming, Mario Cuomo,

John F. Kennedy, Henry Kissinger, Newt Gingrich, F. Lee Bailey, George Bush, Bob Hope, Gene Wilder, Dana Carvey, Mel Blanc (voice of original Loony Tunes characters), Michael J. Fox and Steffi Graf.

In Personality, Gemini indicates predispositions for being voluble, quick to dialogue, dexterous, imitative, versatile, clever, curious, inquisitive, adept, quick-thinking, animated, alert, lively, restless, facile, glib, nimble and wacky. On the negative side, it indicates capacities for being dimwitted, scattered, superficial, shortsighted, vacuous, flighty, inconsistent, fickle and mindless.

The Asteroids

The Asteroid Belt occupies an orbital span between Mars and Jupiter that conforms to a rough astronomical/mathematical pattern, called Bode's Law, which predicts planetary orbits in terms of their proportional distances from the sun.

The multiplicity of the asteroids symbolizes the potential to play on any situation, possibility, opportunity or gambit at hand in terms of a host of possible responses: To any stimulus, there is an unlimited *variety* of potential responses. Representing the universe of possibility, the asteroids symbolize potentials for *serendipity, chance* and *coincidence*.

The largest asteroids have drawn enormous attention in recent years as astrological forces in their own rights. In particular, Ceres, Pallas Athena, Juno and Vesta—all named after major goddesses in the Greco-Roman pantheon—are seen to correspond to significant motivations in human life. As the third principle relates not only to what is immediate but also *specific*, these asteroids symbolize relatively specific roles, voices, and potentials of experience. The influences of the four most prominent asteroids are interpreted in Appendix 2, and the symbolic correspondence of Gemini and the asteroids is further discussed in Appendix 4.

Third House

Planets in Gemini's third house of the natal chart draw you to experiences of sibling relationships; challenges of adapting to and *facilitating* your immediate life situation; convenience and coping with the factors of life at hand; teaching of younger children and teenagers; short trips; the special interests, diversions and intrigues of *locality;* familiarity, frequent contact with and relation to the near environment; being in touch with a variety of people; journalism; advertising; developing specific abilities, specific skills and specific forms of knowledge. (Planets in Gemini may effect similar experiences.)

THE FOURTH PRINCIPLE: CANCER / THE MOON

CANCER is the sign of the CRAB. Cancer rules the BREASTS and the STOMACH.

Cancer is the CARDINAL WATER sign of SUMMER, indicating powers of *personal emotional initiative*.

The keywords of Cancer are "I FEEL." The color associated with Cancer is YELLOW-ORANGE.

The Fourth Principle

The moon, Cancer and the fourth house center on the motivation for basic *well-being,* and Cancer can be interpreted in terms of an "instinct for well-being." Similarly a fundamental Cancerian quest is to *feel good.* It has been suggested that the word "good" derives from the root meaning "to hold fast." Whether this derivation is true or not, it gets to one root of this principle: Hold fast to what feels good. The idea of holding fast reflects the crab's symbolism of *tenaciousness.* It also relates to Cancer's traditional association with the conservative's attitude: Hold onto what you've got. The moon and Cancer indicate the motivation to hold onto home, parents/children, the motherland, traditions, memories and friends.

Within the crab's hard outer shell are its soft insides, and this principle refers to the softer affairs of intimacy and domestic life. As the crab's shell signifies the home, Cancer symbolizes home-oriented instincts for privacy, *creature comforts* and fulfilling basic *domestic needs.*

Concerning the fulfillment of basic needs of hunger, thirst, caring and unconditional love, this principle refers to the power of *positive reinforcement*, and so pertains to principles of Behaviorism. This principle indicates motivations of *self-interest* and *personal incentive,* and so symbolizes philosophical underpinnings of private enterprise and capitalism.

Highlight/Sidelight: Psychologically, it is useful to think of the fourth principle as resting on four basic potentials: feelings, caring, self-interest and self-esteem. While all four potentials are more or less equally vital, it often happens that one or another is expressed at the expense of others. For example, just as there is a vivid hard-soft dichotomy in the symbolism of the crab's shell in relation to its insides, this principle suggests a dichotomy between the extremes of hard, self-interested selfishness on the one hand, and soft blubbery feelings on the other. Healthy expression requires all four potentials to be developed on a roughly equal basis.

 Cancer

Cancer's keywords, "I Feel," indicate powers of feeling that, while most marked in children, do not end with childhood. In ruling the stomach, Cancer indicates the power of such stomach-centered feelings as comfort, goodness, security, satiety and well-being. By the same token, it represents the capacity for such "bad" feelings as *dis*comfort, nausea, anxiety and upset. In its never-ending registering of the ebb and flow of feelings, the stomach is the most sensitive organ of the body, and Cancer indicates the power of *sensitivity* to all feelings. It indicates predispositions to be sensitive not only to your own feelings but to the feelings of others; to nuances of feeling; to impressions and intonations of feelings; to the tints and shades of feeling that are highlighted in artistic sensibilities. It indicates the predilection to sensitive experiences of quietude, calmness and gentility. Cancer further signifies the predisposition to bring feelings to whatever you touch, to *personalize,* and to take things personally. It represents the power to imbue every experience with feeling, and to generate feelings in connection with even the most seemingly impersonal or formal of situations. And it signifies the predisposition to experience intensely *any* sort of feelings the moment may bring, thus indicating the fundamental power of *subjectivity.*

In ruling the breasts along with the stomach, Cancer is associated with the two parts of the body most directly involved with food and nourishment. Hence Cancer represents food-related powers including those of growing, cooking and loving food, and likewise indicates culinary instincts. As the cardinal water sign, Cancer symbolizes powers of emotional initiative in *feeding, nurturing, nourishing, caring* and *providing*. All these powers are intrinsic to the care of small children, and in connection with the moon's symbolism of mother, Cancer indicates both *maternal* and *parental* instincts. Sun-sign Cancerians are sometimes called "moon children," and Cancer indicates the power of caring not only for little children but also for the child in oneself. It signifies the power of the personal touch, the caring touch and the loving touch.

The crab's shell symbolizes instincts for protection and self-protection, for safety and security. When exaggerated in personality, these instincts can translate into traits of "withdrawing into your shell," presenting a "hard shell" to the world, and being cantankerous. The crab signifies the most basic instinct of self-interest: protect and take care of your own. Cancer represents the experienced need to provide both for oneself and the nucleus of one's family; and it indicates penchants to being wily, crafty and worrisome in meeting this need.

Homer's Achilles as portrayed in the *Iliad* is charged with Cancerian symbolism. Beyond Liz Greene's interpretation as cited in Chapter 3, Achilles symbolizes an archetype that begins with his emotional reaction to losing his favorite slave to Agamemnon. As a classic Cancerian, Achilles responds to Agamemnon's own Cancerian I-me-mine behavior by experiencing *hurt feelings*. Refusing to lead his Greek armies to battle, Achilles chooses instead to withdraw into his tent (*aka* his shell), where he plays his lyre and wallows in his feelings. Consequently his armies lose in battle, and eventually his beloved friend Patroclus, who has taken his place as leader, is killed. Thus Achilles suffers for his own selfishness. Yet Achilles could likely have prevented Patroclus' death by *forgiving* Agamemnon in the first place. As dramatized in this myth, confronting the need to forgive is a central Cancerian (and lunar) archetype.

A related Cancerian archetype is expressed in the phrase, "I found it, I feel it, it's good." This phrase refers to a motif involving deep feeling-based experiences that give rise to the sense of realizing some strong personal truth. Such experiences need not be sorrowful; they may involve experiencing something powerfully good, some source of goodness. Cancer represents the potential for deeply moving emotional experiences from which there arise bedrock *personal convictions.*

Cancerian instincts are expressed in the Archetypes of the Nurturer, the Cutie, the Sentimentalist, the Sensitive Artist/ Writer/Teacher, Dr. Feelgood, the Artist's Subjective World, the Artistic Feel, Good Vibes, the Softy, the Hard Shell, the Curmudgeon, the Patriot, the Capitalist, the Personal Odyssey, the Personal Crusade, the Personal Experience, the Source, My Private World, It's Mine.

Famous People born with the sun in Cancer include Rembrandt, Peter Paul Rubens, Marcel Proust, Marc Chagall, Ernest Hemingway, Hermann Hesse, Stephen Foster, John Paul Jones, Henry David Thoreau, George Sand, Helen Keller, Mary Baker Eddy, Ann Landers and Abigail van Buren (twins born July 4th), Neil Simon, Frederick Perls (founder of Gestalt Therapy), Stan Grof, John Bradshaw, Elisabeth Kübler-Ross, Thurgood Marshall, Gerald Ford, Bob Dole, Jack Kemp, Phil Gramm, H. Ross Perot, Sgt. Ron Kovic (author, *Born on the 4th of July*), Mike Tyson, Bill Cosby, Tom Hanks, Princess Diana and Ringo Starr.

In Personality, Cancer represents predispositions for being cute, sweet, sensitive, giving, loyal, alive to feelings, domestic, crafty, acquisitive, (self-)protective, tenacious, magnetic, impressionable, for having a subjective flair, for having strong feelings, and for gravitating to sources of good things. On the negative side are indicated capacities for being cranky, crabby, crybabyish, selfish (shellfish), greedy, closed, withdrawn, cantankerous, sourpuss, too subjective, limited by needs, importuning, timid, over-dependent, and mired in one's own little world.

☽ The Moon ☽

The symbolism of the moon, with its age-old suggestions of emotional and maternal aspects of life, encompasses all those things that we talk about in terms of our feelings. The moon symbolizes the child within us, that part of ourselves that in infancy is a bundle of needs for warmth, comfort, security and nourishment; that part of ourselves that develops into the motivation to care for ourselves, yet to care for others as well, whether that other is your own child, another person, your pet rock or a plant. It indicates basic potentials for *attachment* and loss; for intimacy, vulnerability, sensitivity and impressionability, for innocence and naiveté. It indicates the motivation of *incentive* to bring goodness, comfort and well-being unto oneself. Conversely, the moon symbolizes potentials for fear, pain, grief and numerous other negative feelings.

As associated with the mother, the moon symbolizes emotional potentials that originate with the mother-child relationship. These include *nurturing, reassurance, support, unconditional love, care, trust, dependence, loyalty* and kindred basic emotional bonds. It indicates potentials for familiarity and belonging, for devotion, hugging and cuddling, for giving attention and needing attention, and for self-esteem. It signifies the motivation, so magnified in children, to gravitate to sources of nourishment, well-being and good feelings. With its ever-changing phases, the moon represents the potential for changing *moods* and for "mooning" around. Lunar emotionality is suggested in the "moon-struck" daze of the smitten lover as much as in the "lunatic" behavior of the emotionally unbalanced.

As the Earth's only satellite, the moon represents the emotional gravity of our feelings. It symbolizes the sense that, when it comes to our feelings and needs, we are at the absolute center of the universe where everything seems to (or feels like it should!) revolve around us. It indicates the potential for being at the center of one's own subjective and private universe, and also the need for privacy.

Mythologically, the moon is identified with Diana (Artemis) who, while being "Lady of Wild Things" and "Protectress of Dewy Youth," was best known as goddess of the hunt. The moon represents the motivation for "the hunt of life," the emotional incentive for actively pursuing the fulfillment of needs: the pursuit of self-interest. Regarding this pursuit in the wider world, it indicates the potential for *personal appeal.*

Being "ruled by your feelings" is of course a lunar potential. This can mean, among other things, being driven by motivations for self-gratification and immediate gratification. But at the same time, the moon indicates the potential to be comfortably centered within one's feelings, and the ability to respond with sensitivity, caring and a feeling for the need of the moment. It signifies the motivation for developing personal tastes, affections and attachments that are grounded in feelings, and indicates the potential for attachment to pets and small animals.

Negative potentials represented by the moon include panic, desperation, phobia, hypersensitivity, isolation, helplessness, over-dependency, nervous eating, anorexia, anxiety and angst.

Lunar motivations are expressed in the Character or Image of the Homebody, the Cook, the Pal, the Good Friend, the Companion, the Parent, the Child, the Pet Owner, the Day Care Provider, the Artist/Writer's Sensibility, the Temperamentalist, the Emotionally Overwrought/Unstable, the Sensitive Type, the World of Feelings, the Child's World, the Moody Type, the Impressionable One, the Emotionally Volatile.

The moon's placement by house in the natal chart indicates the area of experience where you might be especially subject to old emotional patterns, to moods, and to "going through phases"; where it is most natural to engage your subjective faculties; where you must overcome emotional inertia or drag; where your feelings show; where you feel at home.

Fourth House

Planets in Cancer's fourth house of the natal chart draw you to experiences of home; private, personal and domestic life; deeply personal matters; close friends and bosom buddies; companionship and intimacy; relationships with mother and other primary caretakers; relationships with your own children as well as with small children in general; tending to the emotional and security foundations of your life. (Planets in Cancer and/or the moon emphasized by aspect in the natal chart may effect similar experiences.)

THE FIFTH PRINCIPLE: LEO / THE SUN

LEO is the sign of the LION. Leo rules the HEART and the SPINE.

Leo is the fixed FIRE SIGN of SUMMER, indicating powers of *sustaining* and *creative personal spirit.*

The keywords of Leo are "I WILL." The color associated with Leo is YELLOW.

The Fifth Principle

As the sun represents the life-giving spirit of personality, it signifies all the spontaneous expressions of being yourself. But beyond personality and being yourself, the 5th principle addresses the *drama of becoming* yourself. This principle represents the personal drama of life, and the *story* as personal drama. The sun and Leo symbolize life as an unfolding story of self, and refer to the family as crucible in which character and identity are forged. The sun and Leo indicate potentials for having a special calling, for being special, and for being a unique character. They indicate the progressively more full expression of this unique character through life, and symbolize the philosophy of self-realization.

The kingly character of Leo, along with the sun-as-star, symbolize potentials for glamour, majesty and magnificence, for splendor and royalty. This principle signifies the family as the personal kingdom. The color associated with Leo is yellow, the sun's radiant color.

Highlight/Sidelight: A central potential indicated by the sun, Leo and the fifth house is *recreation:* re-creation. Much as the sun spontaneously creates a world of vital energy in every moment, this principle indicates the potential for the hot *fusion* of the creative process. This potential is realized most universally in children, who as manifestations of creation are constantly engaged in recreating their own worlds. Re-creation is realized in the act of spontaneously expressing self, in acts of pure play, in fun, and in drama. It is realized in any experience, work experiences included, where self is fully invested, where there is some element of creative joy, where the past and future are, for the moment, fused.

♌ Leo

As the riotous frolicking of its kitten cousins suggests, Leo's lion represents the instinct for *play* and *playfulness*. The endless antics of lion cubs likewise symbolize in Leo the power of *entertainment*. Stretching out in regal splendor in the sunshine, then nonchalantly fending off the cavorting of its offspring, the lion represents instincts for *relaxation* and *enjoyment*.

Of all the animals of the zodiac, the lion is the most familial, and Leo indicates familial instincts. A family of lions is called a "pride," and the big cat Leo represents the instinct for pride, for taking intense delight in one's own or another's being. Leo signifies children as "offspring," and represents personal character as offspring of family character. It indicates the predisposition to enjoy the spontaneous personalities of children—of overgrown children, too. Indeed Leo indicates the predisposition to *act* like an overgrown kid, and likewise to seek the warm attention of others. Insofar as the Leo character succeeds in gaining this attention, the power of *self-confidence* is indicated; yet in the absence of such attention Leo indicates the capacity to be unsure of self.

With its imperial roar, the lion represents the preeminent power of expressing self, the instinct for self-expression. Like the sun, Leo symbolizes the vital essence of radiant self-expression, and indicates the predisposition to creative self-expression in story-telling and *acting*—"acting out self." Hence Leo symbolizes dramatic instincts, and likewise indicates the will to self-expression in all forms of art.

Leo's rulership of the heart and spine dovetail with the symbolism of the lion. The "lion-hearted" individual is a person of exceptional courage, and Leo symbolizes the power of courage to be who and what one really is. The spine and heart symbolize powers of will and will-power, of being true to self in the face of adversity, of dignity and personal integrity. With respect to the heart, Leo further symbolizes instincts for being generous and magnanimous *(lionhearted)*, for encouragement *(taking heart)*, for having strong personal feelings *(hearty* likes and dislikes, *heartfelt* sentiments), for earnestness and sincerity (*whole-heartedness*).

Sun-sign Leos are sometimes characterized as acting like kings or queens, and Leo does indicate a predilection to egocentricity. But this trait forms just one facet of Leo symbolism with regard to the archetypal figures of the king and queen. At the heart of these figures is, at least metaphorically, the sun. Just as kings were once thought to descend from the sun, Leo represents a motivation to show oneself to be a shining spirit—a solar creator—in one's own right. Yet in order to shine like the sun, the Leo character must reckon not with the king but with the beast in his nature. Liz Greene speaks of this challenge in connection with Parsifal and the Holy Grail legend:

> Parsifal's insensitivity to his mother, to the Red Knight (whom he kills ... simply to show off), to Blanchflor [a woman whom he rescues and then abandons], and to the Grail King himself ... are embodied in the alchemical image of the lion, the animal form of the king-to-be. This naive clumsiness is ... an integral part of the young or immature Leo ... yet even with this clumsiness, fate chooses him for the vision of the Grail before he is ready to understand it... Whatever the Grail may be ... it seems to come early to Leo, not through Labor but through the natural gifts and intuition of the sign. But then it is lost because ... the ego claims the success for itself. Thus it must be refound ... often through much hardship.[60]

The myth of Parsifal dramatizes the leonine tendency to treat the world as if the sheer aura of will and personality will conquer what is in one's way. Falling into the trap of egocentricity, the Leo figure must learn that the power of personality can only bring happiness when it is united with both a generous heart and the light of the Higher Self. This archetypal pattern is symbolized in Hesse's *Journey to the East,* where the central character, named Leo, is both giving and humble, having succeeded in suborning his ego to a spiritual vision.

Beyond identifications with kings or queens, the central Leo archetype is symbolized by the quest of searching for the Grail itself, as Leo—and the sun—represent the archetype of the *spirit quest,* the challenge to realize and express the self's inner spirit.

The more pure and true the expression, the more the Leo/solar character shows the fire-spirit of his true identity; and so less is the need to show off. The pursuit of the Grail—the quest to express the spirit of personal identity—is the *reason d'être* for the Leo character. The fulfillment of this quest can be seen as a lifelong unfoldment of the predisposition to self-expression.

Leo instincts are expressed in the Archetypes of the Creative Artist, the Temperamental Artist, the Storyteller, the Dramatist, the Teacher as Dramatist, the Actor, the Showman, the Showoff, the Big Kid, the Ham, Leo the Total Party Monster, the King, the Queen, the Prince, the Princess, the Character, the Quester, *Moi.*

Famous People born with the sun on Leo include Napoleon, Benito Mussolini, Fidel Castro (King of Cuba), Bill Clinton, George Bernard Shaw, Carl Jung, Herman Melville, Alex Haley, Garrison Keillor, Danielle Steele, Bert Lahr (Cowardly Lion in *The Wizard of Oz*), Leo Durocher, Casey Stengel, Cecil B. DeMille, T.E. Lawrence (of Arabia), Peter O'Toole, Lucille Ball, Caroll O'Conner, Alfred Hitchcock, Peter Weir, Ken Burns, Jerry Garcia, Mick Jagger, Madonna, Whitney Houston, Andy Warhol, Dustin Hoffman, Robert DeNiro and Robert Redford.

In Personality, Leo indicates predispositions for being personable, warm, expressive, proud, showy, brassy, dramatic, true to self, hearty, entertaining, playful, spontaneous, magnanimous, sincere and generous. On the negative side it signifies capacities for being superior, overbearing, egocentric, full of oneself, the tiresome center of attention, show-offy, haughty, prideful, willful and thin-skinned.

⊙ The Sun ⊙

… And now ladies and gentlemen, making a special appearance in connection with Leo the Lion and the Fifth Astrological Principle, we are proud to present, in all its radiant glory, direct from shows around the world, the CELEBRITY of our crowd of symbolic motivations, LIONIZED in sages' dreams and telling visions—let's hear it for THE STAR of our solar system—THE SUN!!! (Roars, cheers. Enter SUN over eastern horizon.)

The sun symbolizes the star in ourselves, the brilliant, life-giving spirit in every person. It represents the "solar center" of self, the source of vitality, joy—*joie de vivre*—happiness, wonder and delight. For children, such joys are found everywhere, and the sun represent potentials for those spontaneous *surprises* of being that are so wonderfully expressed by children. The sun indicates the potential to be childlike in play and in spontaneous self-expression. In its fusioning, radiating brilliance, the sun signifies the potential for personal radiance, for being genial and cheerful, for having a "sunny disposition," for "beaming," for being bright, glorious and *brilliant*. It represents the motivation for celebrity—stardom—and indicates potentials for adulation, adoration and admiration.

Just as the heart is the central life-giving organ of the human body, the sun is the source of life energy on Earth, and so represents the radiant center of personality and identity. It symbolizes the central light of individual personality, the source of personal spirit and character. Like the heart, the sun represents the center of the true self, the core of personal identity. It represents the motivation to express identity, to *self-realization* and *self-discovery*. The sun symbolizes motivation to the live out one's identity in one's vocation, in one's family, in the personal drama of life, yet also in simple spontaneous acts and words. It signifies the motivation for genuineness—"being yourself"—and similarly the potential for *integrity*, being true to self.

The sun indicates motivations for warmth and affirmation, for *heartlove*. With its glyph formed by a circle with a dot in the middle ($\odot$), the sun represents the wholeness of self, the whole self's response to life, and the potentials for *wholeness* and *wholesomeness*. It symbolizes the motivation for spirited interplay in family life. It indicates the motivation to express basic personal likes and dislikes, and signifies the power to characterize, to draw in a few creative strokes or gestures, the nature of self, others, and personal experience.

The sun was identified with Apollo in Greek mythology. As communicated through the Oracle at Delphi, it was from Apollo that humans sought to discover divine will. In this connection, the sun symbolizes the motivation to know *higher will*, which can be experienced as God's will. The sun likewise symbolizes the light of the Higher Self.

In negative expression, the sun indicates potentials for willfulness, egomania, self-centeredness and blindness to the existence of others.

The solar motivation is expressed in the Character or Image of the Star, the Personality, the Hero, the Self-realized Individual, the Vocation, the Calling, the Person of Integrity, the Happy Child/Happy Person, the Creative Artist, the Show, the Story, the Personal Vision, the Family Spirit, *L'Etat, C'est Moi.*

The sun's placement by house in the natal chart indicates the area of experience to which your spirit is most fully drawn; where you most naturally express yourself and your identity; where you can bring true personal creativity to bear; where you are challenged to find yourself.

Fifth House

Planets in Leo's fifth house draw you to experiences of family and familial-type relationships; affairs of the heart and heartfelt personal relationships; the family crucible and the forging of personal identity; interplay with children; acting and drama; spontaneous and creative self-expression, vocation and avocation; self-realization and being true to self; entertainment, relaxation, recreation and amusement. (Planets in Leo and/or the sun emphasized by aspect in the natal chart may effect similar experiences.)

♍ THE SIXTH PRINCIPLE: ☿ VIRGO/ MERCURY

VIRGO is the sign of the VIRGIN. Virgo rules the INTESTINES, and with Mercury, the NERVOUS SYSTEM.

Virgo is the MUTABLE EARTH sign of SUMMER, indicating powers of *adaptive personal practicality.*

The keywords of Virgo are "I ANALYZE." The color associated with Virgo is YELLOW-GREEN.

The Sixth Principle

On the surface, the symbolism of Mercury and Virgo can seem like the dullest in all astrology. Beneath the surface, however, is a "pearl of great price." This treasure is for the watchful eye, the trained ear, the keen sense to appreciate. The sixth principle addresses powers of responding to subtle differences, *essences* and *qualities* in all matters, including *quality of life.* It indicates the power to *appreciate* qualities of the sublime no less than the mundane, the motivation to find the sublime in the mundane—and to turn the mundane into the sublime. As such this principle refers both to alchemy and the quest for perfection.

Virgo is often identified with the trait of discrimination, but it might be better termed the power of *discernment.* This power can be engaged in all manner of circumstances, from discerning whether water is pure, to what is making a car engine misfire, to what is missing in a wayward teenager's life.

The 6th principle speaks to all the duties and practical necessities that regularly occur in life. These include repair, maintenance, cleaning, sanitation, clothes-making, carpentry and secretarial work, plus those most mundane of daily concerns, dishes and the laundry.

Highlight/Sidelight: In the image of a woman holding a sheaf of grain, Virgo symbolizes vital connection between nature and human nature, and represents the *order of nature* itself. Further, Virgo indicates the power to perceive natural order in human affairs. Hence while Virgo characters can become "order freaks"—compulsively neat—they may also respond to a feeling for natural order in life which is unrelated to the maintaining of surface order. Virgos are inherently concerned with *their own* place in the order of things. On this account Virgo influences serve to attract issues of *fitting in,* and/or feeling out of place. It is a Virgo predilection to reach points in life where questions are asked: Where do I fit in? How do I fit in? What am I fit for?

♍ Virgo ♉

In connection with the sun's passage through Virgo from about August 23 to September 22, the symbol of a young woman holding a sheaf of grain represents activities of harvesting: the cutting, gathering, drying, threshing, milling and storing of grain. These activities represent in Virgo the instinct for *responding to the practical necessities of life.* Virgo indicates the power of recognizing and doing what is *necessary and essential,* the instinct for tending to common concern. It represents the predisposition for being *helpful* in responding to all manner of practical necessity, for *efficiency* and frugality, for *economy* and *conservation.*

In tending to the harvest, the Virgo maiden symbolizes the powers of *service* in all walks of life. Virgo symbolizes the power of *refining* the *techniques, crafts* and *skills* that are essential to performing such tasks, and the power of *practice* in perfecting any skill. Although sun-sign Virgos are often called critical, this trait may be seen as a predisposition to perceive the need for improvement, and similarly Virgo indicates the instinct for (self-) improvement. Whether this instinct is expressed in terms of practicing what one perceives is another matter.

Holding a sheaf of grain—the staff of life—Virgo's maiden represents powers of *nutrition* and *health.* Whole grain here symbolizes powers of health, health-consciousness, and such regular practices as good diet, hygiene, getting fresh air and exercise. Virgo signifies the virtues of *consistency* and *moderation* in daily living.

The intestines, ruled by Virgo, are responsible not only for passing on waste for elimination, but for assimilating essential nutrients in food. By the same token Virgo represents the faculty of *mentally* assimilating the essential details or elements of any matter or circumstance. The keyword "analyze" refers to breaking down something into parts and pieces, and much as the digestive system of the human body acts to break down foods into smaller particles for purposes of assimilation, Virgo symbolizes the power to perceptually break down any matter into discrete parts, pieces and elements so as to mentally digest them. (This symbolism of digestion here gives particular meaning to the image of Virgo characters as "regular guys.") Virgo's rulership of the intestines indicates instinctive concern with practical matters of waste, waste disposal and recycling.

Virgo is traditionally associated with "details," and this sign does indicate predispositions for dealing with details, parts, pieces, minor changes and small increments: the handwork and footwork of life. Yet such instinctive concern can be likened to the work of the wood sculptor, whose chipping, chipping, chipping, brings into relief, tiny step by tiny step, the vital shapes or contours of life. It is when doing the small things brings no relief, either by dint of *obsessing* or because doing the small things becomes intrinsically burdensome, that "sweating the small stuff" loses its vitality.

A summer sign, Virgo indicates powers of feeling that take on subtle meanings in connection with the symbolism of the virgin. Virgo represents the instinct to maintain *purity* of inner feelings, and to reach *clarity* in responding to inner promptings, even while compelled to deal with the realities of external circumstances. Caught between her inner feeling sensibilities and outer circumstance, the Virgo character seeks the twain's meeting, the middle line. She seeks to respond in accordance with her *own* nature and feelings in the context of the outer circumstances she faces. Figures in mythology who express this archetypal inner-meets-outer conflict are not necessarily chaste or pure in the traditional sense. They are often complex, colorful and earthy; and they may be sexually active—"sacred harlots."

Related to the motif of responding to inner promptings in the context of exterior exigencies, Virgo represents the predisposition to attract crises of personal adjustment. To the extent that one's inner sensibilities cannot be reconciled with outer circumstances, a proneness to manifest psychosomatically is indicated. Virgo signifies the challenge to reconcile internal reality with external reality in responding to the many conditions of living with others as well as in matters of employment.

As with Mercury, Virgo symbolizes mental powers of perspicacity, criticism, perceptiveness and precision.

Virgo instincts are expressed in the Archetypes of the Critic, the Writer, the Technician, the Technical Wizard, the Wonk, the Detail Guy, the Tight-Ass, the Mental Dynamo, the Craftsperson, the Skilled Worker, the Health Care Worker/Social Worker, the Health Nut, the Nurse, the Repairman, the Carpenter, the Narrator, the Concerned Teacher, the Naturalist, the Herbalist, the Common Plaint, the Plaintive Song, the Sacred Harlot, the Regular Guy.

Famous People born with the sun in Virgo include Maria Montessori, Mother Theresa, Margaret Sanger, Kate Millett, Mary Shelley, Dr. Samuel Johnson, D.H. Lawrence, Theodore Dreiser, Leo Tolstoy, H.G. Wells, Richard Wright, Alfred A. Knopf, Ken Kesey, Stephen King, Euell Gibbons, Loren Eisley, Walter Reuther, Bill Monroe, Patsy Cline ("Coal Miner's Daughter"), Van Morrison, Chuck Berry, Buddy Holly, Otis Redding, B.B. King, Michael Jackson, Greta Garbo, Sophia Loren and Cal Ripken Jr. (played over 2,000 consecutive regular-season games).

In Personality, Virgo represents predispositions for being thoughtful, perceptive, technical, exacting, meticulous, discerning, concerned, practical, sharp, precise, measured, punctual, dutiful, frugal, conservationist, cautious, modest, deferential, dependable, low-key, holding an ear to the earth, putting the nose to the grindstone, appreciative, "regular," health-conscious, conscientious and helpful. On the negative side are indicated capacities for being picky, pointed, hypercritical, tight-assed, prudish, mentally fixated, tied up in knots, plugged up, hypochondriac, undemonstrative, uninspiring and messy(!).

☿ Mercury ☿

Mercury was the messenger of the Olympian gods, and the planet Mercury is sometimes called the "Messenger of the Senses." Mercury symbolizes classic functions of the mind: registering and assimilating sense impressions, mental retention, memory and perception. It indicates potentials for sharpness and clarity of thinking, for acuteness of recall, for retention of facts and information, for linear, critical and rational thinking. It indicates the motivation for putting thoughts accurately into words, for writing, and for communicating exactly what is meant. As the fastest orbiting planet, Mercury symbolizes "mercurial" potentials including the racing of thought and restlessness of the mind.

In symbolizing faculties of perception, Mercury represents the potential to "see things as they are"—to record sensory messages accurately. Paradoxically, however, it also indicates the motivation to *interpret* sense messages according to individual predilection, and the related potential to rationalize. (As with everything else in natal astrology, such different potentials are subject to expression according to differing modes and circumstances of development, and according to interplay with and affect by other natal influences.)

Because its orbit is so close to the sun (it never diverges more than about 27° away from the sun as seen from the Earth), Mercury suggests the idea of the "mind in service to the spirit." As the sun symbolizes the "fixed star" spirit-center of individual nature, Mercury represents the mind as messenger for the central self, weaving and working one's solar will in and out of the tapestry of external affairs. Mercury indicates the motivation to engage in the task of *mediating* the relationship of self to world.

Reflecting Virgo's symbolism of health, Mercury symbolizes the potential for regulating mental health. While this connection is enormously complex, it appears that this potential is related to the mediating function just noted. If schizophrenia is defined as a splitting of the mind from the emotions, a key function of the mind as represented by Mercury is the maintaining of continuity and consistency between cognitive and emotional dimensions— *cognitive consonance.* As we negotiate our way through life, to recall the theme suggested in Virgo, the mind is charged with reconciling internal reality with external reality. In such mental processes, the mind must often deal with feelings and emotions that cannot easily reconciled with the exigencies of external reality. When such reconciliation can not be achieved or sustained on an ongoing basis and/or regarding affairs of crucial emotional import, the mind can progressively lose its ability to effectively mediate emotional reactions. Mercury indicates the potential for irrational as well as rational thinking.

Mercury represents the primary mental function of *attention*, and the motivation to *attend* to circumstances. It indicates the ability to meet any problem, necessity or issue in life by *paying attention*, and symbolizes potentials for *mindfulness, concern* and *thoughtfulness*. As with Virgo, it symbolizes the ability to sense the order of nature, and one's own place within this order. Evoking Taoist philosophy, Mercury symbolizes the motivation to respond to all circumstances of life in accordance with the ways of nature; the idea that in becoming mindful of nature, any problem can be solved and natural order restored. It signifies the capacity to respect the importance of humble and mundane affairs as part of the natural order of life. Such "Mercury wisdom" is indicated in the Zen saying, "Before enlightenment, chop wood, carry water. After enlightenment, chop wood, carry water."

One Mercury archetype is that of the native American who is able to "read" the subtlest of messages—a hint of scent in the wind, a sound "heard" through the hand held to earth, the sensing of the faintest suggestion of a footprint. In this regard, Mercury indicates the potential for *refinement of the senses*.

As the messenger of the senses, Mercury symbolizes faculties for all manner of monitoring the physical plane: measurement, inspection, sorting, accounting, bookkeeping, referencing, registration and recording. Like Virgo, it indicates the motivation for *preparation*, and for concern with technicalities and fine points.

Mercurial motivations are expressed in the Character or Image of the Narrator, the Commentator, the Spokesperson, the Essayist, the Journal-keeper, the Keen Sense, the Reader, the Working Stiff, the Secretary, the Recorder, the Serviceman, the Technician, the Technocrat, the Recorder, the Utilityman, the Workingman, the Thoughtful/Watchful One, the Hobbyist, the Attender to Detail, the Zen Practitioner, the Mindful One, the Tracker, the Mental Magician, the Alchemist, the Practitioner of Economy.

Mercury's placement by house in the natal chart indicates the area of experience where necessity plays a key role; where you most recognize the need for improvement; where you are most challenged to use your mind; where your thoughts lead you;

where it is important for you to be regularly and actively engaged, in part for the sake of your mental health.

Sixth House

Planets in Virgo's sixth house draw you to experiences of reckoning with and adjusting to the realities of everyday life; dealing with and/or deferring to the circumstances of living and working with others; working out personal and practical problems by paying careful and consistent attention; learning the underside of appearances and reality; developing daily routine and consistency; service to others; duty; employment and fitting into the world; daily practice; perfecting any skill or craft; improvement of self and circumstances; health conditions, health consciousness and healthful practices. (Planets in Virgo or Mercury emphasized by aspect in the natal chart may effect similar experiences.)

THE SEVENTH PRINCIPLE:
LIBRA / VENUS

LIBRA is the sign of the BALANCE. Libra rules the HIPS.

Libra is the CARDINAL AIR sign of AUTUMN, indicating powers of *generating social communication.*

The keywords of Libra are "I BALANCE." The color associated with Libra is GREEN.

The Seventh Principle

The glyph of Venus is the same as that for woman, and Venus represents that part of ourselves classically identified with women. In contrast to the macho symbolism of Mars, Venus indicates classically feminine potentials for the lilting, easy, graceful rhythms of generating *rapport* in social relationship.

The 7th principle refers to manners, etiquette and style, all of which may come at the expense of substance. This principle casts relationship as *partnership,* and indicates the potential for *romance.* The 7th house indicates experiences of friendship, affairs, dates and other social liaisons where the object is to relate and, at least metaphorically, to dance.

Highlight/Sidelight: Venus symbolizes the potential for being *gay*—stylishly lighthearted—and as much as it refers to "gay-ness," so is the Venusian principle prominently (sometimes exaggeratedly) expressed in male homosexuals: gays. Conversely, many lesbians express the traditionally male-identified potentials symbolized by Mars. Yet as with all other principles of astrology (and contrary to black-and-white characterizations made in certain popular books using the names these planets), the principles of both Mars and Venus are androgynous.

 Libra

The sign of the balance, Libra's scales symbolize the power of bringing equipoise and *harmony* to the interactions of relationship, the power of bringing self into dynamic balance with other. Libra indicates instinctive sensibilities for responding to the tos and fros, the highs and lows, the ebbs and flows, the his's and hers, the mine and yours of all relationships. It signifies instinctive response to the moving, dynamic center of balance in relationship, the sensibility for acting and speaking so as to anticipate the back-and-forth swings of any interaction. Pertaining to these sensibilities, it indicates predispositions for being amenable, gracious and affable, and for having the sense of what is apt.

As the cardinal air sign of fall, Libra denotes the power of generating communication in relationship. This power is central to all manner of social affairs, including public relations, making deals and agreements, mediation, and work that involves dealing with the public. This Libran instinct for communication in relationship, while sometimes taken to extremes in the caricature of the ingratiatingly suave salesman with a slightly insane PR smile screwed into place, is expressed more fully in the figure who engages in breezy, lilting and casual comments and conversational initiatives. Libra symbolizes the inherent power to respond through the sense of *relatedness.* It also signifies "flirting instincts" and the predilection to flattery.

Beyond capacities of a purely social nature, Libra indicates the power of responding to balance and harmony in all manner of *aesthetic* affairs. The counterbalancing sides of the scales represent the instinctive sense of balance and proportion in such matters as color, decor, dress, art, dance and music. Thus Libra represents aesthetic instincts, along with related sensibilities of taste, fashion and style. It indicates the predisposition to respond according to the sense of *appeal.*

Like the scales, Libra's rulership of the hips symbolizes the power to swing from side to side, both literally and metaphorically, in interactions of communication and relationship. It represents the power of responding gracefully and in harmony with the actions of another, a power that is manifest in the archetypal act of dancing with a partner. Essentially the same kind of power is central to generating *accord* in relationship, and Libra indicates the instinct for reaching accord. It signifies predispositions for *tact, diplomacy* and *keeping the peace;* for smoothing over what would otherwise be rough places; for finessing touchy moments; and for *negotiating* all manner of situations so as to maintain harmony.

As far as negotiating difficult situations is concerned, it would be hard to find a more archetypally Libran dilemma than that which confronted Paris in Greek myth. As the story goes, Hera, Athena and Aphrodite (Venus) argued amongst themselves as to who was the most beautiful. To resolve the matter, they coerced Paris, who was considered the most beautiful man on Earth, into choosing. In classic Libran style, Paris found it difficult to choose, and tried to finesse the situation by saying that all three were equally beautiful. The goddesses did not accept that solution, however, and subsequently each tried to ply Paris with bribes. Hera promised him riches and dominion over Asia Minor. Warrior goddess Pallas Athena enticed him with the prospect of becoming invincible in battle. But voluptuous Aphrodite held the winning suit (hearts), as she promised Paris love with the most beautiful woman on Earth. For Paris, this was no contest at all, and he gave the nod to Aphrodite's appeal to beauty and love. In the ironic fulfillment of Aphrodite's promise, however, Paris fell for the beautiful Helen, who happened unfortunately to be already married to King Menelaus. In this most famous tale of a lover's triangle are the mythic origins of the Trojan War.

Knowing that taking sides with one goddess would upset the others, Paris ignored a cardinal Libran principle: Don't upset the balance. But Paris was by no means merely interested in keeping the peace, for as a classic Libran character he instinctively responded to the appeal of romance. On the other hand, Libra's scales symbolize the sense that in making choices, we better weigh the *consequences.* Hence Libra represents not only the ability but the challenge to anticipate the consequences of our actions.

In affairs of choice and decision, Libra indicates predilections to see-saw back and forth, to be unable to choose (waffling), to go to opposite extremes, to play both or all sides to the center, and to try to keep both/all sides happy.

On a different score, Libra signifies the predisposition to respond to issues of social justice, and the power of *social activism.* The scales are of course a symbol of justice, and this aspect of Libra can be interpreted in terms of *doing justice to* any issue by weighing factors pro and con. But the balance can also be interpreted in terms of an instinctive awareness of the other side, an inherent openness to the experience of others. Beyond the more superficial values associated with Libra, this sign indicates the power for deep identification with the plight or situation of others. In social relationships, in turn, this power can translate into a proneness to being "too nice," taking the priorities of others before one's own.

Libran instincts are expressed in the Archetypes of the Diplomat, the Negotiator, the Activist On Behalf of Social Causes, the Artist as Social Activist, the Popularizer of Social Issues, the Public Relations Guy/Gal, Life as Art, the Artistic One, the Beauty, the Partner, the Romantic, the *Bon Vivant,* the Man/Woman About Town, the Nice Companion.

Famous People born with the sun in Libra include Jean Millet, Mahatma Gandhi, Desmond Tutu, Dwight Eisenhower, Jimmy Carter, Jesse Jackson, Dick Gregory, Brigitte Bardot (French beauty, animal rights activist), Cheryl Tiegs, Eleanor Roosevelt, Alfred Nobel, Arthur Miller, Eugene O'Neill, William Faulkner, F. Scott Fitzgerald, Jim Henson, Ed Sullivan, Barbara Walters, Truman Capote, George Gershwin, John Lennon, Bob Geldof (musician who organized global famine relief Band Aid concerts), Paul Simon, Bruce Springsteen, Jackson Browne and Sting.

In Personality, Libra indicates predispositions for being appealing, socially communicative, congenial, agreeable, tactful, diplomatic, easygoing, graceful, smooth, suave, flirtatious and aesthetically inclined. On the negative side it indicates capacities for being bland, indecisive, insincere, vain, artificial, superficial, and for swerving to extremes.

♀ Venus ♀

Venus was the goddess of charm, grace, beauty and love, and Venus signifies these same potentials in ourselves. It indicates the motivations of both partners who conspire in romance: the charmer and the charmed, the lover and the loved, the beauty and the *apprehender* of beauty. On this last note, Venus represents the *aesthetic* motivation, the motivation to respond to aesthetic values in all realms of life. In the realm of love, the Venusian motivation indicates the principle of love as aesthetic, as dance,

as a choreographed dyad. This principle was beautifully captured
by Anne Morrow Lindbergh:

> A good relationship has a pattern like a dance and is built
> on some of the same rules. The partners do not need to
> hold on tightly, because they move confidently in the
> same pattern, intricate but gay and swift and free, like a
> country dance of Mozart's. To touch heavily would be to
> arrest the pattern and freeze the movement, to check the
> endlessly changing beauty of its unfolding... Now arm in
> arm, now face to face, now back to back—it does not
> matter which. Because they know they are partners
> moving to the same rhythm...[61]

Venus represents the motivation for *courting* as a dance in
which rhythm, charm, compatibility and harmony all come into
play. The word "charm" derives from the Latin root *carmen,*
"song," and the Venusian potential for charm refers to a lyrical
sensibility in relationship. Regarding another song-related word,
Venus symbolizes the potential for *enchantment.*

In signifying motivations classically identified with women,
Venus represents the potential for responding to values of
compatibility and *rapport.* Traditionally it has been the woman
who, faced with the man's overtures, is charged with asking the
questions: Are we truly compatible? Do we make a good couple?
Are we good with and for each other? Venus indicates the motivation to generate and respond to the harmonies, the symmetries
and the compatibilities of relatedness. On the opposite side of
this coin, it represents the potential to experience *clashes* in
social and aesthetic affairs.

As a feminine archetype, Venus indicates basic social potentials for beings simply nice, agreeable, cordial, pleasant and
sociable, for being companionable and entertaining. It indicates
sensibilities of *social aesthetics* as expressed in grooming, the
way we dress, how we gesture, walk and carry ourselves. Venus
symbolizes the aesthetic sensibility of taste in social entertainment, cuisine and speech. It symbolizes the aesthetic potential
for responding to the dynamics of harmony in art, music, decor
and humor. It symbolizes artistic sensibilities for contrast and
counterpoint, irony and humor, discord and accord.

As the planet closest to the Earth, Venus represents the potential for experiencing closeness—the motivation to "get close," and likewise indicates the motivation for communicating *affection* in social relationship. It represents potentials for being fey, amusing and whimsical; yet it also indicates potentials for generating an artificial style of relating, for utter blandness, for affectation, mannerism and venality.

Beyond social and aesthetic realms, Venus symbolizes potentials of grace and rhythm, timing and tempo in athletics, especially in gymnastics, skiing and figure skating. It indicates the aesthetic potential for sensing balance, symmetry and *elegance* in mathematics, physics and other intellectual affairs.

Venusian motivations are expressed in the Character or Image of the Dancer, the Date, the Guest, the Host, the Mingler, the Partner, the *Artiste,* the Aesthete, the Romantic, the Affair, the Lover's Triangle, the Social Butterfly, the Flirt, *Savoir Faire,* the Model, the Sophisticate, the Romantic Adventurer, the Harmonizer, the Humorist, the Singer, the Entertainer, the Lyricist.

Venus indicates the motivation for generating a *style of relating,* and Venus' placement by sign at birth is suggestive of one's instinctive style of relating.

Venus' placement by house in the natal chart indicates the area of experience where you most need and seek harmony; where social relations are exceptionally important; where you may bring a socially creative sensibility; where you get romantic or aesthetic ideas and visions.

Seventh House

Planets in Libra's seventh house of the natal chart draw you to experiences of "meeting the other," marriage and other partnerships; public relations and being in the social or public eye; the wide-open interactions of relationship that can result in antagonism and the making of enemies as much as in friends and great good times; popularizing or appealing to other's tastes; being caught—or poised—in the middle; challenges to achieve harmonious relationship; artistic and aesthetically related endeavors including affairs of fashion and style; romance and social entertainment. (Planets in Libra and/or Venus emphasized by aspect in the natal chart may effect similarly experiences.)

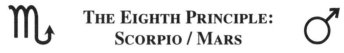 THE EIGHTH PRINCIPLE: SCORPIO / MARS

SCORPIO is the sign of the SCORPION, the EAGLE and the PHOENIX. Scorpio rules the GENITALS.

Scorpio is the FIXED WATER sign of AUTUMN, indicating powers of *sustaining emotional relationship.*

The keywords of Scorpio are "I DESIRE." The color associated with Scorpio is BLUE-GREEN (turquoise).

The Eighth Principle

The symbolism of this principle encompasses most of the potentials that are central to Freud's instinct theory: *eros* and *thanatos,* libido and aggression, pleasure and ego. The 8th is the largest of the twelve astrological principles in terms of the sheer number of capacities it addresses; and Scorpio is the only sign of the zodiac composed of three separate symbols—the scorpion, the eagle and the phoenix.

Mars and Scorpio represent the principle of *survival,* and indicate several different dimensions of survival: survival by reproduction, physical survival, social survival, economic survival and emotional survival. Among the social potentials indicated here are the forging of communal bonds through shared trial and ritual, shared social values, social expectations and social approval, pressure to conform, alienation, estrangement, ingroupness, exclusion and outcasting. This principle refers to capacities of compliance and rebellion, oppression and liberation, offense and defense, attack and counterattack, provocation and retaliation, insult and retribution; to feud, battle, injury and, finally, death.

In connection with the 8th house, this principle indicates experiences that involve resources held in common: budgets, taxes, wills, legacies, marriage agreements, divorce settlements, and lawsuits; corporate, political and social disputes over public resources; the exchange of money for work; debts, loans and mortgages. It indicates capacities for disagreement pertaining to competing interests about social, financial and moral issues; to market value, marketing, corporate bodies, mergers and unions. The 8th principle represents powers of exchange, competition and adversarial relationships in banking, business, labor and law.

With respect to resources held in common, this principle indicates the potential for the communal *sharing* of resources, and so symbolizes philosophical underpinnings of socialism. It also refers to basic political rights, to the corruption of such rights, and to the struggle for rights.

The 8th principle refers to experiences of *major change* in life including puberty, initiation into adulthood, rights of passage, marriage and divorce. Mars and Scorpio indicate potentials for involvement in matters of life and death in medicine, surgery, birthing, biology, the ministry and the military.

Highlight/Sidelight: Both Mars and Scorpio indicate the instinctive drive for mastery and control; yet at the same time this principle speaks to such potentials as Tantra, the acceptance of fate, mysticism and mystical attitudes, all of which involve the apparent surrender of control.

A resolution of this paradox is suggested in the injunction to *walk the line.* The idea of walking the line can be understood in connection with the symbolism of the number 8, wherein the connection between the two loops—symbolizing connection between self and other, between self and the world—focuses on a single point. The implication here is that in our engagements and exchanges with others, there is a natural middle point. Those driven to control seek to move beyond the "natural middle" creating terms of connection that shrink the other side. In so doing, it might be said that they fail to respect the "otherness of other," and ultimately cheat themselves. Conversely, those who give up control too easily are liable to put their fate in others' hands, which creates an equally skewed dynamic of exchange. Between these two courses, the image of walking the line suggests the finding of that point where motives of desire and control are expressed so as to bring about an ongoing depth, fullness and roundness of exchange.

♏ Scorpio ♏

The initial symbol of Scorpio, the scorpion, mainly represents *competitive, physical* and *reproductive* powers, the "down and dirty" of the struggle for survival. In contrast, the eagle signifies the power to soar above the fray, and represents *moral* and *mystical* capacities. The phoenix in turn speaks to depth processes of psychological death and rebirth, and represents transformative powers through which emotional, physical and moral energies are *regenerated.*

The scorpion is an archetype of survival, and indicates the two primary survival instincts as conceived by Freud: sex and self-preservation. The scorpion's stinging tail symbolizes physical *potency* as expressed at the most basic—and basest—levels. Scorpio symbolizes *competitive instincts* as they manifest not only in business and economic survival but in all sports and games, challenges, tests and contests. It represents powers of physical prowess, physical fitness, strength, training and conditioning. Meanwhile, scorpions are known to fight until death when enclosed with one another; it is one of those species that, like the human, is capable of killing its own kind. Thus Scorpio represents the proverbial "killer instinct," the instinct to fight, the ethos of dog-eat-dog and survival of the fittest. It indicates instincts for aggressiveness, gamesmanship, winning and succeeding, the power to conquer, to beat, to dominate, to exploit. The Scorpio instincts for potency and power are at the heart of the remark uttered by sun-sign Scorpio Theodore Roosevelt: "Talk softly but carry a big stick." Scorpios are reputed to carry both a sting and a stick.

Yet survival is not merely a matter of beating up on the other guy, and Scorpio symbolizes social and socially productive powers of survival in business, commerce and politics. Whether in reproduction or in social affairs, survival is a matter of *exchange,* and powers of exchange indicated by Scorpio include the give and take of bartering, bargaining, trading, dealing, selling and buying, mixing it up and getting down to business. Scorpio represents the power of exchange in the *agreements* and *commitments* of marriage, contracts and compacts. It indicates predispositions to exchange in social and economic as much as in physical and sexual intercourse.

In its symbolism of sexual instincts, Scorpio refers to a whole range of capacities associated with sex and reproduction. These include pleasure, lust, attraction, attractiveness, come-ons, arousal, conception, pregnancy, abortion and birth. Scorpio's number, 8, symbolizes the joining together of two people in mystical/sexual *union,* and likewise in Tantric sex. Scorpio indicates predispositions to sensuality, sexiness and seductiveness.

As signified in the keywords, "I Desire," Scorpio indicates the basic emotion of desire. Like Mars, Scorpio indicates the drive to deal in the three basic currencies of desire—sex, money and power—and represents desire as integral to drives not only for sex but for success, fame, fortune, rewards, gains and political power.

Along with desire, the other fundamental emotion represented by Scorpio is anger. While desire is the primary emotional component of sex, anger is the basic emotional component of self-preservation, aggression and fighting. Scorpio indicates powers of desire and anger as combined variously in jealousy, resentment, frustration and greed. Meanwhile, anger is the primary component of another seemingly basic emotion: hatred. And like Mars again, Scorpio indicates the capacity for hatred. Yet Mars and Scorpio also symbolize the archetypal challenge to *fight* hatred and kindred dark, destructive emotions. Scorpio symbolizes the theme of experiencing emotions such as hatred, bitterness, jealousy and revenge—emotions that are bound to dwell within oneself as much as in the outside world.

The destructive force of dark emotions is classically symbolized in monstrous figures characterized by a particularly scorpionic feature: engaging the monster would mean death for one of the combatants. To fight such monsters would mean becoming ever more deeply entangled with their destructive power; there could be no withdrawal. Hence to conquer these monsters, heroes of mythology were challenged to fight in such ways so as to avoid being sucked in by the deadly power of the monster. For example, Gorgons such as Medusa turned their foes to stone simply by engaging them in direct visual contact. Merely to behold a Gorgon was to die. Perseus was able to vanquish Medusa because he engaged her without looking directly at her;

he conquered Medusa by allowing himself to look only at her reflection.

Perseus' vanquishing of Medusa symbolizes the understanding that to conquer the dark forces that we meet in the world, we cannot engage them at the level that they tempt us. As much as Medusa symbolizes dark emotions like hatred, similarly, this myth conveys the injunction to transcend those emotions within ourselves—by avoiding the engagement of *our own* emotions at the level at which they tempt us. (This theme is further explored in Chapter 12.)

Scorpio also represents the simpler hero archetype: the slayer of the dragon, the conqueror of the enemy, the vanquisher of the oppressor, the warrior who defeats the evil without.

Ascending from the level of the scorpion, the eagle symbolizes consummate fitness in the realm of survival; master of the skies, it represents mastery of the physical realm. Although the eagle is a bird of prey, moreover, it is able to soar to the heights, and so symbolizes the ability to transcend baser motives of desire and survival. The eagle represents the power to *uplift* one's sensibilities, to respond to higher moral, mystical and communal values of survival.

Scorpio's eagle represents powers of exchange wherein there is mutual benefit, where the survival of both sides is avowedly connected. It symbolizes the power not only to exchange but to share in the social quest for survival, and represents powers of social commitment, fairness, righteousness, morals, moral conduct, morale and solidarity. The eagle also symbolizes mystical dimensions of desire: the *mystery of desire,* the sense that our truest, deepest desires lead us into the very center of the mystery of life.

Between lower survival powers symbolized by the scorpion and higher powers symbolized by the eagle, the phoenix signifies the power to go through major changes in which the death of the old opens the way to the birth of the new: regeneration. The phoenix represents archetypal experiences of deep change, trial, testing, "dark nights of the soul," and the rising, rebirth and regeneration of new life out of the ashes of the old. Just as Scorpio symbolizes the regeneration of life in procreation, so does it symbolize processes of regeneration within a lifetime—or within a day. Scorpionic powers of regeneration apply not only to emotional dimensions but to financial, physical and moral cycles of collapse and recovery. In Scorpio are symbolized predispositions to the darkest and deepest struggles of life, and the capacity to emerge from these struggles renewed.

Scorpio instincts are expressed in the Archetypes of the Conqueror, the Pirate, the Valiant, the Brave, the Survivor, Faust, Oedipus, Perseus, the Sensualist, the Entrepreneur, the Go-getter, the Swimmer, the Tough Guy, the Party Animal, In Your Face, the Fighter, the Powerful, the Researcher, the Biologist, the Commitment, the Socially Involved, the Phoenix, the Reborn, the Dark Night of the Soul, the Taxman, the Blues and the Blues Singer.

Famous People born with the sun in Scorpio include Martin Luther, Feodor Dostoyevski, Marie Antoinette, Captain James Cook, Robert Louis Stevenson, Daniel Boone, John Philip Sousa, Eugene Debs, Elizabeth Cady Stanton, Theodore Roosevelt, General George Patton, General George Rommel, Auguste Rodin, Pablo Picasso, Georgia O'Keeffe, Martin Scorcese, Burt Lancaster, Charles Bronson, Katherine Hepburn, Hillary Clinton, Richard Burton, Mahalia Jackson, Neil Young, Joni Mitchell, Bonnie Raitt and Roseanne Barr.

In Personality, Scorpio indicates predispositions for being competitive, achieving, assertive, feisty, plucky, physical, enterprising, engaging, driven by desire, strong, sharing—or else secretive, communal—or else reserved, convivial, irreverent, sensual, mystical, and for "getting down to it." On the negative side, it signifies capacities for being crude, contentious, disputatious, obsessed, oppressive, manipulative, corrupt, immoral, greedy, controlling (control freaks) and power-hungry.

♂ Mars ♂

In Roman mythology, Mars was the god of war and combat, and like its namesake the planet Mars symbolizes human potentials for aggression, violence, victory—and mortality. As with the symbolism of Scorpio, Mars represents both "lower" physical and competitive potentials and "higher" moral and mystical potentials. It indicates survival-related motivations for risking danger and injury, physical bravery, moral bravery and guts. Yet it also indicates the potential for physical or moral weakness, for being taken advantage of, for taking advantage, for deceit, manipulation, corruption, stealing, murder and other crimes. The perpetrator and the victim are both part of the Mars principle.

Mars represents the motivation for physical *action* and *self-assertion.* Like Scorpio, it represents the drive to survive in terms of *competing, achieving and succeeding.* Mars indicates the drive of *ego* and the motivation to exert *control* over one's affairs. Inasmuch as achieving success and economic control over one's life requires entering into trade-offs and agreements, Mars symbolizes the inevitability of adopting *values* (for good or ill) in the quest to survive in the world.

The classic archetype of the warrior, Mars represents the motivation to *prove* oneself, and refers to ritualized tests and trials of strength, competence and achievement. It indicates the motivation for self-control and the gut potential for *excitement.*

Just as the glyph of Mars (♂) is the same as that for male, Mars speaks to that part of ourselves that is classically identified with men. Mars represents the voice that says, "I want," the drive to pursue getting what we want, and the drive to fulfill our desires. Even more than Scorpio, Mars symbolizes the source of individual desire, the origin of each person's eros, passion and desire nature. It symbolizes the seat of passion and desire which, as with Scorpio, can be conditioned by the "Big Three"—sex, money and power. But the higher implication of Mars (as uniquely configured in the birth chart) is that each person's desire nature is ultimately individual, and not easily realized. It represents potentials for the *frustration* of desire, for depression, fixation and alienation. Regarding the pursuit of desire, Mars signifies the urge to enter and swim in the river of life; and it symbolizes the meeting of fate.

Martian symbolism is expressed in the ethos of the *martial* arts. While the primary meaning of the word "martial" centers on the motivation of self-defense, the philosophy of the martial arts incorporates elements of mysticism that are also central to the symbolism of Mars. Emphasizing flow between opposing forces, the interaction between active thrust and passive reception, and working *with* rather than against the physical force of another, the Martial realm includes receptivity as well as assertion, compromise as well as demand, and flow as well as force. Similarly, just as the dominant party in any uneven relationship must eventually give way (if only to death), Mars symbolizes the strength of going with changes rather than trying to fight them. In personal relationships, a kindred mystical potential is reflected in the idea that what is hated, judged or resented about another is actually an (undeveloped) part of oneself.

Mars indicates the potential for action and involvement on behalf of what is seen as right and morally imperative. It indicates the potential for *respect*—and self-respect. With regard to self-assertion, it indicates the basic motivation to *argue*.

Mars indicates the source of *soul* within us, the potential for soulfulness, and for expressing soul in singing the *blues*. It represents motivations for *honesty,* for walking the line, hanging in there, hanging out, carousing and partying.

Martian motivations are expressed in the Character or Image of the Warrior, the Hero, the Doctor, Blood and Guts, the Martial Artist, the Antagonist, the Opponent, the Swashbuckler, the Competitor, the Athlete, the Jock, the Party Animal, the Pusher Man, the Grunt, the Businessman, the Union Man, *El Macho*, the Pleasure-seeker, Animal Magnetism, the Lover (with Venus), the Soul Mate, the Mystic, Stranger in a Strange Land, Walking the Line, Get Down, the Righteous One.

Mars' position by zodiac sign can be interpreted in terms of your instinctive mode of self-assertion. The sign Mars was in at birth is also descriptive of your desire nature.

Mars' placement by house in the natal chart indicates the area of experience in which you are challenged to struggle to get what you want—and to know what you want; where you are challenged to assert yourself; where you are drawn into involved exchanges with others.

Eighth House

Planets in Scorpio's eighth house draw you to experiences of committed relationships; deep involvements and deep connection to others; athletics, competition and contests; business; earning a living; money and financial affairs; economic survival; contracts and wills; rentals; sharing space; resources held in common; death and taxes; getting into the middle of the fray; diving into the river of life; mystical connection and mysticism; depth and death-rebirth experiences; sexual and occult affairs; research and investigation. (Planets in Scorpio and/or Mars emphasized by aspect in the natal chart may effect similar experiences.)

 ## THE NINTH PRINCIPLE: SAGITTARIUS / JUPITER

SAGITTARIUS is the sign of the CENTAUR-ARCHER. Sagittarius rules the THIGHS and, with Jupiter, rules the LIVER and the GALL BLADDER.

Sagittarius is the MUTABLE FIRE sign of AUTUMN, indicating powers of *adaptive social spirit.*

The keywords of Sagittarius are "I ASPIRE," "I UNDERSTAND," and "I SEE." The color associated with this sign is BLUE.

The Ninth Principle

Both Jupiter and Sagittarius signify the principle of magnitude and enlargement. Jupiter is the largest but also the least dense of the planets, as it is made up mostly of hot gasses. Between its huge size and its metaphorical hot air, Jupiter symbolizes motivations for expansion and inflation. In social relations, this principle translates into inclinations to superlative, exaggeration and hyperbole: "super" everything and fabulous anything; the magna, the mega, the max and the most; the grandest, the greatest, the highest and the farthest. This principle refers to anything conceived on a grand scale, to mega-projects, spectacles, sensations and extravaganzas. The 9th is the principle of the Big Plan and the Grand Design, and refers to the larger picture in which we all play *roles* and have *higher purposes.* Jupiter and Sagittarius indicate the principle of relation to the larger whole. Both Jupiter and Sagittarius indicate the motivation for participating in and understanding *intercultural* affairs.

The 9th principle refers to all systems of organization, including systems of transportation, education, government, law, philosophy, theology and metaphysics.

Highlight/Sidelight: Sagittarius has been said to "rule," or symbolize, the Native American. Although this suggestion is belittling in its reductionism, it is nonetheless interesting on several counts. First, the horse came to represent to many Native American cultures something of what it represents in Sagittarius: a huge expansion of power. Second, just as Native American culture was thoroughly tribal, Sagittarius represents tribal instincts. Third, the spiritual religion of many Native American cultures was imbued with metaphysical essences of Sagittarian nature.

Centered in the vision of the "Great Spirit," Native American metaphysics evokes the presence of a *comprehensive organizing principle,* and the *spirit of unity* in the universe. Transcending in some aspects the egocentric conceptions of paternalistic deities in other religions, the Native American ethos of the Great Spirit conveys a sense of living in direct relation to the whole universe. Appealing to a naturalistic God in the "Big Sky," such conceptions harmonize with astronomers' visions of the Big Bang, Einstein's vision of the Grand Unified Field—and Sagittarian visions of encompassing higher design.

♐ Sagittarius

The symbol of the centaur-archer represents the power to *increase* and *expand* human powers beyond their "natural" limits. Both the centaur and the archer symbolize "super"-human abilities achieved through the power of *coordination.* As the centaur-archer coordinates the body of a horse with the head, trunk and arms of a man, Sagittarius symbolizes the power of coordinating and channeling tremendous forces of nature, such as waterfalls, combustion, electricity and horses, to greater human purpose. Much as the harnessing of the horse increases the scope of human power beyond organismic limits, Sagittarius symbolizes the instinct to expand the scope of power through *collaboration* of multiple efforts so as to transcend the limits of the individual acting alone.

The archer complements the centaur in representing "super-power." While the centaur indicates the augmenting power of coordination and collaboration, the archer signifies powers of *calculation, aim* and *design*, and for *planning* and *engineering.* Sagittarius represents the power of *organization,* the predisposition to organize efforts according to prearranged design and purpose.

The archer's upwardly-pointing arrow—the glyph of Sagittarius—symbolizes the ability to ascend and cover great distances. Likewise, both the equestrian might of the centaur and Sagittarius' rulership of the thighs represent powers of *transportation* and *long-distance travel.* The sign of the centaur symbolizes instincts for self-transport in hiking, mountain climbing, skiing, bicycling, cross-country running and horseback riding. Relating to these activities, it represents the predilection to go beyond what is close and familiar, and further indicates the predisposition to partake of the language and culture of far-off places. Sagittarius is associated with "flights of the mind," and the archer's arrow represents the power to ascend ever higher and go ever farther, in mental and metaphysical as well as in physical and socioeconomic ways.

The myth of Phaeton conveys a Sagittarian archetype in which ascent—fiery ascent—becomes self-destructive. Phaeton, a mortal son of Apollo, aspired to the greatest of adventures: to guide the sun-god's chariot across the skies. But Phaeton guided his horses recklessly and flew too close; the chariot burst into flame, fell from the sky and set the world on fire. In reaching for the stars Phaeton—and Sagittarius—represent the all too human liability to overreach, to overdo, and to try to achieve or attain too much.

Short of flying to the sun, Sagittarius indicates the power of inspirational response to challenging situations. It signifies the inclination to enjoy the sense of *freedom to move* in everyday life. It indicates the predisposition to ambulate, circulate, envision and transport. It indicates the *theatrical* instincts of magnifying human reactions for predesigned social effect—the spirit of theater.

As the fire sign of fall, Sagittarius places the symbol of fire in connection with powers of social nature. In this regard it represents the power of *social spirit* as expressed in all manner of cultural, societal and organizational contexts. Sagittarius indicates the predisposition to *participate* in organized social and cultural affairs, and represents *tribal* instincts of identifying with larger social wholes: teams, extended families, clans, fraternities, sororities, races, religions, nations, socio-cultural and ethnic groupings. It symbolizes the spirit of the tribe, the spirit of the *we,* the spirit of social *unity.* Sagittarius represents the predilection to adopt a spirited sense of social purpose, among other things in the context of *career.*

Signified by its keywords, "I Understand," Sagittarius indicates the predisposition to understand interrelationships that make any whole system viable. Long identified with the concept of "higher understanding," it represents the power to comprehend interrelationships in social organizations, politics, economics and law. It indicates the power to understand and interpret symbols and *meaning* in the context of cultural trends and socioeconomic relations, and in connection with symbolic configurations such as are expressed in religion, philosophical systems and astrology. It indicates powers of *codifying* and *systematizing.* And it signifies the instinctive ability to grasp interrelationships as conveyed in systems of natural science, engineering, business and finance.

Sagittarian instincts are expressed in the Archetypes of the Adventurer, the World Traveler, the Man/Woman of the World, the Big Businessman/Financier, the Wheeler-Dealer, the Prime Minister, the Team Player, the Director, the Supervisor, the Theatricist, the Visionary, the Far-seeing, the Superhero, the High Flier, Phaeton, the Flamer, the Supernova, the Shooting Star, the Cultural Aficionado, the Cultural Symbol, the Symbolist, the Big Project.

Famous People born with the sun in Sagittarius include Ludwig Van Beethoven, Henri Toulouse-Lautrec, William Blake, Emperor Nero, Mary Queen of Scots, General George Custer, Strom Thurmond, Alexander Dubcek (Premier, symbol of free Czechoslovakia, 1968), Benigno Aquino, Charles de Gaulle, Winston Churchill, George Schultz, Andrew Carnegie, J. Paul Getty, William F. Buckley Jr., Charles Berlitz, Charles Schulz, Walt Disney, Woody Allen, Steven Spielberg, Frank Sinatra, Jim Morrison, Jimi Hendrix, Tina Turner, Bette Midler, Katarina Witt, Alberto Tomba, Larry Bird, Bo Jackson and Don King.

In Personality, Sagittarius indicates predispositions for seeking to comprehend the larger picture, for being philosophical, calculating, far-seeing, straightforward, frank, pointed, direct, fiery, outspoken, enthusiastic, freedom-loving (in the sense of liking room to move), adventurous, purposeful, broadminded, extravagant, magnanimous, theatrical, bluff and hyperbolic. On the negative side, it signifies capacities for being imperious, blunt, outrageous, bombastic, barbed, pompous, long-winded, calculating, overweening, dictatorial and bossy.

♃ Jupiter ♃

Jupiter was the chief and most powerful of the gods, and wielded the power of the thunderbolt. Similarly, the planet Jupiter symbolizes potentials for wielding *higher powers* and for experiencing higher powers in diverse realms. Jupiter represents higher powers of society and culture, higher powers of social organization, higher powers of the physical world, and higher powers of the metaphysical world.

With reference to realms of society, culture and social organization, Jupiter indicates the motivation to ascend to socio-economic power, and to wield powers that are made possible by systems of social organization. It signifies the motivation for attaining a *vehicle* through which we may ascend in the world: *career* vehicles, financial vehicles, vehicles of transportation, social vehicles, and even criminal vehicles like rackets or scams. It likewise indicates the motivation for experiences that are made possible by such vehicles, including long-distance travel, the learning of complex systems of knowledge, and partaking in major cultural affairs.

Jupiter represents the motivation not merely to wield higher power for one's own purposes, but to progressively expand powers available for the good of others and society. It indicates the motivation to *contribute* to society, to *benefit* common social causes, and symbolizes the potential for the sense of *mission* and *purpose* in life. Jupiter is traditionally called the "Great Benefic" and indicates magnitude not only of size and power but of benefit that can be given or received through the higher organization of society. Hence it indicates potentials for social welfare, patronage, scholarships, grants and endowments. It indicates motivations for *benevolence* and *philanthropy*. It represents the motivation for *boosting*—boostering—self and others upward in the world.

Akin to Sagittarius, Jupiter symbolizes the principle of higher understanding with regard to all "powers that be." It signifies the potential to learn, teach and contribute to the understanding of all larger systems. It indicates the motivation to teach meaning, to instill higher understanding, and to be centrally concerned with education.

In connection with metaphysical realms, Jupiter symbolizes the motivation to apprehend Higher Power as such is conceived to reside in God, Allah, Jesus, the Great Spirit, the Great White Light, or in any other religious/metaphysical conception. Characterized as the "higher mind," Jupiter represents the philosopher in ourselves, and symbolizes the motivation to conceive of higher powers in religion, astronomy, psychology, astrology, physics and the "New Physics." It represents the potential to sense the presence of higher powers in the universe, and so to experience *awe*.

In the physical realm, Jupiter indicates the motivation for high-powered experiences in the context of travel, adventure, and in feats and peaks of physical achievement. It indicates the potential for ascending to peaks: mountain peaks, peaks of endurance and other peak experiences.

Cited as the "principle of expansion," Jupiter symbolizes various potentials related to expansion: expanding of horizons, expanding activities and capabilities, and expanding philosophical world-views. It represents potentials to wax philosophical, to hold forth, to expound, to explain at length. It equally symbolizes the dangers of self-inflation, self-aggrandizement, of too-rapid increase, unwise expansion and *excess* in everything from covering the world with shopping malls to consuming too much food.

As the largest yet least dense of the planets, Jupiter indicates the potential for experiencing *buoyancy*.

Jupiterian motivations are expressed in the Character or Image of God, the Awesome, the Great and Powerful Wizard, the Philosopher, the Metaphysician, the Educator, the Mentor, the Guru, the Professor, the Godfather, the Godmother, the Social Benefactor, the Philanthropist, the Missionary, the Big Deal, the Big Wheel, the Bigwig, the Career Man/Woman, the Lawyer, the Skyscraper, the Pontificator, the Big Windbag, the Booster, the Benefactor, the Ally, the Alliance, the Team Player, the Team/Tribal Partisan, the Aunt/Uncle/Grandfather/Grandmother/Cousin.

Jupiter's placement by house in the natal chart indicates the area of experience where you may develop expansive, boostering attitudes; where such attitudes come into play with respect to career and your path in life; where both your vision and your philosophical attitudes are centered. Jupiter's placement by house suggests the area of experience where benefit, luck and/or the sense of expansion may develop as a function of connection to others and the large world.

Ninth House

Planets in Sagittarius' ninth house draw you to experiences of life as an adventure; higher understanding and organized systems of knowledge; metaphysics and philosophy; higher education; larger social issues and cultural affairs; career challenges; publishing; long distance travel; "extended relationships" such as those involving other cultures, long distances, step-family and in-laws; climbing the metaphorical mountain; higher aspirations; symbols and the interpretation of meaning; ethics; freedom of movement and consciousness; ambiance. (Planets in Sagittarius and/or Jupiter emphasized by aspect may effect similar experiences.)

♑ THE TENTH PRINCIPLE: ♄ CAPRICORN / SATURN

CAPRICORN is the sign of the GOAT. Capricorn rules the KNEES and, with Saturn, the BONE STRUCTURE.

Capricorn is the CARDINAL EARTH sign of WINTER, indicating powers of *generating practical thought.*

The keywords of Capricorn are "I USE." The color associated with Capricorn is BLUE-VIOLET.

The Tenth Principle

While Capricorn is commonly identified with the goat, the symbol is more fully symbolized by the "goat-fish": the head, upper body and front legs of a mountain goat joined to the tail of a dolphin. As with the symbolism of Sagittarius, two beings are fused together so as to symbolize complex human capacities. But whereas the centaur-archer of Sagittarius combines two beings into more than the sum of their parts, the fusion of the goat-fish seems something of an exercise in futility: Neither the tail of the dolphin nor the bony legs of the mountain goat are suited to their counterparts' habitats. Each form is useless to the other.

This contradiction is resolved in connection with Capricorn's rulership of the bone structure. Capricorn symbolizes the concepts of *structure, form* and *function,* and the principle that form determines function. The goat-fish symbolizes the power to assume form so as to accomplish function.

This principle refers to all the structures and forms by which society functions: institutions, government, bureaucracy, hierarchy, rank, rule, requirement, office, position and policy. This principle pertains to the highly structured institutions of the police and the military; to the formalization of administrative functions in documents, legal rulings and the enforcement of law; to punishment and judgment. It refers to all relationships of ruler and ruled, legality and illegality, legitimacy and illegitimacy; to the Establishment, the State and the Authorities. Saturn and Capricorn symbolize the Reality Principle and the principle of *Objectivity.* (This does not mean that Capricornians are bound to be inherently more objective than others—only that they are inclined to come across in such a manner.)

Highlight/Sidelight: In that Capricorn carries the image of being a no-nonsense, goal-oriented and pragmatic type, it can be surprising to learn that such apparently unlikely characters as Elvis Presley, Janis Joplin, Anais Nin and Paramahansa Yogananda were born with the sun in Capricorn. The "Elvis factor" here—earthy sex appeal—is symbolized by the goat-god Pan, as discussed below. But there is also the implication of baring one's soul in *whatever* dimensions of life one might be drawn to.

Capricorn and Saturn indicate the predisposition to create *reality grids,* or reality constructs, that effectively define for the user the laws of life. These laws are not usually intellectual creations; they are born of direct experience. Depending on the primary experiences through which these reality constructs are formed, they can be as purely amoral as moral, as purely self-serving as spiritual. Once established in the Capricorn character, moreover, such reality grids take on the hard sheen of Truth, Truth that s/he is compelled to impart to others.

♑ Capricorn 🐐

As symbolized by its keywords, "I Use," Capricorn represents instincts for *how things work,* the power to become practically adept at all manner of workings within the human universe. Capricorn indicates *mechanical instincts,* the predilection to operate machinery and the workings of technology, to apply practical know-how to any structured process. It symbolizes the power of *functioning,* and represents the predisposition to develop the capabilities to function in the context of jobs, procedures, orders, laws and instructions. Capricorn represents the sensibility of *functional relation to the whole* and indicates the instinctive ability to function in the context of such structural wholes as banks, schools, hospitals, towns and states. It indicates powers of management, execution, professionalism and expertise. Capricorn also represents powers of manufacturing and construction.

The mountain goat symbolizes reaching the heights of *accomplishment,* and the goat-fish symbolizes the kindred power of *determination* to accomplish a task. While this power naturally translates into the personality trait of being determined to accomplish the tasks one takes on come hell or high water, it does not translate into a generic willingness to take on any task that comes along. The Capricorn character is wont to be quite choosy about what mountain s/he is willing to climb, and what structure he or she is willing to work in.

One of the most colorful and appealing dimensions of Capricorn is symbolized by Pan, the Greek shepherd deity who had the horns, legs and ears of a goat. Pan the Piper-Shepherd is a vigorous, lusty character antithetical to the image of the drone beholden to the machinery of society. A god of Nature, Pan symbolizes Nature's *lust for life,* and the virility born of living by the *laws of nature.* Pan represents *earthy wisdom,* Earth mysteries, instinctive insight into Natural Law, and the power to *utilize* natural processes and natural laws toward vital end-goals.

While Capricornian Pan embodies a vigorous earthy vitality, both Capricorn and Saturn are symbolized by a character in whom such vitality is missing: the Old King. The Old King represents any figure who has outworn his authority. This archetypal character symbolizes patterns of experience pertaining to father figures in general, to one's own father, and to anyone who rules on the principle of effete paternalistic authority.

In mythology and history, kings were thought to have derived their authority from either God or the sun. In either case, the sources of the king's authority were seen to be ultimate, divine, spiritual. In the figure of the Old King, however, the ability of the father figure to tap into such spiritual sources has dried up. Instead, he wields authority simply on the basis of tradition and position—the principle of authority voided of any vital basis of legitimacy. Hence the archetype of the Old King presents the challenge to overthrow the Old King—the father figure—in order to reestablish a true basis for authority. This means rising to the challenge not only of usurping the authority of the father figure but of *generating spiritual and practical bases for exerting one's own authority.* In challenging authority figures, the question must be answered: On what real basis do I, or can I, assume authority? Failing to address this question, Capricorn signifies the predilection to wield authority blindly and arbitrarily—to *be* the Old King. Inasmuch as the Capricorn's instinct *is* to assume authority, however, this sign more generally indicates the drive to establish authority in one's own right.

Capricorn indicates the instinct to assume not only authority but *responsibility*—to make sure that things work. As much as the predisposition to take on responsibility is developed early on, Capricorn indicates the predilection to become prematurely serious: as children, little adults.

Capricorn instincts are expressed in the Archetypes of the Manager, the President, the Executive, the Old King, the Hierophant (Tarot), the Great Ambition, the Unforgiven, the Scapegoat, the Undeterred, She Who Picks Herself Up By Her Bootstraps, the Machiavellian, the Utilitarian, the Authoritarian, the Hermit, the Mechanic, the Can-do Guy or Gal, Makes-Do-With-Nothing, Tough-Guy Glamor, Pan, the Old Goat, the Old Salt, Natural Law.

Famous People born with the sun in Capricorn include Isaac Newton, Johannes Kepler, Louis Braille, Albert Schweitzer, Benjamin Franklin, Paul Revere, Horatio Alger, Howard Hughes, J. Edgar Hoover, Richard Nixon, Gamal Abdel Nasser, Mao Zedong, Joseph Stalin, Ali Bhutto, Martin Luther King, Kim Dae Jung (Korean human rights activist jailed for many years), Dian Fossey, Jack London, Don Shula, Humphrey Bogart, Mel Gibson, Cary Grant, Elvis Presley, Janis Joplin, Nicholas Cage and Robert Stack.

In Personality, Capricorn represents predispositions for being matter-of-fact, responsible, goal-oriented, accomplished, hardworking, hard-nosed, street-wise, tough-minded, mechanical-minded, vigorous, worldly wise, earth-smart, hardened, lusty, salty, self-deprecating, self-abnegating, skeptical, persevering, pragmatic, disciplined, and for laying down the law. On the negative side are indicated capacities for being cold, authoritarian, dismissive, cynical, judgmental, Machiavellian, ruthless, rigid, arbitrary, relentless, paranoid, and for being a skinflint: cheap.

♄ Saturn ♄

Saturn was the father of the major Olympian deities, and the planet Saturn symbolizes a host of motivational potentials that are classically associated with the father. These include *responsibility, obligation, authority, judgment, the rule of law, decisions, self-discipline, hard lessons taught and hard lessons learned, profession, honor, position in the community,* and *work in the world.*

As conveyed in the word "saturnine," Saturn has come to be identified with gloomy, grave and taciturn characteristics—qualities that often accompany heavy responsibility. But Saturn was once associated with happy and prosperous times in connection with the ancient celebration of the Saturnalia. This holiday, which early Catholics intentionally supplanted with Christmas, centered on the winter solstice, when the fruits of the year's hard work were to be enjoyed. Saturn was the god of seed and of sowing, and the saying, "As you sow, so you shall reap," applies well to the Saturn principle. Called "the Reaper," Saturn represents the principle that the universe brings to account both the credits and debits of our actions, and that this accounting is manifest over time. In the fable of the ant and the grasshopper, the ant is a Saturn character who will enjoy the winter solstice while the unwise grasshopper will suffer. Saturn symbolizes the father-identified motivations for hard work, self-discipline, and taking the inevitable tests of time.

In its symbolism of the father, Saturn represents the motivation to take and assume responsibility in all areas of life. As with the archetype of the Old King, this planet symbolizes patterns of experience in which the individual is confronted with the failure of others to take full responsibility. This pattern of experience is liable to begin with one's parents, and relates centrally to the Saturnian inclination to *blame.* Yet it also forms the basis of the challenge to assume responsibility both for oneself and for external matters that one considers important. Saturn indicates the motivation to assume responsibility for oneself in the very process of taking responsibility for external concerns. It indicates the motivation to take responsibility for what one must, to make decisions in life, and to face the consequences.

Among the many epithets applied to Saturn is that of the Bridge. As with the symbolism of its rulership of the bone structure, the Bridge symbolizes the motivation to build and use structures to accomplish lasting ends. Indicated here is the motivation for achieving objectives that will bear the weight of real-world stresses. Saturn indicates motivations for perseverance, realism, determination and serious-mindedness.

Counterbalancing Jupiter's symbolism of expansion, Saturn symbolizes the principle of contraction. It similarly signifies potentials of constraint, restriction, *limitation* and *boundaries*. It symbolizes the *crystallization* of what is definite and unavoidable, and indicates the necessity to deal with the hard realities and facts of life.

Saturnian motivations are expressed in the Character or Image of the Father, the Professional, the Sober and Serious One, the Adult, the Judge, the Unforgiving, the Policeman, the Bureaucrat, the Authority, the Buck Stops Here, the Worker, the Workaholic, the Hard Reality, the Law, the Facts of Life, the Establishment, the Rules, the Tests of Time, the Decision, the Expert, the Accomplished One, the Work, the Accomplishment, the Law Unto Himself.

Saturn's position in angular relation to other planets at birth may be interpreted among other things in terms of the experience of the father, and the role of one's father in one's life. For ways of interpreting Saturn's placement by sign, see Chapter 15.

Saturn's placement by house in the natal chart indicates the area of experience where you are challenged to put in a lifetime of work to concretize what you consider most important; where circumstances may seem especially difficult and/or constricting; where you must work to rectify chronically difficult conditions; where you are challenged to develop long-term goals; where you may learn your most difficult lessons or run into the greatest obstacles; where circumstances may require long-term effort.

Tenth House

Planets in Capricorn's tenth house draw you to experiences involving your position in the social order; your most visible role, function or place in the community; work/profession; jobs that have a relatively high public profile; the intentional or unintentional attainment of public visibility, reputation, honor (or dishonor) and renown; accomplishment and expertise; observing social forms; publicly witnessed responsibilities and obligations. (Planets in Capricorn and/or Saturn emphasized by aspect may effect similar experiences.)

♒ THE ELEVENTH PRINCIPLE: ⛢ AQUARIUS / URANUS

AQUARIUS is the sign of the WATER-BEARER. Aquarius rules the ANKLES and, with Uranus, the BRAIN and the ELECTRICAL SYSTEM.

Aquarius is the FIXED AIR sign of WINTER, indicating *communicative* powers oriented to *integration with community and collective life.*

The keywords of Aquarius are "I KNOW." The color associated with Aquarius is PURPLE.

The Eleventh Principle

The symbol of Aquarius is the water-bearer, but it is an air sign, and so represents powers of communication. Similarly, while the parallel waves that form Aquarius' glyph resemble waves of water, they might better signify streaks of lightning. Altogether, the symbolism of Aquarius and Uranus is charged with *electricity.* This principle refers to all electronic inventions including computers, radios, televisions, telephones and satellite systems. In turn these inventions symbolize the human powers of communication and information processing which they facilitate.

Aquarius' 11th house is traditionally associated with "friends, hopes and wishes." This idea can be rephrased in terms of the *experience of hopes, wishes and mutual interests that link us to friends.* The 11th house refers to potentials for progressive change and reform that develop through *communities of interest* —whatever those interests might be. The 11th principle signifies efforts to promote change in concert with new ideas and current waves of opinion. This principle encompasses powers of personal and public opinion, operating by consensus, reform movements and community relations work. Aquarius and Uranus symbolize the principle of life as a series of *events,* life as subject to affect by ever-changing interstices of factors, and life as a phenomenon of the ever-changing *now.*

Highlight/Sidelight: Uranus is known as "the Awakener," and the influences of Uranus are seen to catalyze sudden realizations that change our entire picture of life. Reflecting the positive spin this epithet carries, Richard Tarnas writes that Uranus "always awakens and liberates whatever it touches."[62] In pointing to sudden wake-ups, however, Uranus also indicates the potential for shake-ups: sudden, unexpected events that are as liable as not to be disruptive and upsetting. In connection with the symbolism of electricity in this principle, the phenomenon of lightning striking is both a symbol and example of such events.

In our times, and especially in America, sudden change has become a virtual fact of everyday life. Clearly not all this change is liberating, nor is it all for the good. But as with so much else in astrology, the potential for sudden awakenings can be good—and liberating—largely as a function of how it is individually developed. The more one identifies with Uranian attitudes that embrace the process and possibilities of change, in short, the more we can become activists for positive change, and likewise the more that sudden awakenings will tend to be experienced as exciting. Conversely, when one resists change, the more that the process of waking up in this new age is liable to be experienced in terms of traumatic shake-ups.

♒ Aquarius 🏺

If Sesame Street had been playing way back when, the ancients might have chosen Big Bird to represent Aquarius. As it was, they probably picked the water-bearer because—like Big Bird—it is a classic symbol of *cooperation*. Aquarius represents the instinct for cooperation, and the instinctive sense of universal *interdependence*.

In many ways Aquarius could also be represented by the honeybee, as Aquarius indicates powers that are vividly evident in the collective behavior of these bees. Such powers center on *networking* and *intercommunication* as well as on cooperation. Aquarius symbolizes the power of having one's "antennae" out so as to be constantly in touch with "what's happening." In personality, this kind of power translates into being "tuned in," gregarious and predisposed to "buzzing around." Aquarius indicates powers of collective communication that include being in the know, keeping up to date on current events and *reporting* such. A classic Aquarian image is that of Headquarters—the hive—where everyone thrives on the energy of communication, of being informed and up-to-the-minute. Aquarius indicates predispositions to ride the waves of current events, current opinion, current trends and current information.

Beyond Big Bird and the bees, Aquarius signifies some of the highest values of collective life. An archetype of *communitarian* values and behaviors, the water-bearer symbolizes capacities for humanitarianism, egalitarianism, volunteering, unselfishness and altruism.

As its keywords "I Know" denote, Aquarius indicates powers of knowledge, powers to which electronic inventions are integral. Aquarius symbolizes powers of *computing,* programming, feeding back, storing, transmitting and receiving all manner of information. It indicates the instinctive ability to *integrate* pieces of information into coherent pictures, ideas and *scenarios.* As the word *science* derives from the Latin root *scire,* "to know," moreover, Aquarius symbolizes "scientific instincts" for making *correlations,* for recognizing interconnections between phenomena, for *hypothesizing* about such correlations, and for *experimenting.* Aquarius symbolizes the power of taking an experimental approach to life.

As symbolized by lightning, Aquarius represents powers of making connections in unexpected, interesting and unusual directions. It indicates instincts for *exploring options,* for thinking of *alternatives* and new ideas, and for being open-minded. In its rulership of the ankles, it represents the predilection to *flexibility*, to being able to turn in any direction, to try out any available course of thought or action. Yet as a fixed sign it also represents a proneness to fixity, and signifies the capacity to lock into self-limiting networks of closed-circuit closed-mindedness. Aquarius represents the power to become totally integrated into circuits of thoughts, attitudes, friends and communities of interest, whether such circuits are closed or open. It has been suggested that Aquarians can be the most conventional *or* the most unconventional of people, and indeed this sign simultaneously represents the seemingly opposite powers of conventionality and unconventionality. As well, Aquarius indicates the power of ideology, wherein one's knowledge of a given matter is invested with a fixed set or circuitry of ideas and opinions. Aquarius is the sign of the

ideologue, and it is no accident that the three Aquarian presidents
of the United States—Lincoln, Franklin Roosevelt and Ronald
Reagan—were arguably the three greatest ideologues that office
has yet seen.*

Mythologically, both Aquarius and Uranus are symbolized by
Prometheus, who stole fire from the gods and bestowed it on
humans. Fire here symbolizes the Aquarian power of knowledge,
which redeems humans from the darkness of ignorance, and
allows humans to become as gods. Yet in delivering the power of
fire to humanity, Prometheus incurred the wrath of Zeus, who
retaliated by causing Pandora's box to be opened, and so a host
of troubles to be loosed upon the world. Thus knowledge is
represented as a very mixed blessing.

The linking of knowledge and suffering in this myth symbolizes the painful awareness that for whatever godlike powers
knowledge can bring, human beings are not gods. We are vulnerable, we suffer, we get sick, we die. Gaining the knowledge of
the gods inevitably brings increased *awareness* of *existential
reality.* Hence Prometheus/Aquarius symbolize knowledge in
terms of becoming *conscious* of the human condition: existential-
ism. This Aquarian power of consciousness pertains to the ability
to explore the relativity of one's own existential condition as
much as that of the world at large. As the awareness of existential reality brings *existential uncertainty,* further, Aquarius
symbolizes the sense that we can do anything—or nothing—to
change our lot. This sign symbolizes the power to become aware
of the *ramifications* of change; change on the collective level
with respect to science and technology, and on the individual
level with respect to the dizzying existential options that have
become available to many. In the knowledge that we, like the
gods, have the world before us, the question of just what to do
presents us with unendingly complex alternatives.

Prometheus also symbolizes the instinct for *liberation* and
emancipation, for bringing freedom through knowledge. In
stealing fire from the gods, Prometheus/Aquarius symbolizes the
same figuratively: the power to *demythologize* any area of human
endeavor and experience by recasting it in terms of powers
known to humans through the lights of knowledge, consciousness

---

* See Chapter 14.

and science. Equally, Aquarius indicates the predilection to live as the gods: to attain *global reach* in experience and knowledge, and to engage in high-energy activities.

Aquarian instincts are expressed in the Archetypes of the Now Individual, Prometheus, Promethean Man, the Humanitarian, the Computer Jock, the Technologist, the Reformer, the Liberator, the Liberated Man/Woman, the Ideologue, the Eccentric, the Inventor, the Explorer, the Experimenter, the Newscaster, the Telejournalist, the Innovator, the New Idea, the Lightning Change, the Energizer, What's Happening, What's Going On, Get With the Program, the Busy Bee, the Superstar.

Famous People born with the sun in Aquarius include Charles Darwin, Charles Dickens, Sinclair Lewis, Frederick Douglass, Susan B. Anthony, Thomas Edison, Charles Lindbergh, Jackie Robinson, Rosa Parks, Angela Davis, Betty Friedan, Germaine Greer, Abraham Lincoln, Franklin Roosevelt, Ronald Reagan, Ayn Rand, Bob Marley, Lavar Burton, Babe Ruth, Hank Aaron, Michael Jordan, Tom Brokaw and Oprah Winfrey.

In Personality, Aquarius represents predispositions for being emancipated, flexible (within a given network), gregarious, universally friendly yet impersonal, cool, voluble, oddball, eccentric, quirky, eclectic, innovative, opinionated, plugged in, current with what's happening, activist and informed. On the negative side are indicated capacities for being fixed, absolutist, erratic, remote, aloof, dehumanized, know-it-all, unreachable and dogmatic.

♅ Uranus ♅

Uranus was named after the god of the skies and heavens who, with Gaia (Earth), was progenitor of most of the major gods and goddesses of mythology. But beyond his generative acts, Uranus plays a markedly small role in the affairs of the gods: He is soon murdered by his son Saturn and thus quickly disappears from the lexicons of mythology. To be killed by Saturn is a fine irony because, as Richard Tarnas points out, Uranus (Ouranos) in mythology is *himself* "the father who is rebelled against, while in astrology, Uranus is clearly the rebellious figure and Saturn is the stern archetypal Father who is the focus of that rebellion."[63] Hence as with Aquarius, many astrologers have pointed to Prometheus as a more natural symbolic correlate to the planet Uranus, finding nothing in the symbolism of the god Uranus to cultivate.

There is however one interesting mythological connection between the god Uranus and Prometheus. Consistent with the values of this principle, Uranus presided over the realm of the heavens, and so intrinsically symbolizes the potential for *enlightenment*. Prometheus seems to have been acutely aware of this Uranian potential when he was given the task of making Man. According to *Bullfinch's Mythology,*

> Prometheus ... made man in the image of the gods. He gave him upright stature so that while all other animals turn their faces downward and look to the earth, he raises his to heaven and gazes on the stars.[64]

In making Man in the image of the gods, Prometheus invested Man with the ability to be both enlightened and *intellectually energized* by the sight of the heavens. Uranus further represents the motivations for *reform, transformation* and renovation, motivations that are stimulated by the sight of higher lights.

Uranus was discovered in 1781, at the time that the phenomena of electricity were first being explored by such figures as Franklin, Galvani and Volta. As with Aquarius, Uranus symbolizes all electrically related potentials of human nature, such as the metaphorical *Light Bulb* as Bright Idea, and the computer as a model of the brain. The glyph of Uranus is shaped like an antenna, and suggests the idea of a person being a transmitter-receiver, open to communications instantaneously and omnidirectionally. Uranus indicates potentials for communicating news, ideas and information, and for lightning-like *flashes of insight.* Zap. It symbolizes potentials for sudden breaks from the past, and for taking sudden new directions.

Uranus was discovered during an era that was revolutionary not only in science but in political developments as well. The discovery of Uranus happened during the Age of Revolution, coinciding with both the American and French Revolutions. Uranus is known as the "planet of revolution," and signifies potentials for revolutionary ideologies of emancipation, egalitarianism and democracy. It symbolizes the motivation to invent and communicate popular, new and radical ideas, waves of fashion, fads and rumors. Uranus represents the potential for revolutionary change of all kinds, for *galvanizing* interest in up-to-the-moment, highly energized developments. It represents potentials for invention, innovation and *discovery*.

Uranus is the only planet that rotates in a north-south direction on an east-west axis. This phenomenon symbolizes the ability to see things from different, unconventional and even oddball angles. Identified with the characters of the Iconoclast and the Maverick, Uranus indicates the motivation to wake up, shake up, shake down and shake out the status quo. It represents potentials for sudden, erratic, nonconformist, highly unusual, "wired and crazy" and experimental forms of behavior; and for haywire thinking that springs from circuitry gone awry.

Related to the symbolism of the brain, Uranus represents motivational potentials for intellectual forms of thought wherein new interconnections are continually happening. As the "planet of electricity," it represents the potential for highly charged, surprising and electrifying communications. It further symbolizes the power of picking up vibrations, thought waves and kindred intelligence "out of the air" in direct telepathic communications.

Uranian motivations are expressed in the Character or Image of the Iconoclast, the Revolutionary, the Maverick, the Crackpot, the Nut, the Oddball, the Intellectual, the Community Activist, the Rebel With a Cause, the Zealot, the Movement Organizer, the Scientist, the Dynamo, the Fad, the New Wave, the New Movement, the New Thinking, the Reformer, the Latest Invention, the Light Bulb, Communications Central, Four Telephones Ringing.

Uranus' placement by house in the natal chart indicates the area of experience where you might go through sudden, unexpected, disruptive and revolutionary change; where you are most open to new, unusual and experimental forms of experience; where you most need freedom to explore and learn; where you are inclined to seek openness and freedom of attitude; where you are likely to meet new people and make new connections.

Eleventh House

Planets in Aquarius' eleventh house draw you to experiences of current events, popular movements, waves of social change, and new or eccentric ideas; integration in collective and/or community life; communications with co-workers, friends and acquaintances; connection to groups and groupings based on common interests; collectives centered on a single theme, purpose, or idea; challenges to open to new ideas and reform; scheduling. (Planets in Aquarius and/or Uranus emphasized by aspect in the natal chart may effect similar experiences.)

 ## THE TWELFTH PRINCIPLE:
PISCES / NEPTUNE

PISCES is the sign of the FISH. Pisces rules the FEET, the LYMPHATIC SYSTEM and the PINEAL GLAND.

Pisces is the MUTABLE WATER SIGN of WINTER, indicating powers of being *emotionally adaptable to collective phenomena.*

The keywords of Pisces are "I BELIEVE." The color associated with Pisces is VIOLET.

The Twelfth Principle

As Hamlet said, "nothing is good or bad, but that thinking makes it so"; and so does the twelfth principle speak to the power of thought in *imagining* reality.

A winter sign, Pisces represents powers of thought as *psychic* potentials. One such potential was elegantly exhibited by Albert Einstein, whose sun sign was Pisces: Einstein *visualized* the phenomenon he was addressing to the point of reaching ecstatic states of contemplation. He sought to enter the mind of God. "I want to know how God created this world," he said; "I want to know His thoughts."[65] Between God and science, good and bad, truth and illusion, this principle addresses the power of thought to perceptually create one's universe.

The beginning of the Christian Era coincides with the beginning of the Piscean Age,* and just as the symbol of the fish was

---

* Each of the great zodiacal ages lasts roughly 2200 years.

adopted by early Christians, with Jesus called "the fisherman of souls," this principle symbolizes the realm of the soul and the divine, of faith and belief. As the 12th sign, Pisces completes the astrological circle, and refers to all endings of cycles, to transcendence and transition into what is beyond. Hence this principle refers to the perception of what happens after death, to the soul's ascendance into the hereafter, and to reincarnation.

In symbolizing the ending of one cycle as the beginning of a new one, Pisces also symbolizes the repeating of cycles in our finite world. Among the cycles indicated here are sickness and healing, waking and sleeping, addiction and recovery. The imagery of the ocean evoked by both Neptune and Pisces symbolizes the whole in which all life communes, the web of life, the subtle gossamer threads connecting all life, and ecology. Pisces and Neptune indicate potentials for perceiving *sublime order* and *cosmic resolution.*

Highlight/Sidelight: Michel Gauquelin's findings concerning the 12th house—correlations of planetary placements in the 12th house with exceptional career success—fly in the face of traditional interpretation. Relevant to these findings is a poll of self-made millionaires and billionaires among the Fortune 400 conducted by *Forbes* Magazine. This poll showed that there were considerably more Pisceans among self-made millionaires and billionaires than any other sun sign.[*] Giving lie to the image of Pisceans as artistic, sensitive *schlemiels,* winning the self-made-billionaire contest links Pisces with high success.

Inasmuch as Piscean influences can be correlated with a success mentality, it may be because these influences engender the predilection to become fully enveloped in a *mythos*—in a mode or current of thinking. The rub is that Pisceans are inclined to become absorbed in *any* mythos. Just as some Pisceans might become enveloped in the mythos of art or religion, others might become enveloped in the "mythos of success."

---

[*] According to the poll, 11.3% of the self-made individuals were born with the sun in Pisces, whereas the next most successful sign, Aquarius, accounted for 9.4 %. *Forbes* Magazine, Oct. 16, 1995. pp. 380-382.

♓ Pisces

Pisces' fish symbolize the power to *align* thought with the flow of *collective currents,* to "school" thought and action in line with prevailing currents of collective life. As the mutable water sign of winter, it represents the power to emotionally adapt to collective milieux, to become *immersed* in enveloping mediums or environments. The watery milieu of Pisces symbolizes any milieu in which consciousness can become immersed, including television, the Internet, business, religious and work environments, hospitals, retreats and schools. Pertaining to another milieu of immersion, Pisces indicates the predilection to gossip. It indicates the motivation to immerse oneself in belief systems, idealized images, illusions and oceanic states induced by drugs or alcohol, and in any other world that is capable of swallowing, sucking up or totally absorbing consciousness.

Pisces' fish and their oceanic habitat signify the flow of imagery from unconscious realms, and so indicates *imagic* instincts. The fish represent the power of imagery to stimulate the imagination in such phenomena as advertising, mass media, cartoons, comics, film and myth. Pisces symbolizes the proverbial power of myth.

As the keywords of Pisces, "I Believe," suggest, the capacities of thought indicated by Pisces are a function of what is believed, imagined or visualized, and Pisces represents the power of visualization. While the psychic powers indicated here can translate into self-delusion and warped belief, they can equally be translated into the clear perception of highly complex phenomena.

Pisces' symbol shows two fish swimming in opposite directions, but also tied to one another. Herein is a representation of paradox, and Pisces symbolizes the ability to perceive and accept paradox. In this regard it symbolizes the relationship between intrapsychic reality and outer reality, inasmuch as exterior currents of collective life and interior currents of psychic imagery run in opposite directions. Somewhat akin to its opposite sign, Virgo, Pisces represents the power—and the challenge—to allow both these currents to meet in consciousness, to center oneself between the inner and the outer. One such centering power indicated by Pisces is *meditation.* Yet it also represents the instinct to tap into unconscious and *libidinal* sources, to give liquid expression to vivid imagery emanating from subconscious realms—no matter what the outer context may be. Pisces indicates predispositions to being libidinous, fanciful, off-color and offbeat.

The glyph representing Pisces has been said to derive from the Egyptian hieroglyph signifying "psychic regeneration." The two arcs with the line between them suggest the two sides of the brain, with the line connecting them representing psychic activities of meditative, dream, prayer and healing states. Pisces' rulership of the pineal gland, the seat of the "third eye," further represents psychic powers of "second sight," of psychic visions and hallucination.

Between the emotional and psychically intuitive powers represented by this sign, Pisces indicates the ability to see many things that may not communicated in words. The color associated with Pisces, violet, lies at the end of the visible spectrum and shades into the invisible range of ultraviolet. Similarly Pisces, the last sign of the zodiac, symbolizes the instinct to perceive invisible and transcendent realms. As much as perceiving is believing, this transcendent power of perception pertains to belief in—or perception of—such phenomena as God, heaven, miracles, reincarnation, life after death, angels, spirit guides, nature spirits/devas, ghosts and extraterrestrials.

In ruling the lymphatic system, Pisces symbolizes the dissolution of toxins in purification and healing. Relating again to the symbolism of the sea, Pisces indicates the instinct for psychically absorbing self in oceanic flows of consciousness (beginning with sleep) that aid the body's healing and self-cleansing processes. In symbolizing purification and cleansing, however, it also symbolizes the capacity for polluting, for pollution of both self and the environment.

In connection with the sea, Pisces symbolizes the experience of *fertile chaos,* and indicates the power to thrive on the chaos and wildness of nature. Conversely it symbolizes the capacity to be *overwhelmed* by chaos, and to succumb to oceanic tides in life. It has been suggested that by way of preempting the threat of being overwhelmed, some Piscean characters develop tightly controlled belief systems. Similarly, some Pisceans are thought to do well in tightly structured environments.

In mythology, Pliny's tale of the boy and the dolphin conveys a classic Piscean archetype. In this little story, a boy was befriended by a dolphin, and rode daily on its back. One day the boy swam out to meet the dolphin, but drowned before he could find his companion. The dolphin carried the boy to shore, where it stayed with the boy, until the dolphin itself died.

Turning a twist on the theme of oceanic engulfment, the dolphin was engulfed in its relationship with the boy. Like the ocean, the dolphin symbolizes the archetypal intent to dissolve self/consciousness into something that transcends self. But this myth also symbolizes the sense that self can become totally absorbed in small things as well as large—in any figure or figment of life. So it is that Piscean characters are as prone to become workaholics as alcoholics, plant-lovers as religious devotees. The dolphin in this myth further symbolizes Piscean capacities for self-sacrifice, for losing ego boundaries, and for *compassion.* It symbolizes a proneness to be so totally enveloped in certain states of consciousness so as to be effectively *in denial* of reality. And it represents the inherent attraction to situations of *rescue.* Pisces symbolizes the archetypes of both the rescuer and the one rescued.

Pisces is associated with Dionysus, god of the vine. Myths of Dionysus link wine and intoxication with both insanity and divinity, and in so doing link three ecstatic states of being symbolized by Pisces. Dionysus also symbolizes the capacity for communion with different faces of nature: wild, serene, pure, savage.[*]

In Personality, Pisces represents predispositions for being dreamy, dreamy-eyed, otherworldly, floating, elusive, fanciful,

---

[*] Edith Hamilton writes of the Maenads, worshippers of Dionysus:

"They went to the wilderness to worship, to the wildest mountains, the deepest forests, as if they kept to the customs of the ancient time before men had thought of building houses for their gods. They went out of the dusty, crowded city, back to the clean purity of the untrodden hills and woodlands. There Dionysus gave them food and drink: herbs and berries and the milk of the wild goat. Their beds were on the soft meadow grass; under the thick-leaved trees; where the pine needles fall year after year. They woke to a sense of peace and heavenly freshness; they bathed in a clear brook. There was much ... ecstasy ... in the wild beauty... And yet, always present, too, was the horrible bloody feast."   — Edith Hamilton, *Mythology*, p. 57.

libidinous, sensitive, off-beat, imaginative, compassionate, idealizing, elfin, sprightly, and living in two worlds at once. On the negative side it indicates the capacity for being evasive, escapist, dissolute, nihilistic, self-pitying, addictive, unreasonable, self-deluding, ungrounded, prone to go through money like water, misguided and in denial of reality.

Piscean instincts are expressed in the Archetypes of the Dreamer, the True Believer, the Devotee, the Savior, the Saved, the Seer, the Lush, the Imaginative Genius, the Space Cadet, the Image-Maker, the Martyr, the Prophet, the Visionary, the Ridiculous, the Sublime, Don Quixote, Puck, the Media Icon, the Gossip, an Ear into the Other World, the Cartoon, the Nature Lover.

Famous People born with the sun in Pisces include George Washington, Mikhail Gorbachev, Harriet Tubman, Albert Einstein, Alexander Graham Bell, Linus Pauling, George Friederich Handel, Pierre-Auguste Renoir, Andrés Segovia, Meher Baba, Edgar Cayce, L. Ron Hubbard, Ralph Nader, Ansel Adams, Dr. Seuss, Jack Kerouac, John Steinbeck, John Irving, Gabriel Garcia Marquez, Lawrence Welk, Ed McMahon, Jean Harlow, Elizabeth Taylor, Edward Albee, Zero Mostel, Billy Crystal, Patty Hearst, Anais Nin, Nat King Cole, Harry Belafonte, James Taylor and George Harrison.

♆ Neptune ♆

Neptune was the god of the seas, and like Pisces Neptune indicates the motivation for *communing* with oceanic realms. Of these there are three: the realm of the unconscious, the realm of collective life, and the cosmic realm.

Pertaining to the unconscious, Neptune symbolizes potentials for communing with unconscious currents through *dreams, fantasy, imagination* and *daydreaming*. Neptune is the Dream Weaver, and represents the motivation for "bathing in" dreams, for allowing the imagery of dreams to suffuse consciousness, and for intuiting meaning in this imagery. It indicates the potential for psychic visions, revelry, floating away in fantasy and *inebriation*.

Like an internal "fantasy faculty," Neptune symbolizes the motivation to *channel* image-laden material from the murky depths of the unconscious into the stream of consciousness. It signifies the potential for *projecting* unconscious feelings and attitudes into the world around oneself, so that the perception of one's environment, and of others, takes on the colorations of what is actually emanating from within. Inasmuch as unconsciously projected contents can be positively charged, it indicates the potential for *idealization.* Conversely it indicates the potential to allow one's consciousness to be totally colored or infused by the external environment. It represents the potential to dissolve ego boundaries and lose sight of where self ends and other begins. Neptune further represents potentials for sublimation, intellectualization, and the achievement of *resolution,* processes through which inner motives are *transmuted.*

As symbolized by the murky depths of the ocean, Neptune indicates the capacity to be deceived by shadowy realms, illusion and distorted perception, for balloon-like inflation of the real into the unreal, for hallucination, impossible dreams and self-deception. It indicates the motivation to transcend ordinary reality, and to seek oceanic states of consciousness through drugs and alcohol; and it represents *mind-manifesting* potentials associated with psychedelic drugs.

Pertaining to the realm of collective life, Neptune indicates potentials for "swimming" in collective currents of thought and belief. It signifies the faculty by which we become attuned to collective ideals, attitudes, myths and icons, and allow the imagery and emotional content of such collective phenomena to progressively suffuse consciousness. This potential can be developed as much in terms of becoming divinely inspired to work selflessly on behalf of the needy as becoming completely absorbed into the *mythos* of Hollywood. It further indicates the power to *perceive* the prevailing currents—and subtle undercurrents—of collective life, and to make conscious choices based on such perception. Yet it equally represents the potential to become submerged in such currents, and to be caught up in the confused, nebulous and illusory imagery of shallow collective reality.

With reference to the cosmic realm, Neptune represents the spiritual motivation to perceive transcendent dimensions of being, and the motivation to achieve transcendent states of consciousness such as universal love and the "peace that passeth understanding." It symbolizes the motivation to seek self-transcendence through such activities as prayer, meditation and fasting as well as through drugs; to receive divine guidance; and to perceive subtle and/or symbolic phenomena as presented in astrology, the *I Ching,* the Tarot and psychic readings.

As the psychic and spiritual faculty within us, Neptune represents powers of psychic suggestion, hypnosis and faith healing. It indicates potential psychic gifts for ESP, channeling, precognitive dreams, psychic intuition and psychic sensitivity. It indicates spiritual potentials for experiencing God, divine visitations, angels, salvation and redemption, reverence and renunciation, seclusion and cloistering, self-abnegation and resurrection, and ultimate concern. Neptune symbolizes the motivation for spiritual enlightenment and wisdom, and even more than Pisces it represents the potential for the dissolution of ego in spiritual consciousness.

As with Pisces' symbolism of healing, Neptune signifies the oceanic power to wash away old hurts and heal old wounds. It symbolizes the potential to turn old difficulties and debilities into compost for new growth and eventual new cycles of experience.

Neptunian motivations are manifest in the Character or Image of the Imaginative Inspiration, Psychic, the Visionary, the Hypnotist, the Spiritualist, the Spiritual Mystic, the Cultist, the Silver Screen, the Shadow, the Sublimator, the Sublime, the Dreamer, the Fantastic, the Sacrifice, the Martyr, the Selfless One, the Drug Addict, the Alcoholic, the Recovering Alcoholic/ Addict, the Self-Deluded, the Long Suffering, the Idealist.

One way of interpreting Neptune's natal placement by sign is in terms of generational tendencies. For example, collective penchants of the generation born roughly 1943-1956, when Neptune was in Libra, were expressed in the mythos of the Hippie. Immersed in their credo of love, peace, music, Eastern religions and drugs, the Hippies expressed values classically associated with both Libra and Neptune.

Neptune's placement by house in the natal chart indicates the area of experience where reality is subject to greatest perceptual distortions; where self may be perceived by others in radically different ways at different times; where it is especially meaningful to develop spiritual awareness; where spiritual growth can best manifest; where you may develop imaginative gifts and express yourself imaginatively.

Twelfth House

Planets in Pisces' twelfth house draw you to experiences of enveloping collective environments such as hospitals, schools and other total institutions; social service (sometimes interpreted as paying off karmic debt); communion with dream worlds; fantasy life and mythic worlds; personal myths and imagery; imagination channeled into media and/or other collective milieux; suffusion of consciousness by prevailing myths, attitudes and ideals; immersion in illusions and addictions; meditation and healing; seclusion; attuning yourself so as to find your "ecological niche"; spiritual life and seeking spiritual guidance. (Planets in Pisces and/or Neptune's emphasis by aspect in the natal chart may effect similar experiences.)

PART III

CHAPTER 10

GHOSTS IN THE MACHINE

> The experimental psychologist assumes with little ques-
> tion that systematic laws of behavior can be discovered...
> The idea of universal determinism is new and exciting,
> even today. We who regard behavior as determined by
> natural law occupy a unique position.
> — R.C. Bolles, *Theory of Motivation*

What is natural law in psychology?

Not so many years ago, psychologists like R.C. Bolles were
thrilled to formulate natural laws of human behavior in the name
of Behaviorism. As late as 1970, scientists still believed that
continuing experimentation would yield ever-growing sets of
statistics showing human behavior to be primarily a function of
conditions of the environment.

Never mind that their conception of natural law was based in
great part on experimentation with rats.

A thousand years ago, in the most marked of contrasts,
Thomas Aquinas saw natural law as a direct function of God's
law. Portraying natural law according to classic philosophical
and spiritual perspectives, Aquinas thought of natural law in
connection with such questions as just when during pregnancy
the soul enters the body. (He believed the soul enters the body at
"the quickening," when fetal movements are first felt.)

Between Aquinas and Bolles, it would seem self-evident that
the search for natural law in matters of human life should
entertain the broadest range of perceived phenomena. It should
arguably leave at least as much room for conceptions of the
spirit, the soul and the psyche as for statistics derived from
experimentation on rats. Yet in modern psychology, the psyche,
the soul and the spirit have all been rejected as subjects of

mainstream academic study. Seventy years after this rejection, the wisdom of confining psychology to the experimental study of observable behavior is still, at the least, questionable.

At the beginning of this century, William James, the "father of modern psychology," pursued a classic integrative approach to the subject by pursuing parallel tracks of inquiry into psychology, philosophy and spirituality.* Later, Jung picked up James' lofty standard. Affirming that the psyche "in its upper reaches ... resolves itself into a 'spiritual' form about which we know as little as we do about the functional basis of instinct,"[66] Jung sought to understand relationships linking biological, philosophical and spiritual dimensions of life. Unfortunately, Jung, the last of the great depth psychologists, was also among the last to feel free enough to integrate scientific, philosophical and spiritual perspectives.

Even during his lifetime, Jung's work was rejected by the growing legion of academic psychologists, who came to consider Jung's philosophical method obsolete. Indeed it was just as Jung reached the prime of his career that academic psychology came under the dominion of hard science. Although Jung brought a great deal of clinical experience to bear in developing his theories, his work was increasingly ignored for the simple reason that philosophical and spiritual traditions were being run off the academic field of play.

With the ghosts in the machine cast out, the spectral influences of the psyche brushed off by hard-minded scientists, attention turned more and more to measurable mechanics of behavior, to the "machine" itself. Decades after scientists' ascendance to power, however, the relationship of science to psychology is not yet resolved. In 1982, the eminent psychologist Philip G. Zimbardo was unusually candid in describing the shortfalls of the scientific approach:

> Now that cognitive psychology has taken the head once lopped off by radical behaviorism and returned to the body of psychology, we might in the next ten years consider implanting a heart or a soul in the same body.[67]

---

* James' last major work was *The Varieties of Religious Experience*.

The thought in Zimbardo's metaphor is telling. He suggests that "radical behaviorism" is the "body" of psychology not only because Behaviorism was the dominant force in the field through the middle of this century, but because it appeared to be a scientist's dream come true: Behaviorism made possible the quantification of behavior (at least in rats!) by means of neat mathematical equations. Generations of students were taught to think of behavior as a tightly "conditioned" function of environmental variables—obviously far too much so. Overlooking the existence of many other kinds of influences in behavior, the Behaviorists took their theory to extremes. Eventually these extremes became infamous. By the late 1960s, irreverent students of Psychology were marching around like zombie-robots uttering, "I am nothing but a bundle of conditioned responses; I am nothing but a bundle of conditioned responses." Change was in the air.

About 1970, interest in the phenomena of cognition broke as a wave on the psychological scene. As Zimbardo implies, Cognitive Psychology's study of factors of "the head" acted to balance out Behaviorism's lopsided emphasis on environmental factors. Meanwhile, the recent resurgence of interest in biological/genetic factors has effectively returned to Psychological Man his genitals. Academic psychology has not yet, however, achieved comprehensive theoretical integration, essentially because, as Zimbardo said, it has lost its metaphorical heart and soul.

What are the heart and soul of psychology? This is not hard to answer: What could psychology's heart be but philosophy, and what could its soul be but spirituality? And even while doctors transplant physical hearts, can we expect *scientists* ever to "implant" the metaphysical heart and soul of psychology (back) into the body of the subject? Obviously not.

The failings of academic psychology were rarely better articulated than in 1955 by Ruth Munroe:

> In America especially, "psychology" has ... become so infatuated with its methodologies as to apply them pedantically to the detriment of its essential aim—the understanding of people. Deliberate limitation of the *person* to such aspects of his behavior as we can study under scientifically controlled conditions makes it difficult to develop

insights into trends and relationships among trends
beyond our original hypothesis.[68]

While appreciating the value of experimental science, Munroe
advocated for a "philosophico-scientific" approach to psychology wherein understanding "trends and relationships among
trends" might incorporate scientific knowledge without being
subordinated to such knowledge. Forty years after the fact, this
suggestion is still sound. Why can't philosophical methods still
draw on the best of both worlds, acknowledging pertinent scientific data in the very process of synthesizing broader theory?

If we understand that not all natural law can be quantified—
especially in psychology—the real questions regarding philosophy's role do not concern its essential legitimacy—it should be
affirmed from the start—but rather its proper place and its limits.
The important questions about philosophy should concern how,
where and when philosophical methods go beyond offering
insight and understanding about fundamental motivations, and
begin to contradict the facts of science. Of course the same
questions should be turned around: Where and when does
science supersede its legitimate mandate and seek to deny the
existence of dimensions, motivations, trends and interrelationships simply because it cannot measure them?

Like scientists, ironically, many astrologers still tend to think
in terms of cause-effect relationships. And inasmuch as astrologers still fall into the trap of astrological determinism, they too
are liable to eschew philosophical methods, to mistake "conduct"
for "principles underlying conduct." Instead of trying to reduce
philosophy's role in astrology, then, we ought absolutely to
affirm it, to say, "We stand on the principle that philosophy is a
sine qua non of *both* astrology and psychology."

We ought also declare that the twelve astrological principles
are a *sine qua non* of philosophical psychology. As we have
sought to convey, the twelve principles of astrology translate into
higher organizing principles in psychology. Hence the idea
emerges that these principles of astrology may be vital to the
development of "philosophico-scientific" theory in psychology.

As it stands, academic psychology is generally devoid of
unifying principles except for one: the principle of experimental
science. Yet amidst the sprawling fields of academic psychology,

fields overgrowing with ever-new crops of experiments, there are hints, implications and allegations of broader underlying relationships. How radically delicious an idea that astrology provides the means of grounding psychology in the understanding of underlying principles.

To those with eyes to see, the principles of astrology work to integrate whole arrays of diverse but intrinsically related material generated by science into principles that cleave to a higher level of natural law. Yet to place astrological principles in relation to the proven knowledge of academic psychology, we also must shape the meaning of those principles in ways that harmonize with the hard explanations of experimental science.

So let us explore how the symbols, the principles and (last but not least) the influences perceived in astrology come into play as we seek to generate elements of a Grand Unifying astro-psycho-philosophico-scientific theory. Or else, psychological theory for lunatics.

CHAPTER II

PSYCHOLOGICAL THEORY FOR LUNATICS

> Different theorists have taken different starting points.
> Any theory of emotion or any empirical research on emo-
> tion deals only with some part of the broad meaning that
> the term has acquired. Some theorists stress [physiologi-
> cal] factors, some behavioural, some subjective. Some
> deal only with extremes, some say emotion colors all
> behaviour. There is no consensus of opinion; at present
> emotion defies definition. It is impossible to make conclu-
> sive statements about the whole subject merely from ideas
> or research in only one of its aspects.[69]
>
> — T. Strongman, in *The Psychology of Emotion*

Emotion has been an especially difficult subject for academic
psychologists because, as Thomas Strongman notes, they can be
studied from such diverse "starting points"—to widely varying
results. Adopting a more optimistic and positive attitude toward
this diversity of perspectives, Carroll Izard writes: "Clearly,
knowledge of the emotions has been, and will continue to be,
advanced by multiple approaches."[70] But basic differences in
frames of reference stimulate psychologists to ask the most basic
of questions about emotions, beginning with: "Are there basic
emotions?" This question is actually so compelling to academics
that it forms the title of the first section of the most recent
definitive work on emotion, Oxford's *The Nature of Emotion*
(1995).

Contributors to *The Nature of Emotion* fill a relatively broad
spectrum of views. At the radical end of this spectrum, Richard
Shweder calls into question all present academic approaches.
Asserting that we must go beyond current starting points,

Shweder tells us that emotion is largely a function of language and culture; that emotions are:

> ... complex narrative structures that give shape and meaning to ... feelings of the body ... and ... soul[!] ... whose unity is to be found in the ... stories they make it possible for us to tell about our feelings.[71]

And he concludes his chapter with this appraisal:

> Before we can answer questions about 'basic emotions' with any real confidence, far more comparative research is needed unencumbered of ethnocentric illusions, philosophical naiveté and question-begging methodologies... [M]y answer to the question "Are there basic emotions?" is "Do not trust anyone who says they really know."[72]

What might be these "question-begging methodologies" be? Actually, the very posing of the question, "Are there basic emotions?" signals a certain kind of prejudice. The posing of this question from a scientific frame of reference assumes that the most important way of approaching emotions is in terms of *breaking them down* to the quantifiable elements that make them basic. (Whatever "basic" means: Researchers cannot agree on even the meaning of the term *basic emotions*.) One contributor to *The Nature of Emotion*, H. H. Goldsmith, cites this very bias:

> Carving the human personality into smaller domains on the basis of our present knowledge to facilitate scientific analysis involves ... a willingness to accept the strong likelihood of eventually being judged as arbitrary, simplistic, or just ignorant.[73]

To generate a starting point that redresses the fragmenting biases of experimental science, let us rephrase the question by asking, "What is basic about emotions?" Scientists would respond to this query with a litany of usual suspects: Basics of emotion include elements of physiological arousal, affect, cognitive components such as "appraisal," antecedent conditions, temperamental differences between individuals, facial expressions and developmental factors.

Yet isn't it more meaningful to say that what is basic to emotion are actually complex and variable *interrelationships* among such elements? As with everything else in psychology, nothing about emotion can be studied in a vacuum. The analysis of any one phenomenon inevitably leads to intricate connections to a bevy of other phenomena. Respecting such complexity, it seems that beyond breaking down emotions into component parts, it is sensible to study them as processes with many dimensions.

Moreover, the very concept of "the nature of emotion" implies that emotions themselves can somehow be seen as distinct phenomena in nature. But do emotions exist outside or apart from the whole human being? No; they are integral to the whole human condition and cannot be separated from it any more than the phenomenon of rain can be separated from clouds. Hence why shouldn't we be asking: *"What are the basic potentials of human nature and experience* by which we can understand the processes of emotion? Or: What are the *basic connections* that link component elements of emotion in the context of larger principles of human nature?

From a perspective that transcends the laboratory, it is impossible to study emotions without recognizing the existence of interrelationships linking experimentally measured components of emotion to aspects of human life beyond what experimental investigators isolate. Any real-world attempt to understand emotions compels us to acknowledge dimensions of human nature that are ignored in academic psychology simply because they do not fit into academic parameters of study.

Take fear. Certainly there is no emotion more basic than fear. Fear has been studied scientifically at least as much as any emotion. The irony is again, however, that experimentally-oriented studies of fear inevitably draw us to awareness of whole other realms beyond what the experiments address. Because of the multiplicity of interrelationships that obtain, to study fear is to confront a higher level of internal organization than scientific analysis can entertain.

Much of the experimental research conducted on fear is coupled with research on pain, and much of this research is placed in the context of learning theory. Classic findings include the following.

Across a wide range of animal species—including human beings—exposure to pain produces learned responses of fear. These responses typically center on avoidance, and are usually associated with past experiences of pain.

A well-known experiment demonstrating the phenomenon of learned responses of avoidance involving fear and pain begins with the placing of a dog in one side of a large partitioned box. The floor of the side of the box in which the dog is placed is wired for electricity. At given intervals, an electric current is turned on. However, ten seconds *before* the floor underneath the dog is electrified, a red light is turned on. To avoid getting shocked, the dog must learn to jump over the partition into the safe side of the box when the light goes on. Normal (untraumatized) dogs learn very quickly, after being shocked only a few times, to make the leap to safety whenever the red light is turned on. The dog becomes, in other words, *conditioned* to avoid the pain associated with the red light.

The emotional component of such conditioned avoidance behavior is fear.

Experiences of pain often produce powerful sensitization to stimuli that are originally neutral. In the experiment just described, the red light is an inherently harmless stimulus, but quickly takes on intense negative associations to the dogs— associations of fear and pain.

Once an organism has become conditioned by exposure to pain, learned reactions of fear and avoidance behavior are typically long-lived. The persistence of such responses may far outlast the actual adaptive value of the original learning. In our experiment, dogs conditioned to avoid the pain associated with the red light will continue to jump over the wall when the red light comes on, long after the appearance of the light has ceased to be followed by electrification of the floor.

Experiences of fear and pain produce extreme physiological changes. The emotion of fear is marked by sudden and powerful changes in the autonomic nervous system, including dramatic increases in heart rate, blood pressure and galvanic skin response.

Some of the most interesting research involving fear and pain involves exposure to painful stimuli that can neither be predicted nor controlled.

Beginning with the pioneer behaviorist Ivan Pavlov, researchers have demonstrated that fear and pain are instrumental in producing *experimental neuroses* in animals. As Susan Mineka of the University of Wisconsin and John Kihlstrom of Harvard have shown,[74] most of the symptoms that characterize neurosis in human beings can be produced in animals by exposing them to painful stimuli that animals can neither predict (and thereby avoid) or control (and thereby escape). The animal symptoms produced by such exposure include severe anxiety, agitation, panic, passivity, freezing behavior, helplessness (also called "learned helplessness"), depression and marked disturbances in feeding patterns.

Similarities between these animal symptoms and common neurotic conditions in human beings such as anxiety neurosis, chronic depression, catatonia and anorexia nervosa suggest that unpredictable and uncontrollable experiences of fear and pain are at the root of much human neurosis. This suggestion is supported by what we know about early childhood.

As has been recognized by psychotherapists since Freud, the potential for experiences of fear and pain is magnified tremendously in the earliest developmental stages—in the first few years of life. What Freudians have not always understood, though, is that these magnified potentials are intimately related to the absence of consistent maternal/parental care.

Experiments with primates* have demonstrated that the absence of a mother figure, with the consequent deprivation of opportunities for clinging, being comforted, and simply being in close proximity to a primary caretaker, cause powerful fear-related reactions. The effects of deprivation and separation from

---

* The most famous of this genre of experiment were conducted by Harry Harlow using rhesus monkeys. In these experiments, infant monkeys deprived of any semblance of a mother figure through the first several months of life produced adult monkeys with the most severe psychopathological symptoms. Compared to the monkeys who were totally deprived, however, monkeys who were provided with terry-cloth puppet "surrogate mothers" fared far better as adults, as the terry-cloth surrogate fulfilled the infant monkeys' basic need for what came to be called 'contact comfort.'

mother figures include passivity, anxiety, detachment, "anxious attachment" (over-dependence), hostility, passivity, insecurity, distress and phobias. As with experiments that involve direct exposure to painful stimuli, the neurotic symptoms produced by deprivation and separation are profound and long-lasting.

The primates to which these findings apply include human children.

Clinical research by John Bowlby has confirmed that newborn babies have intense biophysiological drives and needs for human contact—being held and hugged, sucking, etc.—in addition to the more obvious needs of food and warmth. Between the ages of one and three, similarly, babies have insuperable drives and needs for clinging, and for voice and body contact with mother or an equivalently special primary caretaker. Stemming from these universal needs (or drives, or "behavioral systems" as Bowlby calls them), prolonged or repeated separation from a primary caretaker results in long-term responses constellated around fear and pain, responses of the neurotic varieties cited above.

Minor traumatic reactions to the absence or unpredictability of a primary caretaker typically recede in the course of healthy development. Fear and pain, however, remain crucial to personal well-being. In appropriate situations, fear and pain emerge sharply into the foreground of consciousness, as they continue to be "useful and adaptive" parts of one's behavioral/motivational/ emotional repertoire.

For those who have been visited by more significant trauma in early life, however, the cluster of chronic emotional responses surrounding fear and pain impinge on the "ability to adapt," and may press with unusual force on consciousness for many years beyond the original trauma. Yet with the help of emotional support from the outside, and usually by dint of conscious effort, such conditioned emotional responses may also gradually fade into relatively harmless regions of memory.

Through this exploration of research on fear and pain, implications of interrelationships linking a variety of different phenomena are unmistakable. When you study fear, in short, you wind up finding inextricable connections to such phenomena as attachment, unconditional love, anxiety, hugs, food and Mom. These connections and interrelationships in turn suggest the existence of a higher organizing principle in human life.

Many psychologists not bound by the strictures of hard science have generated conceptions of such a principle. In his masterwork *Attachment and Loss,* for example, John Bowlby synthesized findings from a broad array of ethological and experimental studies. Approaching fear in terms of its adaptive values, Bowlby's work elegantly integrates phenomena including fear, attachment and loss, basic needs of babies and small children, dependency, safety, security, the comforting/nurturing presence of mothers and other parental figures, separation, anxiety, phobia, sorrow, sadness, withdrawal, depression and mourning.

Aside from Bowlby, theories describing relationships among such phenomena have been generated by psychologists including Karen Horney, Fritz Perls (Gestalt Therapy), Harvey Jacklin (Re-evaluation Counseling), Heinz Kohut and Selma Fraiberg. Yet none of these theories has produced anything close to the impact of Freud's theory of sexuality.

As far from the academic setting as one could get, though, a singularly compelling principle regarding such phenomena has materialized in the pop psychology concept of the inner child.

Let us summarize briefly what the inner child conception does and doesn't do. What it does do is integrate a whole complex of emotionally based capacities and processes, and organizes the understanding of this complex in terms of the perception of a *core motivation.* In short it serves to conceptualize a *part of self,* a dimension of being in which a whole constellation of interrelated phenomena come together. The concept of the inner child likewise serves to *organize the experience* of Mom, anxiety, attachment, loss, childhood trauma, the present experience of feelings, comfort, caring, unconditional love and a host of other phenomena. It also gives voice to higher human potentials including sensitivity, vulnerability, intimacy, and many subtleties of experienced feelings.

What the inner child does not do is say very much about what it becomes when it grows up, if it ever does. The inner child concept says little about *active behavior,* and especially little about the behavior of adults, beyond how such behavior relates explicitly to the experiences and feelings of children. It does not account for the myriad of *individual differences* in how we express and interpret experiences of feelings. Finally, it does not hold out much hope of being verified, in and of itself, as a naturalistic reality. We are unlikely to find a teddy-bear in some nether region of the brain.

It is conceivable, though, that we may someday find the imprint of the moon in some nether region of the brain; and so let us now entertain the idea of the inner moon. As metaphor, we may assert that the inner moon contains the whole of the inner child—and more. As influence, we may describe the inner moon as a dimension of human nature, a "psychic organ" that corresponds directly to the moon as perceived astrologically. Inasmuch as we can legitimately describe astrological influences by means of metaphor and other qualitative terms, we need make no final distinction between the inner moon as influence and the inner moon as metaphor.

To make a start at articulating what the inner moon is and what it does, let us first affirm that like the inner child, the inner moon is a symbolic vehicle for perceiving a core motivation in human life. It is a conceptualization that gives coherence to a dimension of being. Like the inner child, the moon serves to give perceptual shape to the whole realm of life and being pertaining to basic feelings including fear, pain, panic, anxiety, grief, feelings of well-being, unconditional love, caring and security. The inner moon is not in any definite sense the cause of such feelings. As a "psychic organ," however, the inner moon generates a dimension through which consciousness, experience and behavior pertaining to such feelings are organized and integrated.

The dimension of being/consciousness generated by the inner moon forms that part of self that *interprets* experience pertaining to a vast range of feeling-based phenomena, and gives *meaning* to such. It forms that part of the subjective "I" that *expresses* feelings. It forms that part of the subjective "I" that experiences intimacy, sensitivity and impressionability, that part of the subjective "I" that cares unconditionally for one's own children, and that can experience the child in oneself.

Beyond feelings, the inner moon serves to organize the experience of *basic needs* for such aspects of personal and domestic life as shelter/home, security, food, attachment and privacy. The inner moon further serves to *direct behavior* oriented to the fulfillment of such needs. It serves to direct behavior pertaining to personal incentive, the incentive to provide, to get up for the daily hunt, and to chase down what's for supper—as symbolized by the moon goddess Diana, who was the goddess of the hunt. Thus the inner moon serves simultaneously to organize internal experience and to direct external behavior regarding a realm of life in which childhood emotional experience, one's own children, feelings, home, security and well-being, among many other things, are constellated.

The successful "performance" of such functions of the inner moon depends in good part on developmental processes.

Although Abraham Maslow was obviously not an adherent of astrology, he effectively described, in Chapter 3 of *Toward a Psychology of Being,* features of development that affect growth of psychological potentials similar to what we have just described. Specifically, he noted that growth in the ability to experience higher and more subtle dimensions of feeling is not automatic. Things can go wrong. As Maslow put it, the "inner core … is weak in certain senses rather than strong. It is easily overcome, suppressed or repressed. It may even be killed off permanently."[75]

Maslow's perceptions are well applicable to the development of our inner moon. Inasmuch as the lunar potential within us is by definition a function of subtle influences, in short, the development of this potential can be thwarted. Instead of growing stronger and more capable, the faculties signified by the inner moon can effectively be short-circuited by conditions that throw us back into less evolved levels of functioning. All the higher organizing functions and potentials of the inner moon are vulnerable to adverse effects of the very conditions that produce neurosis and pathology.

Cultural factors play a huge role in affecting the development of inner moon functions. For example, wholesale changes in cultural conditions have translated into unprecedented development of lunar functions in the male gender. Until relatively recently, men were not expected to be much involved with the traditionally female provinces of home, food, child care and feelings. But since the late 1960s,* it has become much more acceptable for men to take responsibility for the care of infants and small children, and to engage in cooking and homemaking. Similarly it has become much more "natural" for men to cultivate the lunar realms of feelings and sensitivity. More than ever before, men are encouraged to balance lunar *behaviors* such as protecting self and family, making shelter and getting food—all traditionally accepted as functions performed by men—with traditionally feminine lunar *experiences* such as coming to consciousness of feelings.

Such changes in attitude were well summed up in the comment of a father who was denied joint custody of his child by the courts. Referring to the judge, the man, being interviewed on prime-time television said, "I guess he doesn't recognize that these instincts are also part of men."

In order to explore the implications of the phrase, "these instincts," let us pause to briefly assess the nature of our lunatic theory. The preceding sketch of the inner moon seeks to abstract a single influence that exists as part of a very large and complex set of astro-psychological influences. In outlining the dimensions of this influence, we have sought to outline a macro-organizing principle in human life. But in that the influence indicated by the moon does not exist apart from the other influences perceived in natal astrology, the influence/principle indicated by the moon cannot be fully addressed without reference to those other influences.

In natal astrology, two other influences form integral dimensions of the principle signified by the moon: the zodiacal sign Cancer and the direction of terrestrial space called the fourth house with reference to the natal chart.

The influences of Cancer are so intimately linked to the influences of the moon that it is often difficult to make clear distinctions. Similar to the moon, Cancerian influences serve to direct behavior and organize experience with respect to comfort,

---

* A generation close to the vortex of these changes is that born between 1949 and 1956, when Uranus, the "planet of revolution," was in Cancer. It was as this generation came of age that Cancerian issues of personal life, including food, feelings and home, became foci of rapid change.

personal incentive, well-being, the care of children, and food. As with the moon, the influences of Cancer serve to interpret and express the experience of basic feelings including fear and pain, caring and unconditional love. As compared to the moon, however, the influences of Cancer translate into a more instinctive dimension of influence, which means in part that *Cancerian influences are geared more to vivid expression in both personality and behavior than are inner moon influences.* To cite an isolated illustration, one of the instinctive predispositions engendered by Cancerian influences is the tendency to generate sentimentally charged bonds with others.

As with other planetary influences, the inner moon comprises a dimension of influence that is intrinsically concerned with certain interior levels of organization and functioning. Indeed the inner moon constitutes a core motivation that can only be effectively operative in behavior and personality *by means of* the instinctive powers that are indicated by the zodiacal sign in which the moon is positioned at birth. In being more oriented to internal dimensions than are the influences of Cancer, the inner moon is more concerned with the conscious processing of emotional experience, to making internal experience coherent and meaningful. Hence the organizing functions of the inner moon are more capable of processing and integrating the emotional experience of *what has already happened.*

This last distinction can be illustrated in connection with the healing of traumatic experiences involving the two basic emotions with which this discussion began: fear and pain.

As much as higher organizing functions are short-circuited by traumatic experience, both lunar and Cancerian influences may support compensatory behaviors including smoking cigarettes, overeating, drinking and drugs. Cancerian influences, however, tend more to direct other, more overtly effective, compensatory behaviors, such as gravitating to people, places and things that are perceived to feel good, comforting and secure; and then holding on to such. A classic Cancerian response to trauma is to instinctively seek places and/or people through which there is experienced some distinct feeling of comfort, security and well-being. Similarly, healing oriented to Cancerian influences would center on consistent exposure to giving, caring, unconditionally loving external influences, to a tranquil home, good food and a natural setting. In that such exposure serves to repattern different and new behaviors—as compared to dealing directly with core experiences of fear and pain—this sort of behavioral approach to healing is more in line with the level at which not only Cancerian but (to different behavioral effects), the other zodiacal influences "work."

At the same time, ironically, it is in the nature of Cancerian influences to support the *instinctive avoidance* of thinking about past trauma, just as one would instinctively avoid anything that hurts or make one afraid. The inner moon, by comparison, is uniquely capable of organizing the meaning of one's experience, of articulating experience and making it coherent. Hence the inner moon constitutes the "organ of consciousness" explicitly geared to address core experiences of fear and pain. It is likewise uniquely capable of recalling such experiences to consciousness and thereby accessing the somatic dimension of such emotions. The inner moon forms that part of the subjective "I" that can "relive" traumatic experience, that can articulate and interpret the subjective meaning of such, and that can ultimately release the emotions involved, thereby catalyzing the progressive resolution of traumatic experiences at core levels.

Both lunar and Cancerian influences are imprinted at birth as parts of the overall configuration of astrological influences that is unique to every individual. Like all other signs of the zodiac, Cancer indicates a set of instinctive powers through which *any* of the various core motivations, as indicated by the sun and planets as well as the moon, may be channeled and expressed, depending on the natal configuration. Conversely, the zodiac sign in which the moon is positioned at birth indicates instinctive powers through which the inner moon itself is geared to be channeled and expressed. Thus the natal "moon sign" signifies the *instinctive mode of expression of the lunar motivation,* and as such indicates one of the most basic differences in individual temperament. As a hybrid of two often sharply contrasting influences, the moon-moon sign conveys by itself a surprisingly complex unit of psychological influence.

If the moon is for instance positioned in Aries at birth, the lunar motivation is indicated to be expressed through instinctive predispositions to such powers as independence, self-absorption, fiery intuition, impishness and impatience. With the moon-in-

Aries influence, similarly, the feeling-centered lunar motivation is indicated to be channeled through Arian predilections to fiery, headstrong, hardheaded, impetuous and impatient Aries types of expression. Interpreting this hybrid influence in terms of nutshell personality characteristics, one possibility that arises is that of *emotional impetuosity.* (Illustrating this suggestion, three women born with the moon in Aries are George Sand, Camille Claudel, and Lily Tomlin.)

With this little sketch of the moon-in-Aries influence, we have returned to the traditional astrological province of describing influences in personality. But beyond personality, moon-sign influences constitute *developmental* factors centering on *predispositions to interpret emotional experience.* Hence we may study moon signs as indicators of individual differences in emotional development. Such differences are explored in Appendix 1.

CHAPTER 12

MYTHS OF CANCER, SCORPIONS AND THE NEW AGE

The only real cure for the psychological problems that ail us is to develop new forms of our historic symbols and myths. The development of new myths and symbols would make psychotherapy in all its forms less necessary. People would then seek and experience education rather than re-education, learning rather than therapy.

— Rollo May

Caught between the proverbial devil and the deep blue sea, astrology runs up against the hellish demands of academic science on one side, and the oceanic tides of modern myth on the other.

How does contemporary myth put astrology in a difficult position? Because most of the massive myths *about* astrology in today's world work mainly to the subject's detriment. By comparison, myths of the archetypal genre interpreted for the expressed purpose of conveying astrological meaning are, to extend the deep-blue-sea metaphor, relatively minor streams of thought as far as volume is concerned.

Unfounded, misguided and pejorative myths about astrology are all around us. The very idea that astrology has been disproven by science is a myth of gigantic proportion. Other tidal myths run to the effect that people "have" only one sign; that the whole meaning of natal astrology boils down to little bunches of personality characteristics; that "the stars" supposedly determine our fates. Astrology is ill-served by all these myths.

Myth thrives, for better or worse, on what people imagine and believe. Myths can be based on what is true, or what is not, or what is halfway true. Myths are ways of imagining life; much of what we actually experience depends on what we imagine.

Religion contains a great deal of myth, and one feature of classic religious myths is that they affirm higher potentials in human nature: spirit, soul, conscience, moral compass. "It is not that 'God' is a myth," said Jung, "but that myth is the revelation of a divine life in man."[76] Jung is saying here that religious myth satisfies genuine and eternal motivations within us. Even as we reach the third millennium after the birth of Jesus, various religious myths still feel more satisfying than scientific myths of a meaningless universe.

So while myth is vital—and vital to astrology—the most common myths about the subject are little short of pernicious. And while a small segment of our society has become enlightened to more vital myths, we are still not close to reaching a "critical mass" consciousness of more vital meaning. Nevertheless, the time is coming when astrology will enrich the collective mythic imagination; the main question is how this will happen.

Joseph Campbell portrayed the imageries of mythology as telling us of "powers of the psyche to be integrated into our lives"; and the imageries of astrology should absolutely do likewise. But if astrologers are to tell us of astrological myths that awaken us to vital powers within, our culture must somehow be weaned from myths—astrological and otherwise—that promote unhelpful beliefs in outside powers.

Creating myth for the purpose of realizing vital inner powers does not happen in a vacuum. Instead, it happens in the context of the experiences, struggles and challenges that we face in the real affairs of daily life. The experiences of a single day bring into play myths of all kinds—myths about ourselves, myths about the world, myths about life itself—that are long overdue for revision, or that at least are not as helpful as they could be. So it is that the creation, and recreation, of astrological myths must coincide with the transformation of old, effete myths.

A compelling illustration of this kind of possibility is suggested in the connection between two apparently very different meanings of the word *cancer*. From Sanskrit roots (*karkata*, crab, *karkara*, hard), the Greek word *karkinos* came to denote "crab" and hence the name of the fourth sign of the astrological zodiac. Yet "cancer" also denotes a disease originally marked by "chancres": areas of hard tissue. To most people in modern industrial society, the most important meaning of "cancer" concerns a disease that afflicts one out of every three or four people and takes up billions of dollars in medical treatment and research. Like a vast army of marauders from a hostile foreign power, the dreaded disease cancer has become widely perceived as a phenomenon over which the individual, without the help of the scientific/technological forces of the medical establishment, has little or no control; it is seen as an alien destructive force that, in seemingly random fashion, might invade one's own body. As ravaging as cancer has been to millions of peoples' lives, this kind of perception is apparently justified. But in light of the astrological significance of Cancer, the perception is also strangely ironic.

Considering certain factors of behavior that contribute to its development, the disease cancer is in a sense a tragic *projection* of inherent and instinctive powers of the unconscious—powers that are symbolized by the astrological sign of the same name.

It is common knowledge that the majority of lethal cancer cases are caused in significant part by chronic exposure to some harmful or carcinogenic substance in the environment. Among these carcinogenic agents, cigarette smoke is the most common; also well-publicized are pesticides, toxic chemicals and atomic radiation. Yet one of the most crucial questions that arises regarding exposure to such cancer-causing substances is: How much does an individual's behavior result in the *voluntary* ingestion of carcinogens?

The act of behaving in ways that involve chronic exposure to carcinogens is most compelling with regard to smoking cigarettes. Given the enormous publicity on the relationship between smoking and lung cancer, it is fair to say that the chronic cigarette smoker voluntarily and knowingly invades his own body with cancer-generating substances. Although the issues are much less clear-cut when an individual's livelihood, family income and/or home are integral to the process of exposing oneself to other carcinogens, a basic vital principle applies in both kinds of cases.

What is the "principle" that holds here?

Whether it is conscious or not, voluntary or not, the ingestion of cancer-causing substances entails the abrogation of a "first law" of the principle represented by the astrological sign Cancer: to protect yourself.

Much as the word *cancer* derives from the root words meaning "hard" and "crab," the meaning of the zodiacal sign Cancer relates to the hard shell of the crab as a mythic symbol of self-protection. The image of the crab evokes the power to keep that which would threaten our well-being on the outside, and human well-being depends no less than crab well-being on this power. With reference to the act of chronically ingesting carcinogens, the implication is not that people do not have this power of self-protection; it is that this power has been compromised.

Possible "violations" of "natural laws" indicated by Cancer pertain to many other potentials besides self-protection. For example, it can be said that behavior that produces *discomfort*, that causes *irritation*, or that otherwise results in the deadening of one's *sensitivities*, runs at cross purposes to Cancerian imperatives. To the extent that ingesting carcinogens results in such negative experiences, the obvious injunction is NOT to usurp the inherent power to *care* for yourself, to *nurture* and *nourish* your body, and to react to pain by *avoiding what hurts*.

We could go on indefinitely in this vein, taking vital powers as are identified in Principle 4 of Chapter 9, and seeing such powers abrogated in behaviors that invite the specter of the disease Cancer into one's life. By the same token, we could suggest that the transformation of many cancer-causing syndromes could come about by coming to perceive "Cancer" as a symbol of inherent and vital powers. Where now those instinctive powers are projected into fearsome myths about the external world, Cancer could become a mythic ally within.

What myths might achieve the collective realization of such vital CRAB POWERS? What myths could encourage the mass development of good crabby instincts? How can we learn new meanings of Cancer as *instinctive powers to be developed,* as instinctive powers such as self-protection, self-care, sensitivity and nurturing?

While it may be unrealistic to hope for a wholesale transformation in the understanding of Cancer anytime soon, it is nevertheless true that the symbols of the zodiac are already part and parcel of popular culture, and the right kind of pop culture phenomenon could change the whole way people think about astrology and its symbols. This kind of change can happen in unexpected ways. Witness, for instance, John Gray's bestseller

Men Are From Mars; Women Are From Venus. While making no reference to astrology, Gray nonetheless ascribes vaguely valid astrological meanings to Mars and Venus. More to the present point, Disney's modern classic *The Little Mermaid* projects in the protagonist Sebastian a wonderfully positive role model for crabs. As if created by a fanciful astrologer, Sebastian the Crab is a mythic symbol of fully realized Cancerian powers: feel-good, sweet, cute, nurturing, parental and protective.

This *Is* the Dawning of the Age of Aquarius

The most positively charged myth widely associated with astrology revolves around the idea that we have entered a New Age, the Age of Aquarius. Like other myths involving astrology, of course, myths about the Aquarian Age skim the waves of popular culture without getting much below the surface. That's unfortunate, because the myth of the dawning Age of Aquarius holds substance and meaning that is rather vital to us all now.

To get at this meaning, let us get our astrological/astronomical bearings. According to different technical methods of calculating the "precession of the equinoxes,"[*] the Age of Aquarius either has begun as of the beginning of the 20th century, or it will begin as of about 2170.[**] Averaging these two dates, we could say that the Aquarian Age begins late in the 21st century. But since each astrological age lasts about 2150 years, the entry into the Age of Aquarius from the Age of Pisces is not a one-day-to-the-next affair. Instead, it is a gradual process wherein the "cusp," or transition period, spans as much as 500-600 years.

Astrologically, The Age of Pisces (which began roughly concurrent with the birth of Christ) is characterized by Piscean

---

[*] As noted in Chapter 8, the point at which the zodiac begins is an exact function of where the sun appears on the spring equinox. As measured against the vault of the heavens, this point moves slightly backward from year to year. It is this equinoctial point that has "precessed" through the stellar constellation Pisces to the beginning of the constellation Aquarius over the course of the last 2000+ years.

[**] Cf. Nicholas Devore, *The Astrological Encyclopedia.* NY: Philosophical Library; 1974. Pp. 307-309. Devore cites the year 1906 as the beginning of the Age of Aquarius as calculated according to the actual movement of the equinoctial point, but cites the year 2170 according to the movement of the Earth's poles.

themes and paradigms. As Pisces keywords are "I Believe," for instance, the Age of Pisces is identified as the Age of Belief, or the Age of Religion. Similarly, it is expected that powers symbolized by Aquarius will inform the paradigms of world culture as the Age of Aquarius—the "Age of Knowledge"— comes fully to birth.

To witness the burgeoning of science, technology, telecommunications and democracy around the world, it is undeniable that a global metamorphosis is taking place. In the popular mind, these changes have little to do with the Age of Aquarius. But inasmuch as Aquarius symbolizes the powers inherent in these revolutionary phenomena, the idea of the dawning of the New Age begins to take on different hues of meaning.

Aquarian symbolism speaks to the watershed of changes in our times not only in terms of science and technology, but in terms of basic principles—and challenges—of collective life. Inasmuch as human population growth, coupled with technology, is daily shrinking our world into Spaceship Earth, we are increasingly faced with the absolute NEED to *integrate* our whole planet into an *interconnected community*. As problems of pollution, natural resources, the environment and population proliferate, the human community is reaching a transitional crisis of the first global order. To survive this crisis it becomes ever more apparent that we will need to *cooperate* and recognize our collective *interdependence* as never before. At the same time it appears that the global revolution in communications is facilitating the dissemination of *revolutionary* ideas of all kinds to people around the world.

In that Aquarius represents the full scope of the global paradigm shift that appears to be upon us, it is refreshing to see this symbol actually used to this purpose—which Marilyn Ferguson did in her book, *The Aquarian Conspiracy*. While Ferguson notes that she is unfamiliar with the symbolism of astrology,[*] she nonetheless captures with uncanny accuracy a

---

[*] "Although I am unacquainted with astrological lore, I was drawn to the symbolic power of the ... dream ... that ... we are entering a millennium of love and light—in the words of the popular song, 'The Age of Aquarius,' the time of 'the mind's true liberation'." Marilyn Ferguson, *The Aquarian Conspiracy*. Boston: Houghton Mifflin; 1980. p. 19.

whole range of powers symbolized by the sign, powers that she sees as being integral to a "new principle" for our times:

> While science, in its objective fashion, was generating surprising data about human nature and the nature of reality, I saw that hundreds of thousands of individuals were coming upon subjective surprises of their own... They were reaching out for information ...To meet this apparent need for connection and communication... I began ... a newsletter... The newsletter was a lightning rod for energy ... networks grew. Global communications have encircled our world beyond any possibility of retreat ... the whole planet is alive with ... networks of people poised for communication and cooperation ... the new paradigm gains ascendance... We *are* the revolution. (pp. 19-20)

With passing reference to Aquarius, Ferguson envisions the emergence of a new global paradigm centering on powers of science, revolution, news and information, networks, interconnection communication, "lightning rods [of] energy," cooperation, reform, new ideas, liberation, alternatives, experimentation and exploration. *All* these concepts are integral to the principle symbolized by Aquarius. Spanning much of the Aquarian spectrum, Ferguson's vision integrates values of science and technology with a constellation of higher human—and equally Aquarian—values.

The Scorpions of Oedipus

To the extent that we are truly moving into a new age, we may need a whole new set of classic myths. Or else we must put whole new faces on many of the myths of antiquity. Why? Because in the ancient world so much of peoples' lives, and so their fates, was in fact dark and difficult, fraught with disease, hardship and early death. In the face of so much suffering, it is no wonder that the stories of mythology are charged with tragedy. If we, in contrast, are to seize the fire of Promethean/ Aquarian knowledge, we ought to be using our new knowledge to brighten up, when possible, life and fate itself.

Take the most famous psychological myth of all: Freud's Oedipus. Interestingly, Jungian astrologers seem to have left this

dark tale largely alone, as if content to leave it in the realm of
Freudian psychology. Yet it is a tale strikingly rich in psychological meaning; and with a little fire, anvil and hammer, we might
forge an uplifting myth—a new Scorpio myth—without too
much hardship.

The myth of Oedipus centers on the prophecy that Oedipus,
whose parents were the King and Queen of Thebes, would kill
his father and marry his mother. His father Laius seeks to avoid
this fate, and so sends the infant Oedipus away to be killed; but a
herdsman intervenes and saves his life. Ignorant of his origins,
Oedipus eventually fulfills the prophecy made at his birth, and
remains unconscious of his true relation to the woman he marries
and the man he slays, all until it is too late. When he finally
comes to the realization of his true identity and what he has
done, he tears his eyes out. In the climax of gaining tragic
insight, he cannot bear to see.

Although Freud interpreted this myth in terms of sexually
charged dynamics of mother-love and father-hate, let us follow a
more general lead as also suggested by Freud. Let us entertain
the idea that the myth of Oedipus symbolizes the origins of dark,
ugly emotions in early family life. In this context, the prophecy
and fulfillment of Oedipus' tragic fate represent the unconscious
urge to *play out* such emotions as adults in relation to others who
resemble in some basic fashion one's parents or primary caretakers. Oedipus' blindness to the true circumstances surrounding
his actions symbolizes the adult's inability to see that urges to act
out dark and base emotions are not merely the result of difficult
involvement with whoever happens to give us a hard time. The
myth of Oedipus dramatizes the psychological fact that such
dark urges typically stem from primal patterns of experience in
childhood, experiences in which parents are usually focal.

In at least one respect, then, Freud was on target in choosing
the Oedipal myth as the major archetype for the whole of
psychology. He was right to assert that we must look to early
childhood for the origins of dark emotions. Similarly he was
right to promote the realization that we need to examine early
life in order to resolve such emotions. Yet in choosing the myth
of Oedipus, he also chose to stress the inevitability of twisted
development. In this regard he apparently did not recognize that
as children we all have genuinely *innocent* needs for such things

as unconditional love, reassurance, touching and comfort—such needs as are symbolized by the moon and Cancer. Hence by way of reinventing myth, we cannot simply accept the inevitability of involuted development and leave it at that. The myth of Oedipus cries out for a modern Cancerian counterpoint. We need a Cancerian "myth" about the real basic needs of children, and the role these needs play in healthy development. For that matter, we need a myth emphasizing the importance of fulfilling these needs in every stage of life. Of course, a myth to this general effect is already abroad: the myth of the inner child.

But it was not Oedipus' inner child that was centrally at issue in the doing of his fateful deeds. While (moon-related) emotions of fear, hurt and grief are undoubtedly bound up in the emotional struggles that Oedipus' story represents, we must nonetheless deal with Oedipus, as it were, on his own terms. Rather than fear and pain, the myth of Oedipus leads us ineluctably to emotions symbolized by Scorpio, emotions of desire, anger and hate. Freud chose the Oedipus myth because he was intent on dealing with Scorpionic realms of sex and hate and death.

The myths that Freud created with respect to these realms reflect the bleakness of Greek tragedy itself. Believing literally in the myth of Oedipus, Freud saw little room for ameliorating the human condition. In Freud's world, inner conflicts between hate and conscience, between *eros,* ego and destructive instincts will forever darken the horizons.

And how do such horizons appear in the astrological world? In answering this question, let us first reiterate that all of the dark emotions and powers of behavior stressed in the myth of Oedipus, including cruelty, anger, defiance, vengeance, bitterness, incest and (self-)hatred, belong astrologically to Scorpio and Mars, as does sexual desire itself. Second, let us acknowledge that, at some level, *we are all Scorpios*: We all have to deal with emotional darkness.

Addressing this Scorpionic darkness, astrologers have sketched a myth to the effect that the archetypal challenge symbolized in Scorpio is to confront dark emotional aspects of self, to die to them, and to uplift oneself in a "death and regeneration" process. This theme of death and rebirth is symbolized in the progression of the three symbols of Scorpio: from the scorpion to the eagle by route of the phoenix. As Marcia Moore put it,

> "[I]n Scorpio, the soul descends into an abyss in preparation for its ascent to a higher level of self-knowing... Scorpio people are invariably subjected to periods of trial and testing ... if the process has been successful, they arise phoenix-like out of the ashes of the past...[77]

Yet it is one thing to be told that we must die and be reborn; it is quite another to actually do it. Beyond accepting the relatively fatalistic idea that we are bound to go through dark periods in our lives out of which we *might* rise anew, it would be helpful to see some light shed on how to actually get through the darkness. Liz Greene conveys insight in this direction in her trenchant treatment of Scorpio in *The Astrology of Fate,* specifically in connection with the fighting of archetypal monsters. (See Principle 8, Chapter 9.) But while Greene educates us as to how to fight our monsters, and also points to higher spiritual dimensions of Scorpio, she apparently does not see a phoenix-like progression from one to the other. Instead she concludes her ruminations with the perception of an eternal contradiction strangely reminiscent of Freud's vision of unconscious conflict:

> The lofty aspirations of Scorpio, which ... can lead to a loathing for life, and [Scorpio's] powerful sensuality, which wishes to drown in the world, are extremely uncomfortable bedfellows. Yet they spring from the same mysterious core, half sexuality and half spirituality... The difficult combination of spiritualised eroticism and eroticised spirituality is a handful for Scorpio. It is not surprising that so many Scorpios seem to repress or sublimate one or the other in despair that no reconciliation is possible. [p. 234]

It should probably not be surprising that under the title of *The Astrology of Fate,* Greene's treatment of Scorpio is so ambivalent. To Greene's credit, it may be both condescending and unrealistic to purvey the notion that we should simply confront our inner scorpions and die to them so as to rise to the heights of eagles. But clearly the symbolism of Scorpio evokes the possibility of this progression. The question remains: How?

While this question can certainly be answered in more than one way, the myth of Oedipus, and Freudian psychology itself, each provide elements of a classic process of resolution. The myth of Oedipus shows us that as much as "we have met the enemy, and they are us," our first task is *to become aware* of the relation between the monsters that we face externally and the internal monsters that we have created from the dark matter of our pasts.

Even if we happen to be successful in bringing to consciousness the origins of ugly emotions within us, however, there is no guarantee that we can root them out. As many a long-term client-in-therapy can attest, we may wrestle with our demons indefinitely without really conquering them. As far as the "Scorpio emotions" are concerned, while internal psychological examination may take us a long way, it might still not get us into the light. Inasmuch as anger is at the root of the ugly emotions addressed here, moreover, the possibilities of primally releasing anger and rage are arguably more remote than for primal release of experiences of grief and fear. Too often (and more so than with other emotions), hate and anger succeed only in begetting more hate and anger. Consequently, we need some other way of dying to that which must die within us.

In this regard, it was largely Greene's insight that in order to conquer dark emotions, we must avoid engaging them at the level at which they tempt us. Reflecting this insight, Freud saw the resolution of the Oedipal conflict in terms of eventual *disengagement* from the parents. Even when the experiences of early life are charged with the most foul of emotions, it is liberating to realize that all we may need from life is a standoff with our inner—*and* outer—monsters, a getting-close-to-even. Using another term from Freudian psychology, this path relates to the experience of *ego death.*

If dying to internal monsters does not seem particularly like a victory, it is here that we can translate the Scorpio theme of death and rebirth into a more palatable scenario. While it is true that a psychological rebirth follows the kind of death of which we speak, we can reclaim the happier ending of the classic hero myth by not dying. Instead we may claim victory and live to see another day by this injunction: *Battle the monsters to a draw and then move on to more fulfilling engagements.*

As symbolized in Scorpio, the eagle's way is to realize that the scorpion's battle will ever be what it is; that the best thing to do is to leave the battle behind when possible; and that it is when we seek to leave the battle that we are able to find *renewal*. At bottom, the story of Oedipus is bleak because the protagonist saw no possibility of renewal. In today's world, by comparison, the promise of renewal is all around us, and people seek many paths to renewal. Dying to their internal monsters, many are renewed —"reborn"—as evangelical Christians. Many choose new life partners. Many have affairs; some find new love. Many others find renewed life and love with their chosen partners. Such renewal is a classic challenge of life, as reflected in the question: Is renewal possible with this person? People do find renewal in therapy or self-healing. Many find renewal in sports, fitness programs, getting close to nature, new friends, and new ventures. In all these forms of renewal lies a promise: the rebirth of desire. The eagle within must seek to soar anew.

In all these choices are mysteries for the individual to solve. How deep is the renewal here for me; or am I really just marking time? Am I moving deeper into the mystery of life, or am I still just battling the scorpions? These are questions that require not only self-confrontation but a *mystical* sensibility to answer, a sensibility that is another one of Scorpio's mythic powers.

CHAPTER 13

SPIRITUAL DIMENSIONS OF ASTROLOGY

The message boldly blazoned across the heavens at the moment of birth is not meant to emphasize fate—the result of past good and evil—but to arouse man's will to escape from his universal thralldom. What he has done, he can undo... Man *is* a soul, and *has* a body... So long as he remains confused in his ordinary state of spiritual amnesia, he will know the subtle fetters of environmental law.[78]
— Paramahansa Yogananda

Turning us to the heavens, astrology invokes the realm of spirit. Astrology is not, as the myth would have it, a religion, but it can legitimately be called a spiritual discipline. Yet astrology's invocation of the world of spirit is curious, because it ties spirit so closely to matter. If the spiritual realm is in the heavens, the sun, moon and planets are only way stations in that direction, as much kin to the material Earth as to the spiritual skies. Indeed just as the discipline of astrology balances on the fulcrum between science and philosophy, and between masculine and feminine, so does it balance between matter and spirit. In this regard, there is one other pair of counterparts that astrology balances between: the internal and the external.

In this work, we have mainly considered influences that are studied in *natal* astrology, and we have treated these influences as being what the word "natal," suggests: innate, inborn, from birth. We have done so because from the moment of birth onward, these influences generally appear as if they stemmed from inborn sources. However, it is not strictly correct to refer to them as being inborn. The influences recognized in natal astrology technically originate in our celestial *environment,* not acting on the individual until the baby is outside the womb. Hence they are technically *neonatal* influences. Natal astrology might best be said to deal with "influences of the immediate celestial environment that are imprinted at birth."

The implications of this statement are profound, because inasmuch as we acknowledge astrology's neonatal influences to be environmental, our picture of the balance of factors influencing human psychology must shift from "nature" to the direction of "nurture." If we regard natal astrological influences as functions of the external environment, we might even acknowledge that radical behaviorists were right all along: Human behavior *is* predominantly a function of environmental factors, once the influences of the near cosmic environment are brought into the equation.

This is of course an extreme view. But even while they are "owned," or absorbed, at the very moment of birth, we must recognize that the influences studied in natal astrology partake of both nature and nurture. And in light of this small but critical shift in thinking, we must again ask the fundamental question: What *are* the most basic internal and inborn influences in human nature? Must we again turn to biology and genetics in order to find the most purely inborn dimension of individual selfhood?

Biology will always be central to this equation. But beyond biology, there is one deeper dimension of inborn influence to consider: the dimension of the soul. *Psychology* after all refers to the "study of the psyche," and *psyche* derives from the Greek word for "soul." For those who perceive it, it is the soul that forms the ultimate internal dimension of selfhood.

While the concept of the *soul* as employed here incorporates qualities of being and consciousness such as those Thomas Moore writes of, we refer to a more explicit dimension of being: to an energetic entity that transcends the body, exists before birth, makes itself known during near-death experiences, and ascends from the body after death.

Reflecting the contemporary renaissance in the perception of the soul, the main spiritually-oriented branch of astrology assumes reincarnation as axiomatic. This assumption is not in any way a bow to specific religious doctrines, although it does relate to *perceptions* of reincarnation found in such religions as Buddhism and Hinduism. It should be recognized, however, that a similarly transcendent soul is perceived in one form or another in cultures throughout the world, and likewise that perceptions of reincarnation extend far beyond the bounds of Buddhist and Hindu religions.

Still, the largest area of "spiritual astrology" centers on the study of patterns carried over from previous lifetimes, and the "astrology of reincarnation" relates fundamentally to Hindu doctrines not only of reincarnation, but of karma. As a psychological discipline, however, this branch of astrology must orient itself according to attitudes profoundly different from ancient Hindu traditions, traditions that have become translated into attitudes of fatalistically accepting your lot in life. Honoring the brighter spirit of new-world psychology, by comparison, spiritual astrology can comfortably center on the thesis that we are all challenged to be *activists* for change and evolution, first and foremost in our own lives.

Inasmuch as it can encourage activism, astrology's emphasis on individual nature turns new light on the traditional meaning of *karma*. In Eastern religions, karma is seen largely as a matter of cause and effect: Present conditions are results of past actions. This is obviously a sound principle, and there is much to recommend its application to reincarnation. The way this doctrine is typically applied in Buddhism and Hinduism, however, tends to drain life of incentive and appeal. The injunctions of both *karma* ("right action") and *dharma* ("duty") prescribe that conduct be perfected for its own sake. In the context of universal cause-and-effect, one's actions should be rectified so as to produce good effects, as if the actor himself were inconsequential. Attachment to the results of one's actions is to be forsaken. The only "gain" one should seek is release *(moksha)* from the wheel of karma, from the cycle of reincarnation. As with the myths of ancient Greece and Rome, this doctrine derives from a world in which suffering was the norm.

The Eastern injunction to take the actor out of the act runs exactly counter to modern astrology, which focuses above all on the individual doing the acting. In addressing the sources of action within the individual, moreover, astrology offers the opportunity not merely to change our *actions* for the better, but to change our *motives*. And although the motives for our actions may be tied to past lifetimes, such motives are nonetheless acutely bound up with the here-and-now dimension of present experience. Accordingly, while astrological interpretation may point to experiences from past lives as ultimate sources of present circumstances and experiences, it should be primarily concerned with providing insight into questions regarding the ongoing existential experience of self: Who am I and what am I experiencing right now?

Unlike traditional doctrines that advocate denial of self, the astrology of reincarnation can emphasize the individual as a growing, changing and evolving being. It can affirm a self that individuates as it evolves, and evolves as it individuates. As the process of individuation reaches higher levels, in other words, one's actions become simultaneously more "spiritually correct" *and* more self-fulfilling. Thus spiritual evolution is seen not as opposed to personal fulfillment, but rather as complementary to it. This direction of interpretation is in line with modern-day spiritual teachers such as Paramahansa Yogananda and Deepak Chopra. It likewise reconciles with many spiritual traditions— Eastern traditions included—which emphasize the existence of a *higher self* that is of the essence of God. In describing potentials of the higher self in massive detail, spiritual astrology affirms that essences of God can come in many forms.

A classic and contemporary spiritual perspective on astrology runs something like this: The soul is an evolving entity endowed with free will. The soul chooses, to some extent, the individual context it will embody and the circumstances it will experience. The soul chooses, among other things, one's parents, the place, the time and the general circumstances of birth—the whole context of the newborn life. The soul unites with the chosen body at some time before birth, and in this act of incarnation the consciousness of the soul entity is absorbed into the matrix of the fetus' circumstances. This matrix incorporates astrological, familial, socioeconomic, geographical, cultural and biological dimensions.

The soul is a unique id-entity that has evolved for many thousands of years before the present lifetime. The soul chooses an astrological matrix of influence that will both reflect and accommodate the individual soul nature. Astrological patterns imprinted at birth accord to the soul's particular nature and past tendencies, while simultaneously allowing for development in the present and future. From the past, the soul carries into the current life features of psychological character, embedded patterns of behavior, compelling attractions to issues, themes and patterns of experience. Again, the astrological configuration at birth both reflects and supports these patterns. This configuration, however, does not necessitate bondage to past patterns, nor does it signify predetermined destiny. It shows instead the constitutional psychic pattern of inborn nature *through which the individual soul or entity may grow and evolve*—or remain essentially the same.

The astrological nature of the psychic constitution opens to the development of new values and new patterns beyond the old. It allows for dramatically new expressions to evolve from and through the "same old" pattern. Patterns of experience carried over from the past may be transformed. Accordingly, prediction in astrology should take into account possibilities for evolution at every turn. With evolution as the guiding principle of life not only in the biological but the psychological realm, it is plainly a mistake to use astrology as a tool to support fatalistic attitudes.

The birth chart, which portrays the astrological configuration at birth, is thus a symbolic picture of *evolving selfhood.* The individual may develop the potentials indicated within this configuration at ever higher and more subtle levels. At the most evolved levels, the astrological mandala of the birth chart signifies cosmic potentials that may be expressed in transcendingly pure ways. To the extent that "character is destiny," as the nameless Greek philosopher put it, the birth chart might be read to suggest something of fate. But to read fate therein is to deny the roles of growth, conscious choice, external amelioration of circumstances and other processes by which the development of various alternative and newly evolving patterns of expression might unfold. Within parameters, character itself can change as the soul, and the whole of humanity, evolve.

A classic reading of the birth chart invokes another classic psychological and spiritual tradition: Gnosticism. The meaning of the word "Gnosticism" may be summed up in the phrase, "Know Thyself."

Gnosticism originated in the form of a group of religious sects and philosophies during the early years of the Christian era. Articulating doctrines radically different from Catholic dogma, Gnosticism in its many forms was suppressed. Nonetheless, Gnostic teachings survived into the modern era. The study of Gnosticism was given an enormous boost with the 1943 finding of a sealed urn, hidden in a cave in Egypt, that was filled with ancient Gnostic manuscripts.

Among the teachings of Gnosticism is the emphasis on "knowledge of the heart," and the understanding of Christian gospel in symbolic rather than literal terms.* For example, some Gnostics interpreted the Biblical account of the resurrection of Jesus to indicate not the literal raising of his body from the dead, but rather the immortality of Jesus' soul, and hence the universal phenomenon of the transcendent soul. Regarding knowledge of the heart, classic Gnosticism (from the Greek *gnosis*, knowledge) revolves around the idea that enlightenment is to be found through exploration, discovery and development of the inner self. *Knowledge gained through experience and insight* is the true path to salvation. One Gnostic teacher, Manoimus, wrote,

> Abandon the search for God [outside yourself]. Look for
> him by taking yourself as the starting point. Learn who it
> is within you who makes everything his own and says,
> "My God, my mind, my thought, my soul, my body."
> Learn the sources of sorrow, joy, love, hate... If you
> carefully investigate these matters you will find him in
> yourself.[79]

This is of course not only a spiritual but a psychological doctrine. The implication is that not only God but the whole of experience is a psychological projection of what is within. In *Aion,* Carl Jung neatly described what happens when the individual fails to recognize what is within:

> The psychological rule is that when an inner situation is
> not made conscious, it happens outside as fate. That is to
> say, when the individual ... does not become conscious of

---

* "Unto you it is given to know the mystery of the Kingdom of God; but unto them that are without, all these things are done in parables." Mark 4:11.

his inner contradictions, the world must perforce act out
the conflict and be torn into opposites.[80]

"Fate" is used here not in the sense of impending events, but
rather in the sense of negative experience being a natural result
of unconscious behavior. What is being denied within will
inevitably manifest on the outside, usually in unfortuitous ways.

Although sound psychology, the Gnostic injunction to explore
both the human and the divine within was anathema to the ortho-
dox Church. By way of consolidating its power, the Church held
that the way to God and salvation could only be mediated by the
Church's—external—powers and authorities, and so it denied
much of the value of looking inward. The Church's stress on
external power and authority is all too familiar, as it has not
fundamentally changed through the course of two thousand
years. While the dominant paradigm of Western culture has
shifted in the twentieth century from religion toward science and
technology, moreover, dominant perceptions of ultimate reality
are still oriented toward the world outside. Modern society
continues to stress external standards, external authority and
external appearances. Precious little in the spiritual teaching of
our times offers the understanding that what is seen and experienced outside is in many ways but a refracted reflection of what
is within.

To affirm inherent subjective powers and knowledge of the
heart in the face of external objectified power and knowledge is
as vital—and radical—a perspective as it ever was. Even as the
gods of Objective Reality, Science, Technology and Materialism
now all compete with the Gods of Moses, Jesus and Mohammed
in our times, the need exists as much as ever to learn that many
of the true "gods" that "rule" our lives are very possibly more
mysterious and internal than they are explicit and external.

Applying gnosticism to astrology, the birth chart becomes a
tool by which to learn of our inherent natures, and to seek God
within.

PART IV

CHAPTER 14

INTERPRETATION, TAKE ONE:
A SATURNIAN FORMAT

The planets are the primary focus of the chart.
— Robert Hand, *Horoscope Symbols*

In its study of individual nature, natal astrology focuses on charts—birth charts—that depict the pattern of the solar system and the zodiac at the time of a person's birth, as oriented to the place of birth. In the configuration of planets, signs, houses and other astrological points of interest, each birth chart presents astrology's symbols in a unique complex of permutations. These permutations challenge the interpreter to address not one but anywhere from two to six or seven symbolic units *at a time*. Inasmuch as any one of the symbols of astrology yields multiple meanings, the complex of symbolic combinations encountered in a given chart can be dizzying. Making good sense of it all is a heady task even for accomplished astrologers.

At no matter what level astrology's symbols are interpreted, however, two imperatives should hold. First, interpretation should have empirical foundations: it should develop in connection with a process of careful and systematic observation. Second, interpretation should articulate psychological frames of reference. Articulating psychological dimensions of interpretation is critical to communicating just what is being said, and suggested, and omitted.

Beginning with sun signs, the most common area of interpretation deals with the positions of the sun, the moon and the planets by both sign and house. (These positions are articulated in phrases such as, "the moon in Cancer," Mars in the 8th house," and "Saturn in Sagittarius.") Although studied for centuries, the

247

interpretations of these placements vary widely from source to source, with no particular source standing out above others. Interpretations of sign and house placements often consist of relatively simple characterizations of personality and behavior, with little evident attempt to place such characterizations in psychological context. Few of the top names in the field have tackled this area of astrology in any detail in recent years, leaving a dearth of more sophisticated work on this bread-and-butter material of natal chart interpretation.

It is not surprising that we find so little high-quality interpretation of sign and house placements, for this material is remarkably difficult to do well. Making observations in connection with such placements is like trying to hit small moving targets at a distance.

The generic pitfall of simplistic interpretation is that it equates a given influence with a given type of manifestation: x astrological factor translates directly into y type of behavioral trait. Well, maybe and sometimes. Even more than with sun signs, observations of behavior applying to placements of the moon and planets by sign and house tend to be contradicted by *other* observations.

Since astrology deals with *influences underlying behavior,* let us begin to develop a new form of interpretation by focusing on the underlying influences themselves. For example, instead of interpreting Venus in Scorpio by characterizing a whole personality type, let us identify the influences of both Venus and Scorpio as related units of psychological influence, which together signify a relatively distinct *part of self.* Using the psychological terms and interpretations presented in Parts 1 and 2, we can generate an interpretive format that is fundamentally different from traditional interpretation. To create such a format, let us briefly reiterate the psychological meaning of the three major categories of astrological symbols:

- The sun, moon and planets refer to *motivational potentials* that make up the fundamental psychological forces, the core "parts" of ourselves.
- The signs of the zodiac refer to *instincts, predispositions* and *inherent powers* which manifest both externally (in behavior) and internally (in experience).

• The houses of the birth chart refer to the different types and directions of *experience* to which we may be drawn.

Using these psychological definitions, we can interpret the natal placement of a planet by sign and house as follows:

> Your motivation for _____ [refer to delineation of planet as well as the associated principle] is expressed through the instinct for _____ [refer to delineation of zodiac sign as well as its associated principle]; and you are drawn to experience this part of yourself in terms of _____ [refer to delineation of "Planets in _____ House" as well as the principle associated with the house.]

Using this format, interpretation is initially a matter of choosing concepts appropriate to identifying a finite dimension or aspect of self, as compared to trying to translate the interpretation of two or three influences at a time into an entire personality profile. Making explicit reference to different kinds of influence, this type of interpretation encourages the perception of layers of psychological make-up, layers that would otherwise be mashed together.

To illustrate such features of this format, let us return once again to sun signs. Instead of plunging into general personality descriptions of people born with a given sun sign, this format begins by focusing on the influence of the sun. It can proceed, let's say, with the statement that, "The life-giving source and center of your personality and identity, the star within you, is expressed through instincts for..." Only then would follow the articulation of powers indicated by the sun sign itself. Considering the multiplicity of capacities delineated for each sign of the zodiac in Chapter 9, this format leaves open the possibility that manifestation can unfold in connection with the development of any number of instinctive powers indicated by the particular sun sign. Equally, the articulation of the "sun-as-star" encourages the understanding that there *is* a star in each of us; and further that the vividness of personality expression may depend on how bright the inner star shines.

This format can be used to generate interpretations that are not so different, on the surface anyway, from interpretations found in popular literature: It can easily be used to describe behavior and personality. If, for example, you were born with Venus in Aquarius, it is simple enough to take a key concept offered in chapter 9 for interpreting the Venusian motivation—*social style*—and put it together with some of the more behaviorally descriptive powers identified in the Aquarius section. Hence, saying that the motivation symbolized by Venus will be expressed through instincts represented by Aquarius translates into the statement that your social style (Venus) is instinctively breezy (airy), gregarious, communicative, open to new and unusual ideas, and tuned in to current events. Reminiscent of cookbook approaches, this statement nonetheless places observable behavior in the context of expressing a single underlying motivation. It is distinctly more modest a claim than saying to a person born with this placement, "*You* are gregarious, breezy, communicative," etc. Respecting the multidimensional nature of every individual, it makes good sense that a certain part of self is geared to be expressed according to certain kinds of behavioral instincts, while other parts could be of markedly contrasting nature.

Negative expressions of a given influence can be generated by this format as easily as positive ones. For instance, some pitfalls of Saturn's placement in Virgo can be indicated by choosing less desirable Virgoan powers of personality and behavior: "Your (Saturnian) motivation for responsibility and authority is developed through instincts for being critical, perfectionist and mentally fixated"(!) Compare this with a comment offered for Saturn's placement in Virgo in *The Astrologer's Handbook:* "This position often makes people austere, gloomy and depressed because of the excessive weight of work and detailed responsibility."[81]

Although there are similarities between these interpretations, there are also key differences. Knowing that only some of the more negative capacities of Virgo have been chosen is much different than inferring that Saturn in Virgo indicates a whole—grouchy—type of personality. Our psychological format encourages the recognition that there exists a positive-negative continuum in range of expression, that development and expression could as well turn in positive as negative directions.

Akin to the proverbial blind men describing the elephant, what is described by astrologers depends on what parts of it they happen to touch. Somewhat embarrassingly, astrologers are liable to "touch" on manifestations of a given influence that are mutually incompatible. Returning to Saturn in Virgo, Myrna Lofthus describes individuals born with this placement as "neat and orderly,"[82] while Debbi Kempton-Smith states flatly that "most of them are slobs."[83]

It is a dollar-to-a-doughnut bet that *some* people born with Saturn in Virgo are in fact neat and orderly, while others are factual slobs—and still others are somewhere in between. Yet inasmuch as Virgo pertains to instincts for order, it might be appropriate—depending, of course, on what observation indicates—to focus on the *power* of ordering *as subject to development and expression in different ways.*

Beyond encouraging the perception of differences in development and expression, defining the nature of underlying influences allows for the identification of different psychological genres of influence, which in turn can be helpful in bringing into focus different forms of expression. Identifying astrological influences in different generic terms such as archetypes, predispositions, inherent powers, instincts, philosophical values, and personality/behavioral traits, all generate interesting directions for further exploration.

There seems to be no good reason to try to limit the interpretation of zodiacal influences to any one of these psychological genres at the expense of others. Even the concept of "philosophical values" can work as a focus for interpretation—and for observation. To illustrate this idea, let us return to sun signs and look at three Aquarian "stars" of the American presidency: Abraham Lincoln, Franklin Roosevelt and Ronald Reagan. In noting, in Chapter 9, that these three sun-sign Aquarians were the three most ideological presidents the country has seen, we made a standard interpretive statement in terms of personality. But as we proceed to briefly explore the Aquarian nature of these men—and their presidencies—we will emphasize values inherent in this sign that could not be described in terms of personality at all. In other cases we will emphasize underlying values that are virtually indistinguishable from personality traits.

Abraham Lincoln (born February 12, 1809) is remembered above all for his *humanitarian* values and character. Lincoln conveyed other classic Aquarian values in the *Emancipation*

Proclamation, wherein the *egalitarian* spirit of *democracy* recall some of the highest potentials of the Aquarian principle. Relating to the Aquarian phenomena of electricity, transformation, sudden change and revolution, further, it has been noted that Lincoln acted as a *lightning rod* by which the popular ideas of his time were transformed into electrifying change. Through Lincoln *popular opinion* was *transformed* into the revolutionary act of ending slavery.

Like Lincoln, Franklin Delano Roosevelt (born January 30, 1882), was a lightning rod for revolutionary change. Consistent with his sun sign, the most prominent powers manifested in Roosevelt's behavior, and by extension in the New Deal, were those Aquarian powers of reform, communitarianism, interdependence and experimentation in government policy. (Roosevelt referred to his administration as a "bold experiment ") Through the darkest days of the Depression and beyond, Roosevelt was a symbol of *hope* to millions of dispossessed Americans. He also became famous for his "fireside chats," frequently using the *electronic medium* of radio to *communicate* with the American public.

Like Roosevelt and Lincoln, Ronald Reagan (born February 5, 1911) acted as a lightning rod for revolutionary change. His is a peculiarly compelling study in the relationship between Aquarian personality traits and philosophical values. The "Reagan *Revolution*" gave expression to the Aquarian-symbolized capacities for *popular ideas* and *reform*; for example, his agenda for tax reform served as a lightning rod for popular restiveness. On another account—nuclear disarmament—the Reagan Administration became a vehicle of reform, even though it was not the President's initial intent to do so. Likewise, although Reagan was possibly the most ideological president the country has ever seen (a close race here with FDR), this vehement anti-communist nonetheless served as the vehicle for lightning-swift reform in East-West relations. Meanwhile, the "Star Wars" program reflects Reagan's instincts for *eccentric innovation,* Star Wars being a plan for a *radical scientific* fix. For all his eccentricity—consulting astrologers and whatnot—Reagan was a consummate *media* politician; he was known as the Great *Communicator.*

On the topic of Aquarian sun signs, it is an interesting note of astrological history that the biologist Charles Darwin was born on the very same day as Abraham Lincoln—February 12, 1809. While the life of Darwin might seem to resemble Lincoln's only in its greatness, their lives also reflect one another in the depth of expression of philosophical values symbolized by Aquarius. While Lincoln was the Great Emancipator, the egalitarian and the humanitarian, Darwin's greatness was manifest in the equally Aquarian realm of science. Darwin's scientific genius was in effect to *compute* a vast amount of *information* about the biological characteristics of different species in the development of a profound *hypothesis*, the evolutionary "origin of species."

CHAPTER 15

INTERPRETATION, TAKE TWO: PSYCHOLOGICAL APPROACHES

> I do not feel that it is possible to comprehend a birth chart in a deeper sense without having some grounding in the fundamental principles of psychology. The very basic and apparently simple divisions of man's psyche into conscious and unconscious puts the interpretation of the birth chart into a completely new perspective, offering nuances, subtleties and lines of definite orientation which are otherwise missed.
>
> — Liz Greene, *Saturn*

Looking at natal astrology through the lenses of psychology gives rise to a paradox. On the one hand, implicit in astrology's vision of the self's inherent nature is a sense of constancy. As symbolized in the mandala of the birth chart, astrology presents a self that remains recognizably the same over time. Psychology, on the other hand, is based largely on the principle that life is full of variable internal as well as external factors that, in continually interacting with each other, translate into processes and dynamics of change.

This paradox of constancy amidst change is resolved in the perception that, while natal influences are "delivered" as integral wholes at birth, these influences do not, so to speak, jump on the stage in fully realized character. Instead, the development, expression and experience of internal influences *unfold* in complex ways throughout life. In seeking to understand complex processes of unfoldment, astrologers are challenged to recognize and understand relationships between what changes—or what *can* change—and what stays essentially the same.*

As we have repeatedly noted, astrology is liable to devolve to the promotion of flat, static and largely false assumptions of determinism. While most of these assumptions once centered on prediction of fate and destiny, deterministic interpretation now most commonly takes the form of pre-molded conceptions of character and personality. Such conceptions, often negative in character, seem to leave no room for change: Capricorns are judgmental, Leos are egocentric, Scorpios are secretive, and so forth.

As the revolution in psychological astrology continues, it will become increasingly difficult even for casual students of astrology to ignore the lenses of psychology. Many astrologers have already awakened to the implications of psychology, and this movement can only strengthen. As of now, however, the literature of astrology still varies hugely as to how much, how well and how clearly psychological analysis is articulated.

Nonetheless, is possible to name at least seven basic psychological approaches to astrological interpretation. Elements of these approaches are implied in natal astrology even when such implications are made unconsciously. Awareness of these approaches is critical to making sense of the kaleidoscope of statements found in the literature, and to reforming interpretation altogether. Although practically speaking these categories overlap one another, certain features are unique to each.

Note that *personality* will not be found among these approaches. Natal astrology is so completely related to the many and complex phenomena of personality that it is virtually impossible to delimit personality as a category separate from any part of natal astrology. Just as the whole natal chart represents the whole self, the concept of personality is encompassing.

---

* In contrast to natal astrology, predictive astrology centers on implications of change. While predictive astrology and its many indications of change ought to be considered in explicit terms of psychology, it is not within the scope of this book to do so. It would be interesting, however, to consider many of the temporal influences addressed in predictive astrology in the context of the second sub-genre of the "Growth and Development" model outlined below.

1. Growth and Development

Suggestions regarding growth and development are ubiquitous in natal astrology. Sometimes these suggestions are well articulated; much more often they are not. "Developmental Astrology" is a gigantic field waiting to be cultivated.

Two of the more trenchant ways that astrological influences can be interpreted according to dynamics of growth and development are (1) the *need to develop* vital powers according to the influence indicated; (2) the *predisposition to develop according to patterns in which hurdles naturally manifest.*

The first mode of interpretation centers on the idea that natal influences contain vital capacities *in potential,* but that it is an open question as to how, and how well, such capacities will be developed. This is a radical but also plainly sensible basis for interpretation. In a simple version of this kind of interpretation, the more vital powers indicated by the sign in question are considered in relation to more negative powers. People born with the sun in Taurus, for instance, are often called stubborn. Yet at the same time, sun-sign Taureans are endowed with powers of *productivity* and *industriousness.* They are capable of *plowing* into productive work, and in this regard they can be eminently *tractable.* Now the opposite of tractable is, of course, intractable: stubborn. Hence it is appropriate to say that Taureans are instinctively tractable, industrious and productive as much as they are instinctively stubborn. Presumably Taureans are capable of developing their productive and tractable powers more so than powers of stubbornness. From a perspective emphasizing development, observed manifestations of more negative kinds can be seen as the failure to develop more vital behaviors associated with the same sign.

The whole of natal astrology can be placed in the context of lifelong development. This type of approach assumes that we are called on to learn and grow in core ways throughout life—and that we are able to. It implies that people are capable of taking responsibility for their own continuing growth, and encourages them to do so.

In this approach, every sign placement indicates challenges to develop basic vital powers of behavior in the particular "house direction" in which the planet in question appears in the natal chart. For example, I am one of those slobs born with Saturn in Virgo (see Chapter 14). Saturn also appears in the 9th house of my natal chart. Regarding Saturn's Virgo placement, I have never been a neat and orderly person—quite to the contrary in fact. Pertaining to Saturn's placement in the 9th house, however, my specific response to *astrology*—astrology as a 9th house "system of higher understanding"—has been to progressively develop those very Virgoan powers of ordering, clarity, refinement and improvement. Nowhere else in my life have I experienced anything resembling such a basic need for improvement and order; yet with respect to my experience of astrology, such a need is foundational. (Still working on it.) To the extent that this particular Virgo power—ordering—has carried over into my whole "personality" seems to be largely incidental.

As this illustration suggests, the house placement of a planet provides a "house," or area of life experience, in which the developmental challenges indicated by the sign placement of the planet in question achieve a particular context of meaning.

The "need to develop" approach is casually used by good astrologers all the time. For example, Lois Rodden tells us that success in profession is a function of "the extent to which we assume the role symbolized by the MC* voluntarily and constructively."[84] Success is implied here to be a function of the degree to which more vital of the powers indicated by the sign on the MC, or midheaven, are developed.

The second sub-genre of growth-and-development interpretation hinges on the perception that natal influences promote recognizable patterns of growth to which developmental challenges are integral, and wherein such challenges must be surmounted. This form of interpretation typically points to the emergence of developmental patterns in childhood, and follows such patterns far into adulthood. Implicit in this approach is the idea that by learning about challenges inherent in given patterns of development, we can better overcome them.

Patterns of development are central to archetypes as interpreted in Jungian astrology, and are equally central to interpretation of natal aspects. The interpreting of aspects according to this

---

* For an explanation of the "MC," see Appendix 3.

approach usually focuses on angular connections involving the sun, moon and Saturn.

To illustrate, let us consider people born with the "moon in difficult aspect to Mars." In natal astrology, this phrase refers mainly to people born with the moon forming either 180° or 90° angular connections to Mars. As interpreted in connection with repeated observation, it appears that people born with the moon in such aspects to Mars are inclined to encounter developmental issues centering on *emotional self-assertion,* * relating to a "too little-too much" imbalance. On the one hand, such individuals are developmentally prone to become too timid for their own good—unalloyedly receptive and even subservient to the needs and desires of others. Yet they may also develop the tendency to be aggressively defensive in response to perceived efforts at domination by others. While in some contexts they may act subserviently, in others they are liable to become inordinately self-assertive and to take advantage of others, all the while oblivious to the needs and desires of others. Hence people born with such moon-Mars influences are challenged to find balance between self-assertiveness and self-secure receptivity. Such a balance might take many years to achieve.

2. Childhood Influences

Although it is in good part an offshoot of the growth-and-development model, a second paradigm of interpretation correlates astrological factors at birth to circumstances of childhood that are critical to the development of psychological issues and problems. Depending on various astrological indications, childhood circumstances are also interpreted as positive factors in development. In correlating influences to circumstances and conditions of the childhood environment as experienced by the native, this paradigm tends to conceive the astrological dimension of influence to be a kind of "cosmic egg," implying that astrological influences color the entire natal environment of the newborn. According to this thinking, astrological influences are reflected simultaneously on both internal and external—envi-

---

* While lunar aspects generally refer to experiences prominent in childhood, aspects involving Mars suggest issues that become especially prominent in adolescence.

ronmental—levels. In one version of this approach, the birth chart reflects the condition of the parents' relationship, and of the parents' lives themselves, at the time of the "native's" birth.

Parental influences are highlighted. The most common version of this kind of interpretation centers on interpreting the moon's natal sign position and aspects in terms of the role or experience of the mother; and Saturn—or alternatively the sun—in terms of the role or experience of the father. With respect to the Moon-Mars example discussed above, the "too little-too much" pattern is seen here as a kind of inheritance from a mother whose *own* quotient of receptivity versus self-assertion was imbalanced and/or unpredictable.

Interpreting influences in terms of childhood circumstances brings up a chicken-and-egg issue. Which comes first, a set of circumstances, or the child's (predisposed) experience of such? From one point of view, the child's circumstances exist independently of how one responds to them. This perspective effectively places responsibility for development on circumstances themselves. Alternatively, the child's *experience* of circumstances can be considered most critically as a function of innately organized factors. From this latter perspective, the objective circumstances of childhood are subordinated in favor of the idea that we organize and interpret our experience according to internal predispositions. Emphasized here are predilections to *attract experiences* unto oneself. When astrological influences are interpreted primarily in terms of such predispositions, the implication is that the child *creates* the pertinent experiences *in collaboration with* the parents. Such emphasis on internal predispositions can sometimes appear to be unfair. But, especially in later life, this perspective is helpful in promoting individuals to take responsibility for, and thus change, their ongoing patterns of experience.

In reality, it is not usually either possible or necessary to make hard distinctions between the realities of childhood circumstances and predispositions to experience such. Instead, it is useful to understand that internal predispositions *play into* circumstances, and that it is through such interplay that long-term patterns of experience are formed. In all but the extreme range of cases, childhood sources of lifelong patterns of experience can be seen as a process of internal predispositions interacting with, and consequently bringing into bolder relief, aspects of the child's environment that might otherwise, and to others, be less prominent. Even in circumstances that would objectively be described as difficult, individuals tend to focus on different aspects of what is experienced as difficult.

3. Learning

This model features the ways in which natal influences interact with general environmental conditions so as to shape the possibilities of what *can* be learned.

Since natal astrology is presumably the study of inherent influences and not of generic environmental factors, this type of approach is almost never to be found in astrology. Yet such factors as culture, geography and socioeconomic status are bound to affect the development of astrological influences. Take for instance the situation in America's inner cities, where adverse conditions of the physical, social and economic environment obviously affect the development and expression of such Mars/Scorpio powers as survival, toughness, aggression, anger and frustration. Almost by definition the conditions of urban environments serve to emphasize the learning of those very Mars/Scorpio powers of behavior that are endemic to inner city life. By the same token, such environmental conditions impact hugely on opportunities for individuation. Conditions of constant danger, deprivation, poverty and abuse are bound to impede the individual's chances of realizing *any* of the higher or more individual possibilities of growth and development that a natal chart may suggest.

Considering this sort of interaction brings into high relief the principle that internal factors cannot properly be assessed without knowledge of external conditions.

Interactions between inherent influences and environmental factors can be articulated in the context of the trial-and-error model of learning. This approach centers on the principle that while astrological influences—especially zodiacal influences— translate into predispositions to developing powers of behavior indicated by that sign, changes in conditions and circumstances may conspire to send one, as it were, back to the drawing board—to learn *other* powers of behavior indicated by the same sign.

In an interesting illustration of this kind of approach, it has been chronicled that Bill Clinton was something of a firebrand liberal when he was first elected governor of Arkansas, and that he attempted to ram a liberal agenda down the throats of a conservative rural state during his first term in office. When, in consequence, he was defeated in his first bid for reelection, he faced a huge "learning crisis." Changing as a result, he became in many ways the spitting image of a moderate willing to compromise, and it was from this new centrism that he relaunched his political career. Yet remarkably, Clinton went through a similar "learning curve" in his first term as president when, after starting out once again by pushing for liberal causes, his penchant for compromise became a virtual caricature of itself.

For anyone familiar with Clinton's natal chart, it is clear that along with Leo influences (Leo is his sun sign), the emphasis of planets in Libra is striking. Primary powers indicated by Libra include negotiation, compromise and identifying with the other's point of view. This last can lapse into development of the trait known as wishy-washyness. Yet Libra also indicates a predilection to (typically liberal) social activism. Witnessing the way that Clinton has responded to the challenges of his office with respect to his Libra-placed planets, one gets the strong impression that while Clinton developed Libran powers of social activism early on in his life, these powers were negatively reinforced on the job. Through considerable experiences of what can be considered trial-and-error, Clinton learned what became for him the more successful Libran powers of politics-by-compromise, negotiation, and identification with others' points of view.

4. Jungian

Interpretation associated with Jungian psychology articulates a number of different psychological dynamics. Yet perhaps the theme that best captures the essence of Jungian astrology—and Jungian psychology—is that of *individuation*. Central to Jungian approaches to both disciplines is the injunction that we come to realize, in ever more subtle and profound ways, who we are as individuals. In Jungian analysis, moreover, the process of self-realization centers on recognizing within oneself the existence of *unconscious intents* that ultimately define us as individuals. The perception of unconscious intent is key to archetypal interpretation.

Archetypes in Jungian astrology are typically presented in terms of "archetypal characters." These characters are identified either in the form of specific gods and goddesses—Jason, Chiron, Aphrodite, Pluto—or in more generic terms—the Trickster, the Hero, the Old King, the Believer. In either case, such characters all hold some kind of inner intent of which they are often not fully conscious. The protagonists and their stories show us the implicit intent to play out and dramatize the very patterns of experience they signify. As noted in connection with Aries in Chapter 9, the myth of Jason and the Golden Fleece portrays the intent to embark on an adventurous quest; but also to betray self by failing to listen to one's heart.

As is typical of archetypal themes, Jason's unconscious intent is marked by irrationality and compulsion. It is charged with what Jung called the *daimon,* or animating spirit, that compels the protagonist to play out a particular pattern of experience with the kind of damn-the-torpedoes zeal that is heedless of consequences. By no means, however, are all archetypal intents self-destructive.

Whatever the nature of the inner intent, Jungian analysis presents the challenge to fully realize its existence. The Jungian approach equates the inner intent with an aspect of self, a deeper motivation, that seeks to reveal itself. It emphasizes the process of *coming to awareness* of the inner intent as the key step in coming to terms with self. This theme of "confrontation with the archetype" can be summed up as, "This is part of me; this is what I must meet in myself." Basic aspects of self that have been repressed, denied or ignored must be recognized, owned and reclaimed. The "intents" of such aspects of self are often seen to run at cross-purposes to the ways that we have been conditioned to think and behave by family and society. But Jungian analysis does not cast others or "the world out there" in the role of the villain. It may be troubling to recognize the nature of buried aspects of self, but it is nonetheless ultimately liberating.

The psychological process conveyed in Jungian astrology centers on the relation between consciousness and what, while integral to the inherent nature of the individual, is unconscious.

5. Self-Realization-Humanistic

With his emphasis on self-realization, Jung has been called the father of humanistic psychology. But in conceiving of self-realization in terms of unconscious intent, Jung emphasized the idea of becoming what we *must* be. Mainstream humanistic psychology, in contrast, casts self-realization more as a matter of realizing higher potentials—becoming what we *can* be.

Within the literature of astrology are to be found a variety of indications of higher potentials. One set of indications of this kind regards what are known as "favorable aspects." In short, planets in 60° and 120° angular relation to one another at birth, and to some extent those conjunct one another, classically indicate *gifts* and *talents* that are inherent in potential. The implication is that such gifts and talents can be progressively cultivated, developed and fulfilled. Planets in favorable aspect to Venus, for example, are often interpreted in terms of artistic gifts that may be developed.

Meanwhile, the name most associated with humanistic astrology is that of Dane Rudhyar. In books such as *The Astrology of Personality* (1936) and *Person-Centered Astrology* (1973), Rudhyar developed a broad and complex psycho-philosophical approach to the astrology of becoming. He placed much of this approach in the in the context of *holism*. Simply put, holism refers to the continuing process by which parts interact in dynamic relation to the whole. Inasmuch as the birth chart presents a mandala of the wholeness of individual selfhood as made up of many parts, astrology is intrinsically a holistic discipline.

But Rudhyar's metaphysics of astrological holism goes far beyond the idea of a person as a self-contained whole. As he wrote in *Person-Centered Astrology,* the astrological pattern at birth:

> ... establishes the individual's life-purpose and its basic relation to all other wholes in the universe. This organic whole—the individual person—is essentially no different from the infinitely greater and vaster organized whole, which we call the universe—the individual is this whole, focused at a particular point in space and in terms of the particular need of the exact moment of its emergence into independent existence...[85]

For Earth-bound mortals, Rudhyar's metaphysics can be a bit
much. Still, Rudhyar's astrology was vital to the development of
the discipline, and his conception of holism serves to integrate a
subject that is otherwise prone to become fragmented. Yet oddly,
it is perhaps in the realm of prediction that Rudhyar's holistic
approach has been most successfully applied. This application is
most commonly found in connection with interpretations of the
transiting (currently affecting) influences of a given planet in
relation to the whole cycle of that planet. For example, Saturn
takes about 29 years to complete its cycle through the zodiac,
and a whole-based interpretation of Saturn transits places the
meaning of a single transit in the context of the entire Saturn
cycle.

6. Karmic-Evolutionary

In one version of this type of approach, principles of growth
and development are in effect applied across lifetimes. From
such a perspective, the birth chart represent karma, or patterns of
behavior and experience carried over from past lifetimes. These
patterns are bound to be encountered again in the present lifetime, and it is up to the individual to recognize the patterns,
resolve the underlying issues, and open to more enlightened
ways of being. The classic spiritual approach makes *karma,* the
baggage carried from the past, inseparable from *dharma,* the call
to bring behavior in line with universal law. The astrological
concept of dharma carries a fundamental injunction: whatever
unresolved patterns of experience you have brought into this life
constitute the very work you are here to do; so go to it.

In this approach, compulsions to patterns of behavior, as interpreted in karmic terms, are turned inside out so as to indicate
evolutionary challenges. In setting our minds to enlightened
change, in other words, the very failings that have inveigled us
for so long can be turned to our spiritual evolution. If, for
example, a Neptune influence translates into the inveterate
compulsion to believe in illusions, your challenge is to quench
your need to believe, and perhaps turn this aspect of self into a
well-developed imagination. Treated with sensitivity, this kind of
thinking can be truly helpful. A perceptive reading of old and
self-defeating patterns can yield penetrating insights not only
into what is old, but what can be new.

Conversely, when astrological interpretations of karma are presented stripped down—devoid of implications regarding evolution and the possibilities of growth—they are liable to lapse into negativity. Such interpretations are prone to focus on patterns of experience and behavior whose main effects are, as many have put it, that they bum you out.

7. Pathology and Healing

Astrology is full of implications of pathology, and the prospects for correlating astrological influences with pathological potentials are multiple and diverse. Yet if astrological influences are to be studied and interpreted in terms of pathology, they must simultaneously be placed in the context of healing. As with astrological indications of karma, the pathological potentials of astrological influences are not so fixed and determined that they cannot be developed and expressed positively. As with karmic patterns, dark manifestations are inversions of bright manifestations, and in principle the dark potentials of psychopathology are transformable through processes of healing. Interpretations oriented toward healing are becoming increasingly common. One of the best is Melanie Reinhart's *Chiron and the Healing Journey* (Arkana). In this work, the author entertains pathological manifestations as integral to the Chiron* influences, yet uses pathology to illustrate potentials for healing.

Interpretation of the natal chart can be generated in simultaneous connection with one or more of the psychological approaches outlined above. In fact it is possible to develop interesting *formulaic* interpretations of those mundane facts of natal astrology—sign and house placements of planets—in the context of any one of these approaches, or through a blending of two or three different approaches. To illustrate such possibilities, let us consider Saturn's placement by sign.

As we get into this exercise, note that some of the terms of psychological interpretation will resemble the terms of Saturn's influence *per se*. This happens because the principles studied in

---

* For a brief explication of Chiron, see Appendix 2.

astrology translate naturally into psychological principles. The influences of Taurus, for example, translate into principles of growth and development. The influences of Pluto invite interpretation in terms of the (Jungian) *daimon.* Theoretically, all the influences and principles of astrology could be translated into principles of psychology and psychological interpretation.

Saturn symbolizes potentials for contraction, restriction, limitation and constraint; similarly Saturn is singularly identified with the capacity for experiencing *difficulty* in life. It signifies potentials for hard work and the learning of hard lessons. From a "patterns of development" perspective, Saturn invites interpretation on the one hand in terms of the predisposition to experience patterns of constraint and difficulty, and on the other in terms of the developmental challenge to work hard to change the conditions of those same difficulties.

At the same time, Saturn is called the "Lord of Karma." As such, Saturn obviously invokes the Karmic/Evolutionary model. According to this model, Saturn's indications of ingrained patterns of difficulty and constraint can be interpreted as being carried over from previous lifetimes—the results of actions in past lives. Yet Saturn can also be considered the Lord of Dharma. If as Lord of Karma Saturn represents patterns of difficulty that we have brought on ourselves up to this point in our evolution, as Lord of Dharma it indicates *the work ahead,* the work we must do in order to rectify the patterns of difficulty we have brought into this life. Hence Saturn can be interpreted in terms of the work ahead, the work of a lifetime.

Alternately, in that the limitations and constraints that we face early in life take the form of circumstances over which we have apparently little control, Saturn can be interpreted according to the Childhood Influences approach. Taking this tack, Saturn's placement by sign and house indicate experiences of childhood circumstances of difficulty and constraint that condition problems of adult life. Simultaneously, what are experienced as difficult circumstances in childhood should also be understood in terms of the *predisposition to attract* such experiences of difficulty and constraint.

Turning interpretation back in the direction of the first-cited interpretive genre of growth and development, Saturn's sign placement can be interpreted to indicate *the need or challenge to work to establish structures, conditions, and attitudes through which the instinctive powers* (represented by sign placement) *can be fully and vitally expressed.* Here Saturn represents the *need to develop* conditions and structures as indicated by its sign and house placements; and those placements simultaneously indicate areas where developmental difficulties and constraints may manifest.

The "trick" here is not so much how to combine these interpretations, but rather how to apply such formulations directly to Saturn's natal placements. To accomplish this trick, it is meaningful to consider the circumstances surrounding whole mini-generations of people born with Saturn in given signs. Saturn takes two and a half years to transit a sign.

Consider Saturn in Cancer. The more senior generation of the Saturn-in-Cancer population was born between June 1944 and August 1946,[*] when masses of children were affected by wartime privations of fathers off in, and returning from, the service; and with mothers working outside the home. The next period of Saturn in Cancer births was the early 1970s, a period of great cultural and emotional chaos not unlike the war years. Of course, the early 1970s were also war years. Yet there were important differences in circumstances facing these two generations, and on this account it might be appropriate to develop and apply different variations of interpretation to each generation.

Taking a cue from circumstances with respect to the senior Saturn-in-Cancer generation, we can infer that conditions of difficulty collectively affected Cancerian development of security, unconditional love and emotional nourishment. Similarly, we can correlate Saturn in Cancer to difficulties regarding the fulfillment of basic emotional needs. Accordingly, it is meaningful to interpret the Saturn-in-Cancer influence in terms of the *challenge to work to establish conditions and structures (such as*

---

[*] The outer planets, sometimes called "generational planets," take on the order of years to transit through a single sign, and it can be instructive to look at collective conditions experienced by the entire generation born during that transit. Jupiter spends about one year in a sign (Jupiter's transits are the basis of Chinese astrology), Saturn roughly 2.5 years, Uranus 7 years, and Neptune and Pluto from 12 to as much as 20 years.

family structures) through which sustained feelings of well-being can be experienced.

In looking at circumstances surrounding whole generations, it is important to collate and assess experiences as communicated by numerous members of a given generation. So it is that many people born with Saturn in Leo report difficulties regarding how they were encouraged—or not encouraged—to express themselves and their inner identities. Relating to such reports, we can interpret Saturn in Leo in terms of predispositions to experience circumstances of family life as limiting free self-expression, and as restricting the development of self-identity. Similarly there is the indication of attraction to experience parents as laying heavy expectations on the "native" to be something he or she may not be. For these people, the "work ahead" would be to establish conditions and attitudes that promote creative and free self-expression, and to build structures that conform to a true expression of identity. Creating one's own family with a new set of values, and finding work that is truly self-expressive, emerge as good lifetime goals for this placement.

While we have taken Saturn as the initial focus for generating formulaic interpretations, sign placements can themselves be used as the primary foci for interpretation, for example regarding issues of growth and development. Through the lens of a given sign, we can see the challenge to develop basic vital powers of behavior as a function of whatever planet is placed in that sign. The lens of a single sign can also be interpreted to indicate *areas of developmental impact*: areas of life in which challenges to develop new attitudes and behaviors are central. In this regard it is provocative to explore sign placements by asking questions keyed by that sign. For planets in Cancer, questions about one's mother—and the *experience* of one's mother—are obvious candidates. For planets in Libra, we might ask: Where, and in what relationships, has it become important in your life to compromise, negotiate and be diplomatic? For planets in Aquarius: What new ideas, technology, trends and/or movements have come into play that have impacted on you?

The asking of such open-ended questions can serve to stimulate thinking about development of sign-indicated powers and capacities. To the extent that the answers to such questions reveal negative "areas of impact," they provide keys to exactly what powers and dimensions of being are most ripe for growth, development and "wholling."

CHAPTER 16

RETROGRADE PLANETS

I think of myself as a sensible person, not someone who hears voices, or follows them, but this voice sounded so loud and clear and came from such a deep place in me, that it seemed like the voice of a stranger. I had to listen.

"It doesn't make sense," the doubting part of me kept saying. Reasonable responsible middle-aged women do not hear voices—and they certainly don't follow them. No wonder the sensible part of me panicked. It had taken on a lifetime task of protecting me and felt secure, thinking it had done a good job. Even if protecting me meant keeping me stuck in old patterns, at least they were familiar patterns.

I don't know why, but another part of me trusted the voice. The part that doesn't have to ask a lot of questions or need reasons for doing what it wants to do—it just knows. I knew I had to go [and live with an Amish family].   — Sue Bender, *Plain and Simple*

Few symbols carry such provocative psychological implications as the little ℞ that sometimes appears next to the glyph of a planet on a birth chart. This notation signifies that at the time of birth, the planet in question was in *retrograde* motion. Retrograde motion is a regular occurrence in which a planet appears to move backwards through the zodiac. A planet "goes retrograde" as a result of its orbital motion relative to the Earth. Just as a slower-moving train appears to move backwards from the point of view of a faster-moving train, planets appear to move backwards through the zodiac from our point of view on Earth. Every planet moves into periods of retrograde motion within the course of two years; most "go retrograde" every year. Periods of retrogradation last for as little as three weeks at a time (Mercury) to as much as five months at a time for the three outermost planets. Most people are born with at least one retrograde planet.

The psychological implications of retrograde planets are diverse. Their influences appear to exert long-term effects on processes of growth and development. They contribute to some of the most complex dynamics in personality, and promote life-long challenges of coming to terms with the "inner self." They support the development of great intuitive power, but by no means do they guarantee such development.

When planets are retrograde at birth, their influences are not channeled in the same way that influences of the sun, moon, or planets in direct motion are channeled. Retrograde planets indicate influences that are not accessible to consciousness—and thus to consciously motivated behavior—as influences of planets in direct motion are. Instead, retrograde influences are turned inward, generating a particular kind of *subjective* and *subconscious* intrapsychic dimension.

Although it is possible to become conscious of retrograde influences within us, we cannot access these influences in consciousness without changing dramatically what it means to be conscious. Retrograde influences effectively "pull" consciousness into deeper subjective, intuitive and non-rational realms.

Since the psychological dynamics of retrograde planets are so complex, we must forego consideration of most astrological factors that affect the dynamics of retrograde planets, except to say that *their influences tend to find expression through the parts of ourselves that are indicated by other, direct planets to which the retrogrades make strong aspects.* For example, when a retrograde planet is in a major angular relation to the sun at birth, the retrograde planet's influence is typically channeled into expression as a function of its connection with the solar motivation.

The influences of retrograde planets tend to create three different, though related, types of psychological dynamics. These dynamics translate into three different modes of development, experience and expression. While every individual born with retrograde planets can be described to one extent or another in terms of all three modes, individuals typically develop and express themselves more according to features of one mode or another. We can call these modes the *introspective*, the *creative* and the *projective*.

Mode 1: Introspection

Retrograde influences both invite and compel introspection. These influences encourage introspection because they tend to feed into consciousness by means of thoughts, feelings, impulses and reactions that cannot as easily be assimilated by consciousness in relation to outward circumstances as can the influences of direct planets. Retrograde influences generate subjective planes of consciousness that complicate the efforts of consciousness to achieve consonance and cohesion in experiencing the outer environment. Indeed retrograde influences change the whole process by which we achieve the sense of congruence and equilibrium with the world outside ourselves.

Retrograde influences serve to blur distinctions between inner and outer. Turning consciousness to a subjective and deeply internal focus, retrograde influences serve to internalize the experience of people, circumstances, and events, wherein experience becomes part of an interior subconscious world, or *whorl*. This subconscious dimension of experience supersedes what would otherwise be a more clear and direct experience of the external context.

Instead of facilitating the conscious addressing—or simple ignoring—of exterior circumstances, retrograde influences generate subjective, internal reactions and attitudes to external affairs that may or may not be consciously articulated. To the extent that this dimension of subjective experience is not fully integrated into consciousness, cross-currents of thought and feeling may develop, some emanating from consciousness, others from the subconscious plane. Since there is no clear dividing line between conscious and subconscious realms—consciousness runs on a continuum into subconscious and unconscious planes—it is difficult to say at what level one can become aware of such cross-currents.

The emergence of internal cross-currents in experience almost always begins in childhood, concurrent with the development of the conscious ability to articulate experience. Instead of being clear about what one thinks and feels, the tendency is to become "of two minds" with respect to the issues and people current in one's world. Becoming "mixed-up" in what one thinks and feels about others, it becomes chronically difficult to affirm or even to articulate one's attitudes. This mode of development often involves confusion both about one's attitudes toward others and about what path of behavior to pursue oneself.

Thus the influences of retrograde planets contribute to ongoing unresolved experience. They promote dissonances in experience that can become magnified into major, though not well-perceived, issues of subconscious or semiconscious conflict: inner conflict. Although retrograde-related issues may begin in explicit connection with outer circumstances, retrograde dynamics transcend circumstances: We carry the internal conflicts engendered by these influences wherever we go. Regardless of changes in external circumstances, conflicts between conscious and subconscious thoughts, feelings and (self-) judgments become ongoing themes.

Retrograde influences often serve to create *inner dialogue* in which unresolved experience takes on auditory dimensions. Many people born with Jupiter or Saturn retrograde report the presence of inner voices that jabber away incessantly, with varying degrees of coherence—and to varying degrees of maddening effect! Contributing to experiences of almost surreal nature, such inner voices typically seem to generate jumbled dialogues in which different points of view are "heard" simultaneously.

Whether experienced in terms of inner voices or on a more subtle level, inner dialogue can be seen as a central *purpose* of retrograde influences, in that such dialogue challenges us to reflect on ourselves, on our experience, and on our deeper motives.

All planets, in corresponding to core motivational influences, indicate, as Rob Hand put it, *intentionalities* within us. The implication is that the influences of both retrograde and direct planets hold some intrinsic subjective intention—the unconscious intents of Jungian astrology and psychology. Yet in the introspective mode of development, the "intentionalities" of retrograde influences cannot be known independently of the very introspective processes that these influences generate. In the introspective mode, one's deeper motives emerge only through a gradual process of self-reflection wherein seemingly irrational, psychologically problematic currents of the influences in question become, degree by degree, accepted, affirmed and integrated in the evolving experience of life and self. Reaching resolution with retrograde influences through introspection involves fully accepting the existence of the deeper subconscious levels from which they emanate. No matter how "irrational" or unlikely the implicit messages and expressions of these influences may at times seem, and no matter how much self-doubt inner dialogue may cause, it is vital to reach a feeling of comfort with one's deeper subjective responses and reactions. In short, coming to alignment with retrograde influences means fully assimilating and affirming the subjective "I."

Integral to the subjective dimension of retrograde influences are feelings and intuition. Hence successful assimilation of retrograde influences via introspection involves the growth of intuitive power and increasing trust of feelings. As the interior, subconscious, feeling and intuitive frames of reference come to be fully affirmed, retrograde influences may become increasingly expressed in attitudes, beliefs and ideas of colorful, risqué, unusual and even controversial nature. Integrating retrograde influences means affirming these sorts of expression even when the "outside world" might be thought to disapprove. In coming to alignment with and "owning" the subtle inner imperatives that retrograde influences engender, both the choices we make and the ways we appear to behave tend to turn away from established norms.

Those whose feelings and intuitive expressions are affirmed in childhood are bound to have an easier time integrating retrograde influences, and are often able to reach alignment with their inner subjective selves early in life without a great deal of introspection.* Instead of pouring psychic energy into inner dialogue, these individuals are more able to act in accord with their deeper internal imperatives with an implicit sense of empowerment. But as we will see in exploring other modes of retrograde dynamics, the simple fact of being in touch with strong feelings and intu-

---

* As well, retrograde planets forming trine (120°) and sextile (60°) aspects to other planets at birth indicate dynamics supporting easier, more fluid integrative processes in which introspection might be less necessary. Such indications, however, do not always hold, as an "easier" more fluid integrative process might merely wind up translating into a sense of license for engaging in *truly* irrational forms of expression.

itive impulses does not mean that retrograde influences have been successfully integrated. To the contrary, intuitively powerful behaviors can be directed into blind and inharmonious expression. Such expression is itself indicative of inner turmoil and the *need* for introspection. Indeed the failure to engage in introspection tends to result in more arbitrary, one-sided, conflict-producing attitudes and behaviors where conflict is focused in relation not to the interior but the *exterior* world. Hence, while the experience of introspective dynamics may not be easy, introspection is often essential to resolving issues that are generated within the subconscious.

Retrograde influences challenge us to reach peace by finding deeper truths about ourselves; but the truths to be found are typically both complex and initially inchoate. It is left to us, in progressively deeper levels of realization, to see the sense of subconsciously motivated inclinations. Until we do, we may interpret, identify and act on these inclinations in any number of misguided ways.

Issues generated in connection with retrograde influences may have karmic roots. Retrograde planets suggest the existence of parts of ourselves that were expressed in controversial, untoward and/or chaotic ways in previous lifetimes. As carryovers from the past, retrograde influences represent experiential patterns in, and aspects of, ourselves wherein lengthy introspection is required, in effect, to save us from replaying bad and *very* old patterns.

Karma or not, introspection is typically necessary in order to fundamentally realign our internal sense of what feels good— and right.

Mode 2: Creativity

Retrograde influences generate sources of subjective depth, richness and creativity, and anyone born with a retrograde planet owns a well of creative potential.

The creative wells inherent in retrograde influences can be expressed in connection with widely diverse aspects of life: art, music, literature, sports, ice-skating and gymnastics, design, business, cooking and much more. The injunction here seems to be on the order of the Nike commercial: Just do it. Or just *be* it: Retrograde influences can be fruitfully channeled not only in creative pursuits *per se* but in all unplanned and spontaneous forms of in-the-moment expression. Retrograde influences make for entertaining, off-the-cuff manners of being and reacting, and lend themselves to the enjoyment of pleasures that bring existential sensibilities into play, such as movie-going, walking in the woods and sailing.

Creative potentials can develop from retrograde influences with a minimum of soul-searching. The key to this mode of development is (again) being or becoming completely comfortable with one's own subjectivity. As compared to introspectively questioning the whys and wherefores of one's responses to others and to life, the creative mode depends on implicit self-acceptance and the intuitive confidence that if one's responses are like no one else's, so much the better.

The very subjectivity that allows retrograde influences to be channeled so fully into creative dynamics, however, brings certain liabilities. Many born with retrograde planets who are most intensely creative are also cavalier in their subjectively driven actions toward others. For instance Pablo Picasso, who was born with four retrograde planets, was wholly immersed in his subjective/creative process; but Picasso was also quite a tyrant in his personal life. For all his genius, he used his creative/subjective powers with relative disregard for his effects on others. Creativity is a form of power, and unless the sense of power born of creativity is coupled with deepened awarenesses born of self-reflection, it is liable to be become abusive. Hence while channeling retrograde influences into creative modes of expression can be wonderful and productive, introspection is a vital complement to it.

Mode 3: Intuition, Power and Projection

The power born of retrograde influences need not be developed in concert with either introspection or creativity. As with introspective dynamics, retrograde influences can fuel a mode of development in which complicated involvement with the world outside oneself is experienced. But whereas introspection involves a relatively passive relation to other people and the world-at-large, this mode features the *externalizing* of psychic energy that in the introspective mode would be effectively used up in ongoing internal dialogue and reflection. As much as the intuition and subjectivity of retrograde influences can be absorbed into interior processes of introspection and creativity, in other words, the same intuition and subjectivity can be *projected* into exterior affairs. In this mode of development, retrograde influences are channeled into activities and points of view that seem quite pointedly *un*reflecting.

Implicitly ignoring the subconscious pulls of retrograde influences so that they don't "get in the way," individuals who develop via this mode can successfully channel the power of subjectivity and intuition into all manner of tasks and affairs. Retrograde influences contribute to the development of intuitive power as expressed in physical skills such as sports, car mechanics and construction, in business, and in tasks requiring extensive mental concentration such as engineering and legal work. In this mode of development, the task at hand provides the immediate outlet for subjective and intuitively charged motivations.

Still, given the subconscious nature of retrograde influences, the channeling of these influences into total focus on external affairs is not as simple a matter as tapping into some great well of intuitive energy. It is bound to bring complications. Unreflecting externalization of these influences is liable to develop hand-in-hand with attitudes regarding what "the other" does, did or didn't do. Retrograde influences support the projection onto others, or onto some entity in the outside world, of essentially the same inner conflicts and unresolved issues that are internalized in the introspective mode. Retrograde influences support the tendency to identify intensely with attitudes and points of view that explicitly conflict with attitudes and points of view held by others. Many people live whole lifetimes projecting subconscious influences not only into contrarian attitudes but into seemingly *objectified*, externally sanctioned thought-forms. This mode of development supports the tendency to judge and criticize the behavior of others, and/or to adopt polemical positions and moral imperatives. So often in such cases, while the "wrong" is seen to be "caused" by "the other side," one's intense reactions to others and to issues are in reality largely functions of one's own subconscious dynamics.

Strong subjective identification with attitudes and behaviors of a we-they, me-versus-you nature obviously precludes the growth of self-awareness. The power-projection mode of expression is typically marked by streaks of irrationality that are impervious to feedback or questioning. Accordingly, this mode can create intractable problems—for others, at least!—until or unless it is accompanied by elements of introspection.

On the other hand, it frequently happens that people who feel powerless, and who engage in endless internal dialogue, are themselves projecting the *potential* power of their own retrograde influences onto the external world in poor-me ways, and wind up resenting wealthy, successful, or merely happy people out of inner frustration. Unable to come to terms with their own retrograde influences so as to realize the creativity and intuitive power that these influences offer, such individuals are liable to react negatively to counterparts who *express* intuitive power.

In yet other cases, individuals can be blessed from the beginning with the ability to felicitously channel the intuitive power of retrograde influences. Such people might identify strongly with subjective values, veer easily from the norm, hold unusual attitudes and express a vivid intuition. They can be powerful and even controversial without being abrasive. Again, development in this direction is aided by supportive familial and social influences, and also by virtue of being born with retrograde planets forming trine and sextile angles to other planets.

For the rest of us, in whom the process of reaching inner harmony might seem to begin more like a wrestling match, the development of internal self-congruence, creativity and trust of deeper intuitions can always be goals.

MERCURY RETROGRADE

The influences of Mercury retrograde affect the development of perceptual processes, as subconscious elements serve to generate unusually strong spins on perception.

These influences contribute to the growth of remarkably uninhibited capacities for speaking one's mind, and to the blithe expression of oddball, controversial and off-the-cuff commentary. They promote the tendency to issue imaginative, funny and wacky kinds of remarks, and serve to strengthen the intuitive power of saying the original and even irrational things one thinks. Creatively developed, these influences contribute to a talent for generating paisley, multicolored and richly textured perceptions, and so encourage unusual, highly original forms of artistic expression (Vincent Van Gogh, Georgia O'Keeffe, muppet creator Jim Henson, Christo, Madonna). Mercury retrograde influences enhance creative activities in which strong communication of perception is called for. Three such activities are film direction, poetry/fiction, and broadcast journalism. (Film direction: Frank Capra, Alfred Hitchcock, Frances Ford Coppola, Clint Eastwood, Ken Burns, George Lucas, Peter Weir, Wim Wenders, Steve Martin. Poetry/fiction: Herman Melville, Rudyard Kipling, Robert Frost, Gary Snyder, J.R.R. Tolkein, Norman Mailer, Larry McMurtry, Philip Roth, Bharati Mukherjee, Susan Howatch, Ann Tyler, Ken Follett. Broadcast journalism: Larry King, John Cameron Swayze, Howard Cossell, Keith Jackson.)

How this influence is developed and expressed is in part a function of how much others in the childhood environment respect and affirm these individuals in their unusual ways of perceiving and responding. When family members convey perceptions of reality that run markedly at odds with the natives' own perceptions, the perceptions of others may be deeply internalized, creating an inner whorl of conflicting, contrasting thought patterns. Out of this perceptual whorl, natives may spend many years questioning and/or trying to validate conflicting perceptions. This sort of clash can lead to asking such questions as, "Are they crazy or is it just me?" Mental tensions arising from not being affirmed in one's thoughts and perceptions can have profound implications in later development, translating into difficulties with employment, adjustments to the realities of life, and relations with others. Challenges here are to articulate one's deeply felt thoughts and perceptions, and to learn to stand on one's own perceptions, without getting too much involved with what others may think or say.

These influences also contribute, however, to communicating what appears to be an almost brazen disregard for others' concerns, and similar disregard for conventional wisdom in general. In the power-projection mode of expression, people born with Mercury retrograde develop an emphatic inner certainty about their views even when these views are unusual, contrary and even outrageous. This trait can be exasperating to others, especially because these individuals are typically not well able to becoming aware of the obtuse and contrary nature of the things they say, think and do. The influences of Mercury retrograde fuel the expression of pointedly subjective perceptions that are resistant to feedback. People born with this influence often become compelled to communicate highly polemical views. (Lucretia Mott, Alexander Solzhenitsyn, Linus Pauling, Paul Tsongas, Eleanor Smeal, Ralph Reed, Don Imus, Rush Limbaugh, John Singlaub, Newt Gingrich).

More commonly, though, these influences serve to generate perceptions of reality that are uncommonly original.

VENUS RETROGRADE

Venus is found retrograde less frequently than any other planet—7%—and far less frequently than most planets. Besides Venus, the planet found retrograde least often is Mars, at 9%.[86]

Like other retrograde influences, those of Venus contribute to introversion, especially in childhood. Indeed, Venus retrograde provides the classic makings of the social introvert. But dramatic turnarounds from introvert to extrovert are also characteristic, and it is on the axis of introversion-extroversion that this influence generates some of its most vital and interesting dynamics.

In introspective development, early relations with parents may not be normalized. People born with this influence often feel that they must play an artificial role to get along, and tend to react by wanting to withdraw. Or else they respond to what they feel to be artificial expectations by acting contrary. There may be a sense of separation and/or alienation from a parent or from peers. Under such conditions, they are prone to feeling cut off and "socially naked" as they grow, ill at ease in social intercourse.

Those born with this influence who are unable to surmount feelings of being cut off in childhood, may grow to experience intense unfulfilled social needs which, of course, introversion only accentuates. Feeling socially inadequate and/or unfulfilled, they are liable to project themselves in wildly irrational attempts to compensate (Roberto D'Aubisson, Saddam Hussein, Adolph Hitler, Huey Newton, Amy Foster, Tonya Harding, Pamela Smart, David Koresh). Some attract experiences in which dramatic internal realignment in social attitudes and behaviors occurs (George Wallace with respect to civil rights, Ted Turner with respect to liberalism—and hence to Jane Fonda—Warren Beatty and Magic Johnson with respect to promiscuity and/or

HIV). For those who remain more introverted, the experience of being shown "naked to the world" can be overwhelming (Clarence Thomas, Admiral Jeremy Boorda, Hank Aaron during his approach to breaking Babe Ruth's career record for home runs).

Individuals born with this influence are prone to be drawn to relationships of two kinds. First, they may be attracted to (other) introverts—sometimes others also born with Venus retrograde. Second, they may be drawn to others who form an odd "fit" with themselves, where there are marked differences that prevent the growth of real closeness. Often enough, there is a "retrograde," or insular aspect to such relationships. Subconscious compulsions can support patterns of inward turning that inhibit relationships from growing—or growing apart if need be. They might see themselves as playing a special kind of role in their partners' lives in what amount to unspoken pacts. With this kind of dynamic, unacknowledged disagreements between the partners may go on indefinitely. Still, at any time it is possible for communication and direct interaction on mutually vital issues to bring delightful surprises for these characters, as they have the most interesting of underlying experiences to share—if only they would. Those born with Venus retrograde are challenged to become comfortable in communicating their subjective experiences *of* their partners *to* their partners.

More generally, the influences of Venus retrograde engender vividly subjective experiences of relating to others, and as individuals learn to relax into their subjectivity they are able to develop remarkably colorful, bold, and sometimes kinky modes of responding to social relationship. Whether or not they grow up as introverts, these individuals are capable of becoming exceptionally extroverted, and many undergo a metamorphosis, in adulthood if not in teenage years, into the most flamboyant of extroverted social personalities. Developed creatively, this influence encourages a libidinous delight in social provocation. While those born with this influence who become extroverts at an early age are prone to become self-centered, they nonetheless are given to enjoy uninhibited and even outrageous social interaction and repartee (Eddy Murphy, Jack Nicholson, Bob Uecker, Muhammad Ali, Tommy Lasorda, Warren Beatty, Redd Foxx, Bobby Riggs, Magic Johnson). Being (or becoming) completely comfortable with their subjective interior experience of others, these characters are likewise comfortable in baring themselves: Venus retrograde contributes to social exhibitionism.

Venus retrograde influences appear to support the enjoyment of social freedom to an uncommon degree. In introspective development, this predilection for freedom can translate into the ability to go many years at a stretch without forming close partnerships. At the same time, introspective development of this influence contributes to a complete and refreshing absence of social pretense.

The influences of Venus retrograde do not appear to differ in any obvious way from those of Venus direct in terms of promoting expression in the arts, except insofar as the social dimensions of *being* an artist/musician/writer are concerned. Ironically, these influences seem to contribute at least as much to the making of stars of sports as to stars of the arts. (Hank Aaron, Muhammad Ali, Bob Mathias, Jean Claude Killy, Sonja Henie, Mark Spitz, Magic Johnson, Bill Russell, Althea Gibson, Bo Jackson, Deion Sanders.) Again, the social—and psychological—dimensions of *being* a sports star are highlighted. In another irony, while these influences support high levels of vanity, they also promote artistic sensitivity to the vanities of existence (Pearl Buck, Satyajit Ray, Charlie Chaplin, Charles Schulz).

MARS RETROGRADE

Mars symbolizes the motivation to survive, and one of the more common experiences catalyzed by Mars retrograde involves difficulty in either asserting or defending oneself— surviving—in childhood. People born with Mars retrograde tend to attract experiences in which they feel inadequate to assert themselves with regard to abusive parents sexually, physically or psychologically, or against others who either threaten harm or somehow intimidate. Such experiences become deeply internalized, spawning long-term issues about physical and/or emotional strength, and about confidence in asserting self altogether. Well into adulthood, deep-seated experiences pertaining to survival— emotional, economic, social and physical survival—are strong motivating factors, and issues about such are liable to surface at any time.

Challenged to survive and/or prove themselves in childhood, people born with Mars retrograde classically engage in long-term efforts through which they strive to feel strong within themselves. In making such efforts, it is usually necessary to confront underlying fears and avoidance behaviors that may have been present for years. The drive to achieve strength and mastery is often accompanied by development of profound underdog/oppressed sensibilities. Some individuals born with this influence engage in dramatic, turbulent struggles to free themselves—or others—from violence and oppression. (Eliot Ness, Dr. Martin Luther King, Jesse Jackson, Camille Claudel, Jung Chang*). Sometimes the subconscious drive to "get even" spawns the compulsion to irrational actions and exaggerated shows of self-assertion, toughness, strength and power (Lizzy Borden, Al Capone, Saddam Hussein,** Howard Stern). More often, though, this sort of subconscious drive focuses on socially sanctioned achievement.

Mars retrograde influences contribute to exceptional efforts to fulfill some form of the "Mars archetype"—to become warriors physically, emotionally, socially and/or spiritually. These influences promote processes by which a number of different Martian potentials are deepened and intensified. From such Martian depths, some are compelled to fight for moral and politically charged causes (Leon Trotsky, Benjamin Disraeli, Susan B. Anthony, Elizabeth Cady Stanton, Franklin D. Roosevelt, M.L. King, J. Jackson, Bernard Sanders—Socialist Congressman of Vermont—Boris Yeltsin, Melvin Belli, Phyllis Schlaffly, Eleanor Smeal, Linus Pauling, Pope John Paul II). From similar depths, these influences support the development of intense

---

* Jung Chang's *Wild Swans* is an incredibly compelling and beautiful account of three generations of a family's struggle through China's Cultural Revolution.

**Lizzy Borden and Saddam Hussein are two of only five famous people that I am aware of who were born with both Venus and Mars retrograde. The other three are Annie Besant, Bobby Riggs and Jack Nicholson; Nicholson was born six days before Saddam Hussein in 1937. Just as Nicholson wouldn't be a bad choice to play Hussein, Adolph Hitler (born April 20, 1889) was parodied exquisitely by Charlie Chaplin (born April 16, 1889) in the 1940 film, *The Great Dictator*. Both Hitler and Chaplin were born with Venus retrograde.

competitive drive and outstanding achievement in sport (Michael Jordan, Charles Barkley, Wayne Gretzky, Eddy Arcaro, Susan Butcher—winner of Iditarod marathon dog-sled races, Billy Jean King, Pete Sampras, Steffi Graf, Tiger Woods, Lenny Dykstra—"Nails").

The subjective and subconscious dimensions of Mars retrograde influences generate emotional wells, or whirlpools, that draw the native into deep involvement with whatever Mars-related issues happen to be attracted. These issues include sex and sexuality (Freud, William Masters, Truman Capote, Harvey Fierstein); and psychology (Freud, Benjamin Spock, Thomas Szasz, Arthur Janov).

Mars retrograde influences enhance the development of great power and soul in music (Wolfgang Mozart, Ludwig Von Beethoven, Irving Berlin, Andrew Lloyd Webber, Joan Sutherland, Mahalia Jackson, Anita Pointer, Pearl Bailey, Naomi Judd, Otis Redding, Paul Simon, Joni Mitchell, James Taylor, Eugene Fodor, Jascha Heifetz); as well as dance (Chita Rivera, Alvin Ailey, Mikhail Baryshnikov). Akin to Venus retrograde, these influences contribute to colorful and robust strains of expression in personality (Casey Stengel, James Dean, Judy Garland, Carroll O'Connor, Diane Keaton, James Earl Jones, Clark Gable, Jack Nicholson, Dolly Parton, Jay Leno, Howard Cossell).

Note: Illustrations of the influences of the following retrograde planets involve only individuals born with the planet in opposition (180°), in trine (120°), or in quincunx (150°) aspect to the sun.* Because of the relation of the orbits of the outer planets to Earth's orbit, these planets are always in retrograde motion whenever the sun makes trine, opposition, or quincunx aspects to them. (In the one exception to this rule, there are a few days each year when Jupiter, in forming trine aspects to the sun, is not technically retrograde.) By choosing individuals born with retrograde planets in these aspects, the pool of possible choices is markedly diminished, and so makes the individual illustrations more significant. As well, connection to the sun's influence by

---

* Aspects are generally considered to apply here when within 10° of exactitude for oppositions, within 7° for trines, and within 3° for quincunxes. Usage of these orbs is relatively standard for aspects involving the sun and moon.

virtue of these aspects implies that the retrograde influences in question are expressed more strongly and vividly than normal.

JUPITER RETROGRADE

Jupiter symbolizes potentials for experiencing "higher power" as expressed in the one hand in adventure, on another hand in the worldly reach of career roles, and on a third hand in the context of metaphysics, religion and philosophy. The influences of Jupiter retrograde serve to generate deeper psychological dimensions of all three kinds of experience.

When direct at birth, Jupiter influences foster a relatively straightforward quest to expand and increase power in society through career, symbolic achievement and socioeconomic gain. As with Jupiter direct, the influences of retrograde Jupiter can contribute to highly successful careers in Jupiterian fields of law, medicine, politics and big business. Similarly, Jupiter retrograde influences support the motivation to contribute to society in all manner of societal roles. But more so than with Jupiter direct, the influences of Jupiter retrograde serve to attract complicated issues in the experience of the *meaning* of social and career roles. Jupiter retrograde promotes the development of conflicts about one's role and path in life with respect to the larger society, to personal fulfillment, and to the larger purpose of one's chosen career or life path.

In introspective development, individuals with Jupiter retrograde are frequently drawn into internal dialogue about the deeper meaning of career choices, gaining large amounts of money and social status. Confusion or irrational attitudes about the wise use of money may arise. Even while they may be carried along for years in high-powered careers and/or by financial vehicles, those born with Jupiter retrograde may harbor deep questions centering on their careers, wealth and the wielding of power.

Inner dialogue may revolve around questions of personal advancement versus the higher good—or else personal advancement versus *personal* good—what's good for me. In that the introspective mode of development centers on the process of coming to feel wholly comfortable with the inner self, Jupiter retrograde suggests the need to achieve subjective peace of mind regarding one's activities in the larger world.

In development combining varying quotients of the power-projection and creative modes, those born with retrograde Jupiter are capable of developing powerful—though often controversial—visions of personal, political, philosophical, ethical or religious truth (Karl Marx, Jean-Jacques Rousseau, Madame Blavatsky, Eleanor Smeal, Betty Friedan, Billy Graham, Frances Moore Lappé). One pattern of development features a tendency to come into direct conflict with powers that be (Fidel Castro, Robespierre, Simon Wiesenthal, Wilhelm Reich, Ayatollah Khomeni, Baghwan Shree Rajneesh, David Duke, Dian Fossey, Jane Goodall). For those given to introspection, identification with a particular philosophy, religion or system of understanding is rarely a simple matter. Issues typically arise concerning the relative degrees of truth and/or social benefit inhering in whatever larger systems or higher powers they are involved with. Until or unless one comes to peace with a sense of one's role in the larger scheme of things, these influences contribute to "having an argument with God."

Because the Jupiterian motivation is so much a function of powers expressed on the worldly stage, the complicating influences of Jupiter retrograde increase the likelihood of reaching a "crisis in midstream," wherein the individual undergoes dramatic changes with regard to career and the wielding of power in full public view (Alfred Nobel, Mikhail Gorbachev, John Dean, George Bush, O.J. Simpson).

The influences of Jupiter retrograde support creative expression in philosophy, poetry, social commentary and metaphysics (John Keats, William Wordsworth, Walt Whitman, John Lennon, Paul Winter). They encourage the generation of colorful individual philosophies (Ben Franklin, Yogi Berra, Bill Cosby, Alvin Toffler, Caroline Myss—New Age savant, Robert Pirsig—*Zen and the Art Of Motorcycle Maintenance*). They facilitate the search for original and powerful ways to participate in the larger social world (Thor Heyerdahl, Evel Knievel, Alfred A. Knopf, Aristotle Onassis, Lily Tomlin, Bill Cosby, Roseanne Barr, Lavar Burton, David Helfgott).

SATURN RETROGRADE

Central to Saturn's symbolism is the theme of the father, and it is useful to look at Saturn retrograde in connection with themes

pertaining to "the father principle" in psychological development. The influences of Saturn retrograde appear to particularly
affect and complicate the process of internalizing attitudes classically identified with the father.

It is well recognized that, in the course of growing up, we
internalize attitudes of responsibility and discipline, a sense of
conscience, and other "should"-related values in the development of what Freud called the superego. Clearly the role of the
father and kindred authority figures is central to this process of
internalization, and conflict here is a universal possibility.
Whether conflict arises or not, however, the influences of Saturn
retrograde work to make this process relatively less open to
conscious, rational assessment. These influences contribute to
deep experiences of the internalized father, the emotional dimensions of which must be dealt with on their own terms.

To the extent that experiences of the father/authority figure—
or lack thereof—are negative, the influences of Saturn retrograde
are prone to impact in terms of accentuated difficulty in experiencing self-love. With Saturn retrograde, the image of the father
as hard, cold, remote, or absent tends to be particularly powerful.
Similarly, those born with Saturn retrograde often have an exceptionally difficult time with self-judgment, as the internalized
father effectively hammers away in the subconscious. Thus full
self-acceptance is a basic goal to be affirmed. Drawing on the
wisdom of the *Desiderata*, an injunction for those with Saturn
retrograde applies well: "Be gentle with yourself, for you are a
child of the universe."

Yet as with other retrograde planets, these influences support
the progressive development of subjective attitudes and values as
distinct from what has been internalized from without. Instead of
judging oneself, therefore, Saturn-retrograde natives are challenged to develop their own subjective authority. Whether or not
parental influences are generally positive, people born with this
influence are called on to generate an intuitive sense of what is
truly important and worthwhile in life, to make judgments based
on internal rather than external standards. As this subjective
sense develops, expectations of self may come to differ markedly
from standards and expectations that prevailed in youth. Likewise, as Saturn-retrograde natives come to accept themselves,
they may develop an exceptional ability to live life in ways that

run counter to accepted norms. They can also become remarkably more able to live life in the moment.

The process of reaching peace and resolution with this influence has profound implications regarding work and profession. Changes in work/career goals as catalyzed by introspective processes may come about at any time in life. Depending on early development, such changes may result in experiencing the need for greater subjective and creative freedom. Yet the opposite consequence may also occur, in which the individual realizes the need for greater discipline, structure, focus on work, and goal-orientedness.

The subjective qualities of Saturn retrograde favor the development of distinctive creative sensibilities in music (Beethoven, Brahms, Paul Winter, Elton John, Neil Young, Madonna). In literature and humor, creative expression is marked by vivid individual—and sometimes twisted—qualities (Hans Christian Anderson, Maurice Sendak, Jerry Lewis, Richard Pryor, John Belushi, Jerry Seinfeld). These influences support the attainment of excellence in physical artistry (Olga Korbutt, Vitaly Shcherbo, Eric Heiden, Dick Button, Paul Taylor, Pele, Boris Becker). They can also be felicitously channeled into activities where self-awareness dissolves into full engagement with the world outside, such as in sailing and hiking.

Saturn signifies the motivation to fulfill societal functions in all forms of professions and jobs; and the same holds for Saturn retrograde. Saturn retrograde, however, encourages the development of subjective attitudes toward fulfilling such functions— and a subjective sense of what society needs in the first place. In this regard, these influences contribute to subjectively inspired work on behalf of disenfranchised constituencies and causes (Victor Hugo, Harriet Beecher Stowe, Farley Mowat, Cesar Chavez, Elizabeth Kubler-Ross, Peter Mathiesson, Curtis Sliwa—founder of Guardian Angels, Robert Hand). Similar to Saturn direct, this influence supports the motivation to work tirelessly for goals perceived as important.

In the absence of introspective development, these influences can easily be projected in unconscious and judgmental ways. They can fuel a sense of being powerfully convinced of one's own rightfulness. People who develop by the power-projection mode evince an exceptional ability to wield power and authority with never a hint of second-guessing oneself (Daniel Ortega, Che Guevera, Nikolai Lenin, Jerry Falwell, Ross Perot, Richard Daley, George Steinbrenner, Jerry Jones, George Weyerhauser). To the extent that normal channels of assuming power are denied, the power-projection mode here supports a self-empowering alienated outlaw mentality (Jesse James, John Wilkes Booth, Che Guevara, Meir Kahane). Even individuals given to more introspective modes of development are prone to streaks of arbitrariness and authoritarianism in their attitudes and actions toward others. Such liabilities make the development of positive goals all the more vital.

URANUS RETROGRADE

Uranus is the only planet that rotates on an east-west axis, and those born with Uranus retrograde are challenged, by suggestion, to look at the world not only backwards but sideways. Of all retrograde influences, the indications for Uranus retrograde are possibly the most felicitous. At least, inasmuch as Uranus (direct) symbolizes propensities for the unusual, the maverick and the eccentric, Uranus retrograde, with all the subjective values it calls into play, tends to deepen and accentuate these tendencies. So as long as the individual is able to enjoy these propensities, and as long as one's environment supports offbeat and unconventional expression, those born with Uranus retrograde may throw conformity to the winds. These influences encourage the development of exceptional eccentricity, oddballicity, wired creativity and general zaniness (W.C. Fields, Sid Caesar, Dick Gregory, Jim Carrey, Danny DeVito, Chevy Chase, Bette Midler, Charlie Chaplin, Buddy Holly, Randy Newman, Steven Spielberg, Jimi Hendrix, David Bowie, Uri Geller, Timothy Leary, Don King, Lawrence Taylor, Muhammad Ali).

Inasmuch as these influences generate the predilection to see the world in unusual ways, the effects of conventional, traditional and socially correct attitudes in the external environment can be strangely challenging. Faced with a sense of their own eccentricity in a "straight" world, people born with Uranus retrograde must deal with urges to subjective expression that run contrary to what they see as established norms. This issue is usually resolved to the extent that these people can find viable, socially acceptable ways of breaking with tradition, expectations, and perceived social norms. Whether in life style, work, ideas, intellectual pursuits or social behavior, a little craziness goes a long way here. Dance and acting are fine outlets for Uranus-retrograde influences. (Sarah Bernhardt, Mickey Rooney, Peter Sellers, Anthony Hopkins, Diane Keaton, Lou Diamond Phillips, Gelsey Kirkland).

Many with Uranus retrograde do well to find a "circuitry," or social network, in which their more offbeat and unconventional potentials will be welcomed and supported. Others may find outlets in individual activities for which they hold a special, highly charged passion. These influences creatively enhance Uranian potentials for invention, innovation and trend-setting.

The influences of Uranus retrograde fuel the development of eccentric opinions, world views and ideologies, and effectively accentuate "normal" Uranian inclinations to utopian, reformist and/or crackpot philosophies (Henry David Thoreau, Karl Marx, Eugene Debs, Annie Besant, J. Krishnamurti, Georges Gurdjieff, Alvin Toffler, Immanuel Velikovsky, Dick Gregory, Russell Means, Lyndon Larouche, Pat Buchanan). These influences can also feed the development of intensely dark, nihilistic visions of life (Marquis de Sade, Hitler, Nietzsche, George Orwell, William Bonney—Billy the Kid, John Dillinger, Joe McCarthy, Lenny Bruce, Jim Morrison). They can contribute to the development of a whole mentality of chaos and discord, an ongoing experience of being at odds with a crazy, haywire world. Hence these natives may need to be careful of getting carried away with ideas of what they think the world is like. They may need to learn to watch and allow the world to unfold as it will. Conversely, Uranus retrograde fosters the growth of subjective zeal for truly enlightened change, reform and liberation (John Scopes, Oskar Schindler, Nelson Mandela, Desmond Tutu). These influences promote a taste for electric excitement and living on the edge (Ernest Hemingway, Antoine de Saint-Exupéry, Neil Armstrong, Al Unser).

NEPTUNE RETROGRADE

The retrograde influences of both Neptune and Pluto seem to suffuse consciousness to such effect that it is difficult to gain the kind of perspective that makes introspection fruitful. Hence introspective development is perhaps more difficult when either of these planets is retrograde. But the values and processes associated with introspection are no less important.

With respect to Neptune retrograde, the capacity for introspection *per se* is preempted by kind of visual/imagic experience of subconscious contents, as if life was an ongoing movie. Neptune retrograde contributes to a vividly perceptual kind of projection, where what is seen in the world and the people around oneself is so fully colored by psychic material from the subconscious that there may be little distinction between internal reality and external reality. Ego boundaries between self and other tend to be nebulous, and perceptions of others are liable to go through wild cycles of inflation and deflation. Individuals may project whole complexes of childhood experience onto others with hardly a clue that they are in effect rerunning their own old movies. Such psychological projection may be unusually resistant to the development of self-awareness.

The influences of Neptune retrograde are liable to impede coming to terms with childhood Neptunian experiences of alcoholism, religious zealotry and/or mental illness. Even when they can consciously articulate the events of childhood, people born with this influence are not well able to achieve perspective either on the people in their lives or on their own feelings.

One way of dealing with this aspect of retrograde Neptune influences is by the—Neptunian—process of *psychic immersion*. By plunging consciousness into whole new forms of psychological experience, subconscious processes may be catalyzed through which spontaneous healing and "psychic cleansing" can occur. Total immersion in a new "psychic field" helps to wash away deeply ingrained psychic patterns, even without much conscious delving into the matters in question. Being "born again" into new modes of perception is certainly not a classic form of introspection, but the desired results of reaching attunement with the inner self can be similar. The phenomenon of psychic immersion is central to such movements as evangelical religion, AA and ACOA. "Immersion healing" can come through new spiritual identifications, living in different cultures and environments, subliminal healing programs, extended psychological workshop experiences, holotropic breathing and dreamwork. In dreamwork, people born with Neptune retrograde may or may not have an easy time consciously appraising the meaning of dreams, but in either case they have an uncanny ability to relive the images of their dreams. As much as they give themselves over to such reliving, the process of going back and forth between the life of the dream and normal consciousness can itself become a powerful form of psychic immersion.

The influences of retrograde Neptune contribute to being strongly, if also subconsciously, affected by the atmosphere of living/working environments, and so it is important for people born with this influence to consciously consider the "vibes" of their day-to-day environments as real factors in making life choices.

These influences serve to generate wonderfully vivid sources of creativity, and apparently favor expression in all creative forms. Musical creativity is especially highlighted (Mozart, Chopin, Elvis Presley, Dave Brubeck, Glenn Miller, Johnny Cash, Elton John, Diana Ross, Aretha Franklin, Nina Simone, Wilson Pickett, Miriam Makeba, Stevie Nicks). The artistic and literary imaginations are likewise enhanced (Eugene Delacroix, Alexander Degas, J.R.R. Tolkein, D.H. Lawrence, Henri de Toulouse-Lautrec, Norman Rockwell, Ansel Adams). Imaginary, fantasy and/or idealized worlds can be visualized freely. In politics, individuals born with Neptune retrograde have a talent for appealing to the popular imagination (Ethan Allen, Ronald Reagan, Charles de Gaulle). They may be given to work selflessly for some social or spiritual ideal (Mahatma Gandhi, Margaret Sanger, Mary Baker Eddy, Paul Ehrlich). These influences contribute to the ability to embody idealized or sublime cultural images (Marlon Brando, Elizabeth Taylor, Vanna White, Hugh Heffner, Elvis Presley). They appear to contribute to the psychic makeup of individuals who somehow come to live between two worlds (Mahatma Gandhi, Jackie Robinson, Mikhail Gorbachev, Jerry Brown, Henry David Thoreau, T.S. Eliott—banker/poet, Carlos Castaneda).

PLUTO RETROGRADE

Pluto retrograde influences provide sources of deep and powerful intuition that tend to be expressed through intense creativity, or else in blind, compulsive ways. As often as not, some blending of these two kinds of expression is evident.

As with Pluto direct, people born with Pluto retrograde emphasized are drawn to experiences of depth self-transformation. As with Pluto direct, similarly, the influences of Pluto retrograde spawn the development of compulsions that must—compulsively—be played out before they can be fully recognized or dealt with. With Pluto retrograde, this latter phenomenon is perhaps even more pronounced. Indeed, one of the most vivid features engendered by this influence is the growth of compulsions that are all but impervious to examination. People born with Pluto retrograde are prone to develop what amount to blind spots about themselves, and these influences paradoxically contribute to the need to repel anything that threatens to reveal the existence of those very places to oneself. As Bil Tierney put it, "The individual unconsciously resists having his inner negativities scrutinized by both his conscious self and others."[87]

Blind spots can take the form of intense and inexplicable attractions, likes, dislikes, identifications with causes, prejudices and antipathies. Pluto-retrograde influences are easily projected onto the outside world and can manifest in compulsive targeting of, or opposition to, others (Joseph Stalin, Francisco Franco, Charles Manson, J. Edgar Hoover, Jimmy Hoffa, Edward Teller, Strom Thurmond, Rush Limbaugh, Anita Bryant, Jesse Helms)—or even in being the unwitting target of such compulsion and fanaticism (Alger Hiss, Anwar al-Sadat, Yitzhak Rabin, Sharon Tate, Selena, Gianni Versace). For some, these influence translate into the experience of *others* (family members, for example) who themselves seem blind or compulsive.

The more intense, negative and/or opaque the blind spot, the more likely that transformation can come about only by dint of dramatic events. Sometimes a powerful "crash" experience will catalyze a terrific depth catharsis. Sometimes the crash is of the non-reversible kind (James Dean, Jim Morrison, Tim Hardin). This influence engenders attraction to powerful experiences that can breed new and more positive—albeit equally intense—identifications, and new, more positive trajectories.

Far from being intrinsically negative, Pluto-retrograde influences can be developed and expressed in a spectrum of positive ways. Although much that is associated with Pluto pertains to the destroyer role of the Hindu god Shiva, just as much pertains to the creator role, and creative/intuitive development of Pluto retrograde influences can generate colorfully individuated—if also *daemonic*—spirits. Creative spirits born with retrograde Pluto emphasized include Georges Gurdjieff, Leo Tolstoy, Franz Joseph Haydn, George Sand, Pablo Picasso, Maria Callas, Gabriel Garcia Marquez, Buster Keaton, Groucho Marx, Tina Turner, Bob Marley, Diana Ross, Buffy St. Marie, Soupy Sales, Walt Disney, Matt Groenig and Mikhail Baryshnikov.

Developed positively, the retrograde influences of Pluto foster tremendously powerful, pioneering identifications *with*—as well as against—special causes and callings (Martin Luther King, Jr., Elijah Muhammad, Winston Churchill, Korean human rights activist Kim Dae Jung, Sadat, Rabin, Dian Fossey, Mary Baker Eddy, Albert Schweitzer, Gordon Cooper, Yuri Gagarin). People born with this influence are often happiest when they can pour themselves single-mindedly into a project or process. As with Pluto direct, this influence affords intense concentration, and so it can among other things contribute to exceptional achievement in sports (Jack Nicklaus, Muhammad Ali, Gene Fullmer, Jackie Joyner-Kersey, Wayne Gretzky, Joe DiMaggio).

Chapter 17

Planets R Us

> In its most profound and authentic expression, the intellectual imagination does not merely project its ideas into nature from its isolated brain corner. Rather, from within its own depths the imagination directly contacts the creative process from within nature, realizes that process within itself, and brings nature's reality to conscious expression.
>
> — Richard Tarnas, *The Passion of the Western Mind*

Sonja, a friend and client, related an anecdote that lit me up. A friend of hers, who is skeptical of astrology, had asked her, "Do you really think the planets affect your life?" Summing up the whole of psychological astrology as neatly as could be, Sonja replied, "I *am* the planets!"

From the anonymous Stoic of the 3rd Century BC who wrote that the planets are "in us," the subject matter of astrology has made for some interesting relationships between objective and subjective viewpoints. The influences of the planets, paradoxically, are studied as objectifiable influences that derive from the external environment, but are seen to inform subjective dimensions of individual nature. Equally, the subjective "I" who studies these influences inevitably becomes the object of study. I am the planets.

Implicit throughout natal astrology is the idea that subjective reality is a function of internal influences that can be understood as much from subjective* as from objective perspectives. Hence

---

* The concept of subjectivity is used in a somewhat different sense here than in Chapter 16. Yet the implication in both cases is that while subjectivity *can* devolve into solipsistic, self-serving and hopelessly involuted forms, it

while astrology as a matter of discourse in the public domain is dominated by issues of science and objectification, students of the subject are well satisfied to mix and match objective and subjective approaches to astrological knowledge. Like scientists, they observe. They hypothesize. They correlate. They analyze. They collate. But they also perceive; they philosophize; they symbolize; they interpret; they feel; they imagine; they intuit.

Now I want to add another approach, based on what happened to me one bright frigid January day in 1975. I was walking down a dirt road in southern Vermont having an extraordinarily charged dialogue with myself on personal matters. Then, as if out of the blue it struck me as clear as the cold: *My consciousness is tuned to Uranus—in myself.* I was not being affected by Uranus. I was not being controlled by Uranus. Rather, I had in some sense accessed the Uranus (in Cancer) *channel* within myself. The thought I was thinking and the experience I was experiencing was occurring as a function of being tuned into this internal wavelength. My consciousness was tuned to the Uranian part of my unconscious. (How appropriate that the focus of my epiphany was the Light-bulb planet, the Awakener.)

Since that moment, I have become both a monitor and an orchestrator of my planetary consciousness. Many times a day, I spontaneously "take a reading" of the *modus operandi* of my present consciousness. I might think very quietly to myself: That's Venus, or that's the sun-in-Leo, or something of the like. Beyond simply identifying the planetary channel I'm tuned into, I might want to change it. Finding myself in a wistful lunar place when I need to be getting down to work, I might will myself into my Pluto-in-Leo place, which I now sometimes call on for the deep concentration it affords me. Or, I might, somewhat reluctantly, call up Saturn.

Over the years, I have found it more difficult to access some channels than others on a consistent basis. In effect, I haven't known *how* to experience them in order to to call them into my conscious process, or to sustain them there. For example, I was born with Jupiter retrograde, and the "Jupiter channel" has been

applies more generally to the necessary, vital and real colorations of the internal dimensions of individual nature.

about the most difficult for me to consciously access. Apparently because Jupiter was retrograde at my birth, I have been unable to integrate this channel into my conscious thought processes as I have most of the others. But over the years I have learned to tune into my inner Jupiter according to its own requirements. Central to these requirements is that I change my usual mode of experiencing consciousness. With Jupiter, I have learned to intuit a kind of subliminal thought process.

Doing without a given planetary channel completely has not done me well. For example, I did not find the Venus channel in myself until a couple of years after my Uranian epiphany, and being "out of touch with Venus" was not very nice. Before finding Venus, I was rather an antisocial creature. The process of tuning into my inner Venus coincided with the beginning of a long period of adult socialization.

This socialization was in turn part of a larger healing process. Through that healing process I came to deal with my inner moon a lot, after suppressing the hurt, grief and fear that came with that channel for many years. As I healed, I became more able to access my lunar channel without getting a lot of emotional static. When I experience my inner moon now, I'm able to open up to my Gemini powers far more than previously. (I was born with the moon in Gemini.) In healing my moon-in-Gemini channel, I've become a lot more lighthearted, talkative, and prone to zany interchanges.

It was only about 1992 that I finally tuned into Pluto clearly. This was a dramatic event for me. Born with the sun conjunct Pluto (a relatively loose conjunction—the two orbs were eight degrees apart from one another at my birth), Pluto is a key player in my psyche. Gaining conscious access to my inner Pluto coincided with of a key transit of Pluto. Between 1992 and 1994, that is, Pluto "squared my natal sun"—its position in the zodiac in relation to the Earth swung back and forth across the point forming an exact 90° angle to the zodiacal degree in which the sun was positioned at my birth. While I had intellectually anticipated this long-term influence, it was not until the end of 1995 that I fully realized the magnitude of the changes that were catalyzed.

Coinciding with this transiting Pluto influence, I felt increasingly compelled to tap into my internal Pluto. As I did so, I progressively found that I could contain my Pluto channel in consciousness, and actually tune it to deeply creative purposes. These purposes focused mainly on this book: In my Pluto place I found myself intent on penetrating to the core of issues that had nagged me for years. Contacting my inner Pluto also carried over into my work as astrologer, sometimes to beneficial effect, sometimes not. With Pluto in my natal 8th house, I found myself intent on penetrating to the core depths of clients, who in some cases were not asking to have their core depths penetrated. But the broader effect was that I went through a great catharsis, and on the far side of that Pluto transit I find myself being able to tap into my internal Pluto at will. Mercifully, I can usually also leave it be.

Hence while it is common in the field to hear comments to the effect that Pluto is so deep that it can't be known directly, I say "Bosh." It is just a particularly challenging one to know, and to integrate.

Back to network consciousness. At any given time, I seem to have a planetary repertoire of five or six channels that I look to tune into, and that come to me easily, while others are temporarily out of the picture. If I have forgotten about a given planetary channel for a long time, it might take considerable effort to tune it in again.

While I typically experience my planetary channels as discrete from one another, I sometimes tune into combinations of them at once. These combinations are a function of the planets' angular connections with one another at my birth. For instance I was born With Mars (in Cancer in its own 8th house) squaring Neptune, opposing Jupiter, in exact 30° aspect to Pluto, and squaring the axis of the moon's nodes. Depending on circumstances, I might tune into any one of these complex "aspect frequencies," or channel combinations, involving Mars. Whichever combination I tune into produces dramatically different qualities of thought and experience. When, for example, I tune into my Mars-Pluto dual frequency, I might feel strong and fearless, but also crazy. At such times, I can pretty well forget about the softer range of Cancerian wavelengths.

A last note: The urge to monitor my planetary tuning is, I'm sure, a function of Mercury in Virgo in the 9th house: one channel monitoring the others.

As my children used to say, "You're weird, sir." But weird or not, it is all very real to me. As far as I am concerned, I have come to know from the inside out, in the most existential sense possible, the influences symbolized in my natal chart. What wisdom have I gained from this? Internal channel surfing is usually a lot more fun than TV channel-surfing. Keep trying to tune in the channels that are currently difficult to receive, and get to the bottom of what's causing the interference. If the way a certain channel is coming in is not working out, it's possible to change the "attitude of reception" so as to get a different quality of experience. It's a good idea to switch channels before beating any one channel to death. Combinations of different channels bring different kinds of programs. Try different programs, and stay tuned to all the major channels. Be a whole person.

Weird or not, further, I feel confident that all of you out there in radioland tune in to your own inner planets, without realizing it of course. But let us articulate this proposition from a more neutral starting point.

If natal astrological influences are real, these influences could hardly exist *without* exerting effects in, and on, consciousness. It is certainly common for astrologers to consider interactions between natal influences and consciousness. Good Jungian astrologers do so as a matter of course. But like Jungian psychologists, Jungian astrologers address consciousness in terms of becoming aware of whole archetypal patterns—symbolic patterns. As elsewhere in astrology, consciousness of astrological influences is assumed to be mediated by symbols.

But is such mediation really necessary?

What if, as noted in the last chapter, the influences of planets in direct motion at birth *emerge directly into consciousness?* Might not these influences interplay directly in, and with, consciousness? Are symbols absolutely essential to these processes of interplay? Between the lines, many astrologers imply direct links between astrological influences and consciousness. The literature of interpretation is filled with idioms suggesting such processes of interplay. For instance Debbi Kempton-Smith, in describing people born with the moon in Aquarius, writes, "These folks don't have blood in their veins; it's Xerox copy fluid."[88] The suggestion here is that moon-in-Aquarius influences work something like electricity in the veins, with the implication that the electrical phenomenon works its way directly into thought processes—consciousness—and likewise into cognitive aspects of feeling processes.

In addressing this issue, astrologers tend to assume that astrological influences feed into consciousness, and "color" consciousness; yet they say little or nothing about our capacity to be aware of this kind of process in the moment. If astrological influences do affect consciousness, however, it would seem that we must be able to be aware of these diverse internal influences in the moment.

To consider these influences in such ways generates the idea of astrology as the most existential of all possible studies. To the extent that we can be aware of our own natal influences (or channels, as I have called them), and to the extent that we can effectively "play with," or modulate these influences in consciousness, it seems possible to cultivate astrology as a *discipline of consciousness,* a kind of astrological Zen, in which "mere" awareness of internal experience is transformed into something of a contact sport of the psyche. This "sport" calls into play a new level of conscious participation in the moment-to-moment process of being and becoming.

To explore this idea from another perspective, let us consider a pair of astrological quasi-twins: two people born on the same day of the same year, and so born with essentially the same configuration of astrological influences. Assuming times of birth are different, the planets' declination in the skies, and so their placements by house, would be different, as would the entire set of relations between the signs and the houses. The overall planetary pattern would however remain the same, as would the planets' placements by sign.

The individuals in question were both born May 6, 1856. The first is Sigmund Freud.

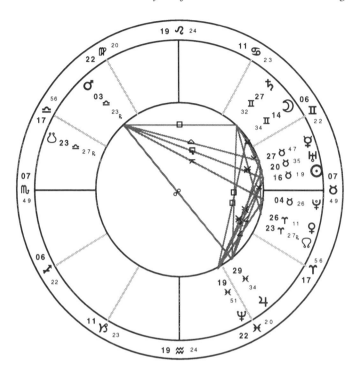

FIGURE 6
SIGMUND FREUD
MAY 6, 1856. 5:23 PM GMT VIENNA, AUSTRIA[89]

Even the briefest glance at Freud's birth chart (Figure 6) reveals a pattern in which almost all the spheres of the solar system are clustered together, and apart from a single other planet. This planet—Mars—was the only planet in rising motion at Freud's birth, while all the rest of the planets were descending.

Just as Mars stands out from the rest of the planets, so is the motivation represented by Mars indicated to stand out in the nature of the individual Sigmund. With reference to Principle 8 in Chapter 9, Mars indicates among other things motivations for desire, sex, sexual pleasure, self-preservation, aggression and death—in short every major potential Freud the theorist held so dear. These indications are augmented by the fact that Freud's "rising sign"—the zodiac sign rising in the East at his birth—is Scorpio, Mars' own "natural" sign.[*]

Now, notice the little ℞ sign below the symbol of Mars on Sigmund's chart, indicating that Mars was in retrograde motion at his birth.[**] Recalling the last chapter on retrograde planets, Mars retrograde at birth holds implications for development in the matter of *subconscious* influences centering on, among other things, sex and sexuality.

In that Freud based his theory of sexuality on the idea of "unconscious conflict," wherein the sexual/aggressive instincts are presumed to be repressed from consciousness, and so to develop in a subconscious realm, it is arguable that in his psychological theory, Freud did nothing so much as *project* the particular complex of his *own* psychic constitution onto the collective experience of Victorian Europe. With respect to retrograde Mars influences in particular, we could develop a case for the idea that both Freud the man and Freud the theorist can be well explained in terms of Mars retrograde dynamics; that indeed Freud's Oedipal theory is a direct function of Mars retrograde dynamics in Freud himself. (This is of course astrological deconstructionism.)

In looking at Freud's world through the lens of Mars, we could point to the particularly *driven* manner with which Freud sought to push his theory onto the world stage, and to *force* his colleagues to unquestioningly accept it. On this note, let us consider the second individual born May 6 of 1856: Admiral Robert Peary, the famous Arctic explorer. As the planetary configura-

---

[*] Along with the sun sign and moon sign, the rising sign is considered to be one of the strongest influences expressed in personality. Yet without the "Mars factor," Scorpio rising could not in and of itself be invoked to explain the singular prominence of the Scorpio-Mars principle as expressed in Freud's theories.

[**] Mars was at the end of its roughly 80-day period of retrogradation at Freud's birth; it completed its retrograde phase and turned direct three days later. (Coincidentally, Carl Jung was born just two days after Mars turned direct.) Pertaining to the standard astrological technique of prediction called "progressions," *the first six years of Freud's life* are highlighted. By the age of six, the influences of Mars retrograde are indicated here to have changed towards a more normal ("direct") mode in which the Martian influences are directly accessible to consciousness. In this regard it is interesting to note how crucial the first six years of life are in Freud's developmental theory.

tion was essentially the same for both individuals, we can again focus on the prominence of retrograde Mars. As did Freud, Peary evinced a classically Martian obsession; not the drive of sex here, but instead the drive of survival and self-preservation. With regard to Mars retrograde at birth, it is not difficult to infer the existence in Peary of a subconscious motivation spawning the irrational "compulsion to exaggerated shows of physical strength, toughness ... [and] achievement."

The explication of Mars retrograde in Chapter 16 begins to provide a lens through which to see not only behavioral manifestations but psychological dynamics pertaining to both these men. With regard to retrograde modes of development, it seems clear that introspection was a major part of Freud's development, while the "power and projection" mode is very much visible in the life of Peary. Whether or not Peary engaged in any real introspective questioning, he was obviously not deterred from projecting himself rather blindly into the expedition that cost the lives of many men.

Born on the same day of all time, Freud and Peary were on the surface very different men. Yet through the single lens of Mars retrograde, it is possible to see a particular dimension of motivation through which each developed into the strangely driven kind of men they both became.

Awareness of these internal dimensions could be most meaningful to living people. For every Peary who might feel too driven to listen to some puny psychological astrologer on the subject of subconscious motivations and internal compulsions, there might be a new Freud for whom *coming to existential awareness* of the Mars retrograde—or any other—influence could be key to feeling or sensing those influences as they emerge into consciousness, and so to *reckon* with those influences in existential consciousness. With the knowledge that such influences can be turned and developed to different possibilities of experience, and the knowledge that we can be active participants in this ongoing development, we can all perhaps turn ourselves toward becoming more wholly conscious actors on life's stage.

Astrology objectifies the subjective nature of every individual, and so allows us to see the forces that conspire in the interior subjective world of others. By the same token it allows us to see in the external world the forces of our own subjective natures. Almost miraculously, then, it allows us to see the subjective and objective worlds as interfaces of each other.

"The Age of Science," said Franklin Le Van Baumer, "made the intoxicating discovery that melioration depends not upon 'change from within' but upon 'change from without' (scientific and social mechanics)."[90] In psychological astrology, however, we come full circle. We find that when we go far enough out— out into the solar system—we return to what is within. We find that what is without comes together with what is within—like God touching Adam, like the stars writing software—at the moment of birth, just as the child emerges from the inside out. We find that coming to awareness of what is within is crucial to both the process and promise of change without.

APPENDICES

MOON SIGNS, EMOTIONAL PREDISPOSITIONS AND PATTERNS OF CHILDHOOD EXPERIENCE

It is commonly recognized in natal astrology that the influences of moon signs play major roles in personality. Not so well recognized, though, are other psychological dimensions of these influences. Inasmuch as the "inner moon" serves to interpret emotional experience (cf. Chapter 11), the instinctive influences indicated by moon signs are powerful underlying factors in how individuals respond to, and in many ways create, the formative experiences of childhood. Beyond factors of birth order and gender, different children are inclined to experience essentially the same childhood environment in different ways, and moon signs are major influences regarding such individual differences.

Moon signs indicate predispositions to interpret conditions and circumstances of the childhood environment, including the "circumstances" of one's parents. These influences likewise serve to attract developmental issues, the resolution of which are key to growth into emotionally healthy adults. Moon signs indicate predilections to develop *patterns of emotional experience* which may be in part dysfunctional. These patterns contain inherent hurdles to growth and development, and to the extent that they are not resolved in childhood, they may be replayed and re-encountered well into adulthood. In the replaying of such patterns, marital partners and other intimates tend to be experienced in many of the same ways as parents and other key figures were experienced in childhood.

The following interpretations are oriented to developmental issues and challenges, and are not intended to apply universally. Although these interpretations are oriented to common dysfunctions in emotional development, they do not assume such dysfunctions to be necessary or inevitable.

Among other kinds of factors, aspects to the moon are bound to affect considerably the patterns interpreted here.

Healthy emotional development promotes expression of virtually all vital powers indicated by the natal moon sign. Developed positively, moon-sign influences contribute to the development of emotionally colored powers of behavior.

The moon's placement in the house of the same number as the sign in question tends to engender similar inclinations, and so house placement influences are put in parentheses.

ARIES (1st House) In a common pattern of development, people born with the moon in Aries experience a parent as oblivious, self-absorbed and obsessed, or else as self-directed and independent. Reflecting such behavior in a parent, these individuals can themselves become emotionally self-absorbed, inaccessible and oblivious to the emotional needs of others. Many born with this moon sign are inclined to develop emotional independence from early on, and tend to hold a low tolerance as adults for staying with a partner.

Yet others—mostly males—born with the moon in Aries are prone to become singularly focused on their (female) partners, even while displaying an air of independence to the world. Repeating an ironically related childhood pattern, they become emotionally absorbed in another much as they did in a self-absorbed parent. To the extent that they are unable to experience the "domestic self" except in terms of absorption in their partners, these individuals are challenged to become more emotionally independent. This moon sign indicates the challenge to express one's feelings even when it may appear to that to do so would be gratuitous—as if feelings were besides the point. But here feelings are the point.

The fiery and independent nature of the Aries moon helps to make life a continuing individual, if also often volatile, adventure. Torch-carriers.

Camille Claudel, George Sand, Oskar Schindler, Albert Schweitzer, Malcolm X, Marlon Brando, Lily Tomlin, Jerry Garcia.

TAURUS (2nd House) As with several other placements, this moon sign generates somewhat different patterns of experience according to gender. As with all moon-sign influences, however, these patterns overlap one another.

For both sexes, the mother figure tends to be strong. For females, however, the mother is often experienced as domineering, possessive and controlling. As adults, these individuals are liable to battle mother meddling in their business, even if mother is many miles away. Similarly, turf struggles with partners and other intimates can be a continuing problem. For those who experience such patterns, a major developmental need is to establish one's own territory, both physically and emotionally. Moving physically away from the mother is sometimes necessary for emotional survival. For women especially, a challenge with this moon sign is to grow new emotional roots.

For males, more often the mother tends to be experienced as solid, a rock of strength, and giving as well; they may be seen as earth-mother types. This kind of pattern contributes to developing an all-enduring, all-accepting emotional strength, and an appealingly earthy emotional nature. On the other hand, males born with this moon sign are liable to be dominated by their mothers, without even knowing it. As adults, likewise, they are prone to allow their partners to call the shots. Many individuals must also learn to control their appetites.

In healthy development, this moon sign supports the ability for unending, tireless and uncomplaining work, and engenders a salt-of-the-earth dimension of character.

Ann Landers/Abigail Van Buren (twins), Rollo May, Arthur Janov, Jesse Jackson, Bill Clinton.

GEMINI (3rd House) Development in early life can be plagued by a lack of emotional communication. Parents may appear to be available on certain subjects or in certain circumstances, and yet totally unavailable in others. The mother can be experienced as being somehow one step removed from the reality of life at hand. The most dominant pattern, however, regards *emotional ambivalence*. Whether because of a split between parents resulting in the presence of two mothers, two fathers, or both, or because a given parent is experienced to have two separate identities, this moon placement generates the predilection to go back and forth in one's feelings, to experience opposite kinds of feelings regarding a given issue or person. To the extent that this *alter ego* type of experience dominates, it is difficult to find one's emotional center.

These individuals are challenged to learn emotional communication. Until they do, they tend in effect to communicate their feelings to the air, in random messages that may or may not be caught by others. As adults, they may attract partners who, like themselves, don't communicate well. Conversely, finding a partner who does communicate well can be a big help in learning communication skills. Getting in touch with feelings is the first step here, as is the *act* of articulating both past and present emotional experience. In so doing, people born with the moon in Gemini can begin to integrate their ambivalent feelings by speeding up the pace of switching sides, dialoguing between the two sides, and realizing how both sides are in some sense "right."

As these individuals get in touch with their feelings—or both sets of-feelings as the case may be—they can become exceptionally lively, colorful communicators. Timing, repartee, zaniness and comedy are features of developed Gemini communications.

Ken Kesey, Howard Cossell, Garrison Keillor, Diane Feinstein, Shirley Temple, Roseanne Barr, Jim Carrey.

CANCER (4th House) Females especially tend to experience the mother as emotionally tense and preoccupied. The mother's needs are often experienced before their own. Both sexes tend to be exceptionally sensitive to their mothers' needs, and may wind up responding to them strongly throughout life, even against their better judgment. From such patterns, women born with the moon in Cancer tend to be attracted to men who are preoccupied, typically with work. This pattern leads females to become tense themselves, until they fully separate themselves, emotionally, from their mothers. Males, in contrast, often experience more unconditional love and giving from their mothers, and can grow to become softies. Yet inasmuch as they are predisposed to respond to their mothers needs, both sexes may find it difficult to voice their own emotional needs as adults.

On the other hand, people born with the moon in Cancer may (like their mothers) grow to become preoccupied with their own needs. In any course of development, however, these individuals are challenged to learn to live with their intense feelings, share them with others when appropriate, and develop relationships of unconditional love. As they do so, they can become exceptionally giving and sensitive individuals. This placement contributes more directly to the unfolding of pure maternal/parental capacities than does the sun in Cancer. They can be very sweet people; also artistically impressionable.

Dr. Benjamin Spock, Elizabeth Kubler-Ross, Liza Minelli, Janis Joplin, Paul Simon, Willie Nelson, Norman Mailer.

LEO (5th House) Akin to the sun in Leo, the Leo moon supports the inclination to act out the need for self-expression. This inclination can be naturally expressed in drama and other forms of "getting on stage" such as teaching, and moon-in-Leo individuals can show real talent in these directions. As this moon sign engenders the classic Leo predilection to become the center of attention, some of these natives are prone to become shameless, unrepentant hams. Self-centeredness is likewise a liability.

Yet while some born with this placement are inherently brassy and showy, others (especially females) are predisposed to seek warmth and attention from others with an almost childlike innocence. For these individuals, getting warm attention from partners in adulthood can be as vital as was the warm attention of parents (especially fathers) in childhood. With the moon in the sun's sign, a central challenge is to break through to a tender, if also sometimes self-dramatizing, heartlove, and by the same token to develop a deep sense of self-love. Often this comes about through affirming love for parents and significant others even after the romance—or childhood—passes. People born with this influence are well capable of developing into uncommonly genuine, sincere and creative adults.

In healthy expression, the Leo moon contributes to warm and spontaneous self-expression, a softer version of the sun-in-Leo influence. It promotes a gift for creative handling of children, and creative gifts in general.

Mahatma Gandhi, Evel Knievel, Tommy Lasorda, Larry Flynt, Clint Eastwood, Jane Fonda, Gloria Steinem.

VIRGO (6th House) The Virgo moon often appears to correspond to childhood experiences of parents or other figures who are old, weak, sick or infirm. A father who is old, sick or weak seems unusually common; mental illness can also be a factor in either parent. As adults, these individuals tend to attract people with infirmities.

The father may be weak in an emotional rather than physical sense, no matter what his position in the outside world may be. He may be experienced as either waiving emotional responsibility, and/or as deferring to the mother. But while the mother often wears the emotional pants in the family, she may be unequipped to play the roles of both father and mother. The upshot of such patterns is that the experience of "chain of command" and other common role expectations in the childhood environment are confusing. These individuals seem often to be expected to keep to themselves, and consequently come to feel that what they do, say or feel doesn't really matter to others. Emanating from such experiences, moon-in-Virgo individuals are prone to feel insecure about their ability to effect needed changes on the domestic/ intimate level. They are liable to communicate inappropriately, as if what they say doesn't matter much anyway.

Hence people born with the moon in Virgo need to learn how what they say and do *does* affect others; that what they feel matters to everyone—beginning with themselves. Once they acknowledge and respect their own feelings, much can be said and done that is needed to be said and done. They have an ability to see things for what they are, and cultivating this ability is vital in dealing with the realities of both childhood and adulthood. To the extent that this ability is not developed, there is a liability to criticize others before one has set one's own house in order. These individuals are challenged to let their actions match their words: If you've got criticisms, you may speak them—but be sure to match them with appropriate and helpful actions. This moon sign also indicates the challenge to discretion in emotional communication, as again there is the predilection to communicate emotions inappropriately.

With healthy development, people born with this influence are capable of tireless application to task, unremittingly helpful attitudes, and developing sophisticated techniques.

John Irving, William Faulkner, William Masters, Deepak Chopra, Dustin Hoffman, Claus Von Bulow.

LIBRA (7th House) This moon sign engenders a predisposition to respond subliminally to communication between parents. Children with this placement tend to internalize dysfunctional communication patterns between parents, and as adults may attract partners with whom they find it difficult to establish good patterns of communication. Hence developing open lines of communication in partnerships is a big challenge.

In the see-saw tradition of this sign, moon-in-Libra influences encourage taking off on emotional trajectories in responding to others, meeting the other person in the middle, as it were, only in passing or going the other way. They are prone to go either too light or too heavy in matching their reactions to the situation. Women are somewhat liable to develop the habit of talking endlessly about their feelings and experiences to others who may appear to be willing to listen, while men are more liable to be oddly recalcitrant. Both sexes are prone to developing a "peace at any price" mentality, while in the process creating a subtle emotional distance. With respect to all these tendencies, this moon sign suggest the challenge to learn to truly listen to the feelings of others, and to *negotiate differences.*

With healthy development, this placement engenders an appealing lilt to the manner of individual expression. Talents in the arts and public sector communications are highlighted.

Humphrey Bogart, Anwar al-Sadat, Richard Chamberlain, Judy Collins, Bruce Springsteen, Tina Turner.

SCORPIO (8th House) The moon in Scorpio indicates predispositions tinged by Freudian themes. With respect to sexual instincts, this moon sign suggests the inclination to engage deeply with the opposite-sex parent.

Males seem disproportionately to grow up with divorced or single mothers. By this and related circumstances, they are inclined to become the "little man" of the house, expected to take on a manly mantle at an early age. As part of emphasized Oedipal dynamics, there is often extra pressure to survive and/or succeed both economically and socially. Toward resolution of Oedipal issues, a real dose of post-adolescent rebellion can be healthy. These individuals are challenged to assert themselves emotionally in order to free themselves from their mothers'— and later their partners'—expectations. For those who eschew the adolescent phase, there tends to be an inordinately swift transition into the activities and persuasions of adulthood.

In both sexes, there is a predilection to ego battles with the same-sex parent, when this parent is present in childhood. This parent may be experienced as strong but ungiving, and/or as emotionally absent.

As with the Oedipal Complex, elements of the Electra Complex are highlighted in females. Whether the father is weak, absent, and abusive—or sweet and good—females tend to become deeply involved with their fathers. Both sexes tend to develop issues centering on emotional self-assertion: balancing the need to assert self with the need for emotional connection. The Scorpio moon generates an internal tension between the need for achieving economic power and emotional assertiveness on the one hand, and the desire to fully engage and share life on the other. This sort of issue usually plays out on the axis of dominance versus submissiveness: self-expectations are either to be either emotionally strong or yielding. The challenge here seems to be one of becoming both strong and yielding, assertive when need be yet also open.

In healthy development, these individuals are able to engage in exceptionally full and deep exchanges with others, and may grow to become unusually capable individuals. This moon sign suggests the inclination to experience a depth of sexual feeling.

George Steinbrenner, Francis Ford Coppola, Phil Donahue, Xaviera Hollander (the Happy Hooker), Warren Beatty, Lenny Dykstra.

SAGITTARIUS (9th House) The Sagittarius moon indicates a predisposition to attract experiences that are difficult to comprehend emotionally. People born with this moon sign are inclined to experience circumstances surrounding the death of or separation from a parent, unusual treatment by a parent, or far-flung conditions relating to parents, as difficult to comprehend and therefore difficult to integrate emotionally. Consequently, these individuals may attract partners who themselves seem emotionally incomprehensible. As they concentrate on learning to understand their partners' frame of reference or world view, they can grow to relate to such partners more fully. Until they do they may have difficulty responding to partners' feelings.

This influence appears to correlate with experiences of parents who are from markedly different backgrounds, or experiences of childhood environments where cultural, ethnic, racial and/or religious differences come vividly into play. These individuals are predisposed to internalize meetings between sharply contrasting worlds, and likewise to internalize childhood experiences relating to larger social issues. Formative experiences may intersect with larger cultural issues including drugs, alcoholism, medicine, mental health and metaphysics as well as the ethos of foreign cultures.

Similarly, the moon in Sagittarius promotes the tendency to bring life experiences into focus—or magnify them—by applying the lenses of larger cultural, religious, philosophical or metaphysical powers. Yet there is also the predilection to get carried away with exaggerated notions that do no particular good. Hence a challenge for these individuals is to view their life experiences through lenses that will uplift without distorting. People born with this moon sign often develop an entertaining ability to enlarge and change the proportions of what they see. They are also inclined to inject theatrical and hyperbolic qualities into their reactions.

Lewis Carroll, Stephen King, Ray Bradbury, Carl Sagan, Billy Graham, Thomas Jefferson, Ted Turner.

CAPRICORN (10th House) In emotional development, this influence generates the predilection to ambivalence toward parents as authority figures. Parental exercise of authority may be experienced as exceptionally solid and well-sanctioned, or else as oppressive, hypocritical and lacking sound emotional basis. Frequently elements of both types of experience are combined. Such experiences tend to focus on the same-sex parent, although the demeanor and the authority of the father are highlighted for females as well as males. The professional status of the father and his position in the world (even if parents are separated) often comes into play in creating lasting expectations. Similarly, there tends to be heightened response to the father's acceptance—or abrogation—of his paternal responsibilities.

A common predispositions for people born with this moon placement is to cast others into the role of authority figures, and then engage in power struggles: Set 'em up and knock 'em down. Projecting authority roles onto others often coincides with shrinking from the task of assuming legitimate roles of authority and responsibility oneself. Such individuals may grow to assume an exaggerated sense of authority in one area of life while avoiding responsibility in other areas; and/or to respect certain figures as authorities while denying the same respect to others. It is important for these people to acknowledge responsibility, first and foremost to themselves. A central question to answer is: What does it mean to be emotionally responsible? Answering this question means, for one thing, learning constructive ways of engaging with others over problems at hand. A related challenge indicated here is to learn to distinguish between feelings and attitudes, as these individuals are liable to project attitudes toward others without realizing or articulating the (usually ambivalent) feelings from which such attitudes stem.

For individuals who do not take themselves too seriously, this influence supports promotes an ironic humor about the ways of the world. The Capricorn moon supports the ability to project oneself with an uncommon air of authority—or else irreverence.

Georges Gurdjieff, Betty Friedan, Yogi Berra, Bobby Seale, Mia Farrow, Richard Pryor, Cher.

AQUARIUS (11th House) The Aquarian moon indicates an internal orientation to experience the emotional content of communications from parental figures as unsettled and erratic. Parents often seem to be bound up in a complex of external activities, relationships and worldly affairs, so that expressions of unconditional love may not be easily perceived. Likewise these individuals are inclined to miss any emotional content in the messages they receive. They are predisposed to experience the family environment as rather haywire, with lines of communication scrambled. From such experiences, people born with this influence grow to become erratic in their own emotional communications, and may come across as detached or unpredictable. As adults they may be attracted to partners who seem aloof. Hence this moon sign brings the challenge to communicate about emotional issues with partners and others, even when the emotional content of their feelings is not clear even to themselves.

With electricity as the medium of their feelings, these individuals have an exceptionally difficult time knowing their feelings.

They do well to become aware of their feeling experiences via processes of communicating. Cultivating groups of friends, "playing telephone," and otherwise engaging in frequent communications on the subject of day-to-day and moment-to-moment status of "what's going on" are valuable means of connecting to their feelings. As adults they are challenged to decipher the "emotional complex" of the environment in which they grew.

This influence supports expression of higher humanitarian and communitarian powers. People born with the moon in Aquarius are inclined to feel very strongly and genuinely the Aquarian values they espouse. This moon sign promotes the tendency to be keenly tuned in to current issues and movements.

Marilyn Monroe, Arthur Miller, Woody Allen, Diane Keaton, Marian Wright Edelman, Fidel Castro, Timothy Leary.

PISCES (12th House) Akin to natal moon conjunct Neptune, the moon in Pisces engenders a predisposition to experience one of the "Big Neptunian Three" in childhood: mental illness, alcoholism and religious fanaticism. In one pattern of development, people born with this moon sign generate an emotional orientation that reflects in quality (if not in kind) the engulfing experiences of childhood. Parental figures may be experienced as being overwhelmed by life, and these individuals often grow to feel overwhelmed themselves, even while on the exterior they can appear to "have it together." In a related developmental pattern, it can be most difficult for people born with this moon placement to deal with the experiences of their feelings as separate from the whole emotional environment in which those feelings arose. There is a predilection to be flooded by feelings that seem to envelop the world around oneself. In adulthood, this predilection can translate into the tendency to project onto others the feelings and experiences that actually emanate from within.

In adult life, the emotional environment of both workplace and home is exceptionally important, and people born with the moon in Pisces do well to the extent that they feel that their environment feeds and nurtures them on subtle and psychic levels. A challenge with this moon sign is to recognize when their environments are not psychically and emotionally supportive, and to seek ones that are. Pursuing spiritual and/or psychological vocations can be especially meaningful. The experience of feelings in terms of spiritual dimensions and contexts can be exceptionally profound, unless the context involved (such as a radical religious sect) is not truly responsive to, or supportive of, individual needs and differences.

The Pisces moon promotes the development of colorful, libidinous imaginations, and a great ability to go with the flow. People born with this moon sign are inclined to become completely immersed—psychically and emotionally—in their personal myths, ideals, fantasies and beliefs. By the same token they are capable of projecting vividly charged myths, beliefs and ideals into the world around them.

O.J. Simpson, Hugh Hefner, Ava Gardner, Michael Jackson, Steven Spielberg, Paul Winter, Fred Rogers (Mr. Rogers), Martin Luther King, Betty Ford, Hillary Clinton.

THE GODDESS ASTEROIDS AND CHIRON

Since the mid-1980s and the publication of Demetra George's *Asteroid Goddesses* (CRCS), four of the largest asteroids—Ceres, Pallas Athena, Juno and Vesta—have attracted a great deal of attention in astrological circles. During the same period, the comet Chiron, which is at present holding an orbit entirely within the bounds of the solar system, has made a surprising ascent to prominence in the field. Although the idea that these orbs could exert influences originally encountered a considerable amount of skepticism, the observation and experience of students and practitioners has progressively validated the legitimacy of these influences in the astrological universe.

As noted in Principle 3 of Chapter 9, the asteroids form an orbital belt that, in terms of both collective mass and proportional position between Mars and Jupiter, can be considered the equivalent of a planet. Being individually a good deal smaller than their planetary counterparts—the largest of the asteroids, Ceres, is 620 miles in diameter—the asteroids refer to relatively minor motivational forces. Still, these motivations are vital and significant.

Identified with major female figures of Greco-Roman mythology, the Goddess asteroids expand the roster of feminine figures in astrology, and evens out the gender imbalance of the mythological clan of planets. Frequently identified with feminist issues, the nature of both the motivations and the patterns of experience signified by the goddess asteroids are indeed classically female, but nonetheless androgynous for that.

⚷ CERES ⚷

Ceres was the goddess of agriculture, and it is from Ceres that the word "cereal" derives. Ceres was the giver of grain to human beings, and as symbolized in the image of carrying an ever-full sack of grain on one's back, Ceres represents the motivation for a certain kind of unconditional giving. It indicates the potential for freely giving of something special that comes from the core self, of giving something with no expectation of return, as if casting seeds on the Earth along one's way. As with Cancer, Ceres is also associated with the growing, preparation and cooking of food.

Along with being identified as the giver of grain, Ceres was renowned for her role as mother of Persephone, with whom there was a great bond of love. But suffering the grief that can be known only to parents, Ceres was devastated when Persephone was kidnapped by Pluto, who swept her off to his underworld kingdom. Ceres wandered the Earth seeking word of her daughter's fate; but since there were no witnesses to the abduction, no one was able to tell Ceres what had become of her daughter. Ceres became ever more distraught, and in her mounting rage and frustration she brought about drought on the land. This created suffering for humans, and eventually the people appealed to Zeus for help. Responding to their pleas, Zeus sent Hermes (Mercury) to order Pluto to release Persephone. But just as Hermes arrived, Pluto succeeded in getting Persephone to eat of a pomegranate, a sexually symbolic act that bound her to him.

In the resolution of their competing interests, Ceres won her daughter for the spring and summer months of each year, while Persephone was compelled to return to Pluto's underground realm for the winter months. In signifying the seasonal cycle of vegetative growth and return-to-seed, Ceres here suggests the experience of waiting for the season of one's fulfillment. The outcome of Ceres' travails regarding her daughter also represents the archetypal joint-custody agreement.

The myth of Ceres, moreover, portrays the unwavering emotional strength and tireless activism of a parent on behalf of her child. In this regard Ceres symbolizes the motivation for being *champion* and unwavering supporter. As portrayed in the myth, Ceres indicates the role of parent (and perhaps especially the single parent) as the tireless advocate of one's child. Yet Ceres also symbolizes the motivation to champion any person(s) or cause that one takes as one's own. It indicates the motivation to champion the cause of children, students or patients in roles such as parent, teacher, nurse and doctor. It symbolizes the potential to invest a special feeling of care for special people or interests in one's life.

Ceres further represents the challenge to champion self: to stand up, stand for, and further your own innocent cause. Ceres indicates the potential for experiencing childhood trials and tribulations, and ironically can indicate a predilection for experiencing a lack of parental care. From the experience that parents really did not champion one's cause in childhood, it becomes difficult to further one's own cause as an adult. Ceres symbolizes resolution of this difficulty by means of identifying with something that transcends self: By championing something or someone else, you can indirectly champion yourself.

♀ PALLAS ATHENA ♀

Although Pallas Athena often appeared as a single figure (later known in Rome as Minerva), the two names of Pallas and Athena represent the fusion of two identities. In one myth, Pallas was said to have swallowed her sister Athena whole out of jealousy, thus incorporating two beings into one. Early myth apparently emphasizes the Pallas figure, and later myth the Athena figure.

Pallas was a warrior goddess who was born full-grown; she was said to have sprung from the head of Zeus issuing a warrior's cry. "Not of woman born," Pallas was much like a man in a woman's body, and signifies a strong orientation both to one's father personally—to being your father's child—and to the *world of the father* in general. Conversely, Pallas represents the "inversion of the mother principle," and indicates the potential to experience the mother as a masculine character with masculine values, and/or the absence of a nurturing female figure.

Brilliant as a strategist and tactician, Pallas was invincible in battle, and so indicates the motivation to win, conquer and prosper in patriarchal society through male tactics. Representing potentials for strong wits, mental toughness and tough-minded intellect, Pallas evokes the image of the feminist who will not just survive, but will thrive in a man's world. Just as the glyph of Pallas resembles the glyph of Venus but with a "diamond head,"

Pallas symbolizes potentials for mental brilliance and invincibility.

Athena, meanwhile, was the patroness of Athens, and was known as the goddess of wisdom. She was the giver of the olive tree, which was seen as the best and wisest of all possible gifts. She was the goddess of arts and artisans. In contrast to Pallas and her hard-edged power, Athena signifies the practical creativity of the craftsman, and further symbolizes the potential for finding and developing *personal truth*. She symbolizes the motivation to speak your truth, ply your craft and make your way according to your own truth in the same patriarchal society whose values the Pallas character accepts unconditionally.

Thus Pallas Athena symbolizes on the one hand the motivation to thrive in male-dominated society by virtue of hard-edged wits, yet on the other the motivation to flourish in terms of your own truth, your own craft or your own way. Emphasis of Pallas Athena in the chart suggests the issue of whether to cleave to the world of the father and succeed by the father's values and tactics, or to pursue life according to your own truth, artistry or wisdom. Pallas Athena represents the potential for making key changes of direction in life, either toward Pallas' "way of the father," adopting typically male means and ends; or toward Athena's "way of the craftsperson," making one's way by virtue of one's own truth or craft. But just as Pallas Athena combines two identities into one, it also signifies the potential for bringing the two archetypes together: bringing strategy, mental brilliance and toughness into the cause of furthering a way or craft that is infused with some inner personal truth.

⚲ JUNO ⚲

Juno was the sister of Jupiter, and in a sense Juno resembles Pallas Athena in that she too incorporates two distinct identities. As with Pallas Athena, the character of Juno changes dramatically from earlier Greek to later Roman myth. In the early classical era when cultures on islands such as Rhodes and Samos flourished, this goddess was known as Hera, queen of the heavens, who was patroness of women and marriage. One of the greatest mythological figures of Greek antiquity, Hera was sister to and the equal of Zeus. Worship of Hera represented the honoring of women in society, and reinforced the dignity of women's roles. Homage to Hera was associated with three major feminine rites of passage: puberty, marriage and widowhood, and Hera symbolizes values inherent in all those roles.

As the mythology of Roman Juno supplanted Greek Hera, however, Juno became known not only as sister to Jupiter but as wife to him, and Juno's identity in later mythology can hardly be separated from that crazy marriage. Juno and Jupiter married because they became infatuated with each other, and it soon became clear that they had committed to each other rashly. Subsequently, Jupiter realized his mistake straight away, and with his insatiable appetite for freedom he abandoned Juno. With an appetite for women that matched his appetite for freedom, Jupiter went on to cavort around the mythic universe striking up affairs with a long series of other females. In marked contrast, Juno held her marital vows as sacred, remained true to those vows—and stuck in them. She carried the mantle of her identity as Jupiter's wife with a sacred sense of honor, even while using her powers in incessant attempts to foil Jupiter's affairs.

Hence while Juno symbolizes the sacredness of commitment to marital vows, and more generally the motivation to *live a commitment through to its end,* she also symbolizes the trials and tribulations of marriage and other deeply committed relationships. In that Juno diminished herself by remaining committed to Jupiter, Juno symbolizes the archetype of giving up one's power in commitments to others. Juno represents the archetypal cycle that begins with giving up one's power, deepens into long-term troughs of *disempowerment,* and comes full circle with the quest to re-empower oneself. In the context of this cycle of disempowerment, Juno symbolizes the potential for an ever-deepening enrichment of the soul. Juno signifies the motivation to take any serious commitment as sacred, and also symbolizes the potential for *enhancing* relationships and other involvements by virtue of soulful commitment.

Negative potentials of experience indicated by Juno include abandonment, persecution, victimization, abuse, exploitation and betrayal.

✧ VESTA ✧

Vesta was the goddess of the hearth. At the shrine of worship to Vesta, a fire was kept burning, symbolizing the undying spirit of the community, and the bond between the individual and the community. When a woman married, she would begin the fire in the hearth of her new home with embers taken from Vesta's temple. The worship of Vesta, and the priestesses, or "Vestal virgins" who tended the sacred fire, became prominent political features of Imperial Rome.

The glyph of Vesta suggests "the fire held within the chalice," and represents the sacred fire of the inner spirit held in the temple of the body. Vesta signifies the potential for *holding the inner spirit as sacred,* and indicates the importance of making *rituals of return* to contact the inner spirit. Vesta indicates the motivation for return to the inner center in ritualized acts such acts as yoga, jogging, walking, cooking and the writing of journals. It symbolizes the motivation for rituals that serve to affirm the integrity of body and mind as well as spirit. Much as the Vestal priestesses of ancient Rome conveyed an aura of symbolic power in performing their rituals, Vesta indicates the potential for becoming a "priestess of the ritual."

As with many of the potentials signified by the goddess asteroids, positive potentials signified by Vesta are often most vividly experienced in their breach. Hence in symbolizing the motivation to hold the inner voice and inner center as sacred, Vesta also represents the liabilities of being *compromised, coerced* and *violated.* And while Vesta symbolizes the bond between the individual and the community, it also represents the power of the community to compromise and *ostracize* the individual.

Vesta symbolizes the archetypal challenge to remain true to the inner self, to act and speak from one's inner center in spite of circumstances. In one pattern of development, the fear of being coerced or compromised gives rise to an attitude of excessive guardedness; and so Vesta indicates the challenge to address fears underlying walls erected in the fear of being compromised. It indicates the challenge to be true to one's inner voice in the midst of worldly affairs.

⚷ CHIRON ⚷

The newest "star" in the astrological universe, Chiron was discovered on November 1, 1977. Curiously, Chiron is actually a comet that, at least for the time being (roughly 500 years) is maintaining a stable orbit within our solar system. An elongated parabola, the orbit of Chiron extends beyond Uranus at one end, but falls within the orbit of Saturn at the other.

A prominent figure in Greek mythology, Chiron was named for the centaur who was renowned as a teacher and healer; he was mentor to several of the great mythological heroes including Jason, Achilles and Hercules. Yet by fateful accident, Hercules wounded Chiron in the knee or thigh. Since Hercules was in part an immortal being, the wound incurred by Chiron was an immortal wound.

Being well-versed in the healing arts, Chiron sought to heal himself. In this healing quest he was said to have spent many years on one of the islands off the coast of Greece, and was said to have developed ever greater wisdom and knowledge of healing processes. But Chiron never did succeed in healing himself, and so became known as the "wounded healer." As the wounded healer, Chiron symbolizes the motivation to heal without what is simultaneously being healed within.

In a common version of the myth, Hercules, the wounder, appealed to Zeus to release Chiron from what had become Chiron's eternal suffering. Zeus acquiesced, and cast Chiron into the stars as the constellation Centaurus. In so doing, paradoxically, Zeus made Chiron whole again. Hence pertaining to the fact that "heal" and "whole" derive from the same root, Chiron represents the motivation to heal into a new wholeness, a greater wholeness that is in some radical way different from the normal sense of being whole. Chiron represents "a wound a lifetime in the healing," and symbolizes the realization of a new wholeness as made possible by long-term difficulty, suffering or sense of woundedness. Of course, such woundedness may be emotional and psychic just as much as physical.

This process of realizing the meaning of new wholeness was wonderfully illustrated by Senator Bob Kerrey during the presidential primaries of 1992. Kerrey, who was born with the sun conjunct Chiron in Virgo (August 27, 1943), lost his leg in Vietnam, yet by this lifetime wound Kerrey became acutely identified with the need for universal health care. As a wounded healer, Kerrey was a key figure in bringing the issue of national health care to American consciousness.

In representing a wound a lifetime in the healing, Chiron indicates the challenge, first of all, to acknowledge one's own woundedness. Without such acknowledgment, one is more likely to play out the role of the wounder; and so Chiron symbolizes the potential to be the wounder as well as the healer. Illustrating this aspect of Chironic symbolism was Roberto D'Aubisson, who was born just five days before Bob Kerrey, so that D'Aubisson too was born with the sun conjunct Chiron. As the rabid leader of the ultra right-wing Arena Party in El Salvador, D'Aubisson was an infamous wounder, widely known as the chief sponsor of the death squads. Fittingly however, he eventually succumbed to his own emotional, spiritual and eventually physical woundedness, dying of cancer in his mid-forties.

Chiron symbolizes the potential for healing not as a return to what once was, but as growing toward a different and greater dimension of wholeness. It therefore indicates the potential to perceive new dimensions of meaning. Chiron represents the motivation to create new meaning out of life, and likewise a new sense of the meaning of wholeness. The glyph of Chiron resembles a key, and represents the key to new wholeness.

Chiron symbolizes the motivation to realize a new or enhanced sense of wholeness in matters beyond wounds and healing, and so symbolizes the potential to perceive *new gestalts,* new wholes, and new configurations of meaning and perception in any realm of life. It signifies the potential for perceptions that diverge dramatically from the norm, and similarly for experiences that constitute major aberrations from norms. It indicates perceptions that are rooted in key, life-changing experiences.

For further reference, Melanie Reinhart's *Chiron and the Healing Journey* (Arkana) is a wonderful work on this topic.

APPENDIX 3

NOTES ON THE NATAL CHART

1. HOUSE CUSPS AND THE RISING SIGN

The house cusps—the lines that demarcate the divisions between the houses—designate the same spatial relationships in every birth chart. The left-hand horizontal line extending from the center of the chart leftwards to the "9 o'clock" point signifies the eastern horizon. (This is of course opposite to normal maps, where the left represents west.) This left-hand horizontal line constitutes the cusp, or beginning, of the first house and forms an initial point of reference. The horizontal line from the center to the right of the chart designates the western horizon and forms the cusp of the 7th house. The vertical line from the center of the chart to the top designates the midheaven (also called the *medium coeli* or MC), the highest point of the ecliptic, and forms the 10th house cusp. The vertical line from center to bottom designates the nadir (the "midnight" of the chart), the point at which setting motion ends and rising motion begins. The nadir forms the cusp of the 4th house. "A "house cusp" refers to the point at which the 30° of terrestrial space indicated by each house begins. (See Chapter 8.)

Owing to the speed of the Earth's daily cycle of rotation on its axis, the points at which the zodiac intersect the directional points indicated by the house cusps depend acutely on the exact time of birth. In roughly four minutes, the zodiac changes its orientation to all the house cusps by one degree. So it is that even the charts of identical twins born just a few minutes apart will show different zodiacal degrees on the house cusps.

House cusps indicate *catalytic points,* points at which the areas of experience indicated by the houses become activated. Similarly, the zodiacal sign that intersects a given house cusp indicates the instinctive powers that are catalyzed in dealing with the "affairs" or experiences signified by that house. The cusp-sign relationship long considered the most important is the sign on the eastern horizon at the moment of birth: the *ascendant,* or *rising sign.*

Pertaining to Principle 1, the rising sign indicates the instincts that serve to generate the individual orientation to life. The ascendant indicates the instincts by which the *individual point of view* and outlook on life are developed. Likewise the ascending sign indicates the predispositions that work to create one's intuitive approach to life, that catalyze the experience of "idea of self" and that generate an intuitive self-image. The ascendant symbolizes the instinctive impulse to act as an individual, to operate from a purely independent perspective.

One of the most popular traditions concerning the rising sign holds that it symbolizes the "mask," or facade, that one presents to the world. Inasmuch as this interpretation assumes the primacy of pretense, however, it comprises a negative potential. The ascendant represents the direction in experience of "self-unto-self," and indicates the potential to show a mask to the world only to the extent that the individual does not feel free to speak and act independently.

Like all house cusps, the ascendant is called a catalytic point here because, like a lighting rod, it serves to attract experience. Hence beyond its influences in personality, the sign rising at birth indicates predilections to attract key individual experiences according to the nature of the instincts represented by that sign.

For example, people born with Virgo rising often attract key experiences regarding employment, while people with Leo rising attract key experiences centering on the realization of personal identity, on family and on relationships of the heart. Cancer rising often serves to catalyze and attract key experiences pertaining to children. Typically such experiences are intense and complicated; and as often as not *the experiences or circumstances that are attracted challenge us to develop central powers indicated by the rising sign.* Thus inasmuch as people born with Virgo rising attract experiences that center on issues of employment, they may actually develop strong Virgo traits in the process of addressing those issues, as compared to developing a "Virgo mask," or personality type, from the outset. By the same token, people born with Leo rising may develop classic Leo characteristics *as a function of experience.* People born with Leo rising tend to experience such issues as identity, self-expression, self-realization and the drama of children as exceptionally meaningful, and so may develop traits such as self-expressiveness in central connection with deep and very genuine internal experience of such issues.

As well, the rising sign indicates key individual attractions to behaviors and activities symbolized by the sign in question. Hence some individuals born with Virgo develop a key individual attraction to the classically Virgoan activity of writing.

As with the ascendant, the signs on the other house cusps indicate instincts through which the experiences indicated by the house in question become activated. For instance the sign on the fourth house cusp (the nadir) indicates the instincts that come into play in dealing with (fourth house) experiences of private life, security, home, comfort, the emotional foundations of self and intimate relationships.

2. PLANETS ON SIGN CUSPS

Sign cusps refer to the locations in the zodiac where one sign changes to the next. The span of sign cusps covers the last 3 degrees of one sign, and the first 3 degrees of the next. Planets located on a sign cusp at birth are channeled and expressed through a combination or blending of the instincts represented by both signs. For example, Mars found in 28° Aries at birth tends to be expressed through a blending of Aries and Taurus instincts, with the emphasis on Aries.

The word "cusp" refers to something that stands out, and planets on cusps tend to be expressed in behavior and personality features that stand out. When either the sun or the moon (or both) are on cusps at birth, these basic parts of self are characterized by an "energetic complexity"—a complex blend—of instinctive powers.

3. INTERCEPTION OF SIGNS

Because of the tilt of the Earth's axis in relation to the plane of the zodiac, it happens that in the intersection of the house cusps with the zodiac, certain houses of the birth chart enclose or encompass greater spans of the zodiac than others. When one whole sign of the zodiac is enclosed within a single house, the sign involved is said to be intercepted. Interception of signs in a chart is evident when one (opposing) pair of signs is found on the cusps of two *consecutive* pairs of houses; while another pair of signs—the intercepted signs—do not fall on any of the house cusps. Interception of signs always involves pairs of opposite signs.

Whether or not signs are shown to be intercepted can depend on the method of calculating house cusps. The most commonly accepted systems for calculating house cusps are the Placidus and Koch systems. No matter what system is used, however, the phenomenon of interception is far more likely to happen at the higher latitudes of both hemispheres.

Intercepted signs are by definition removed from the interstices of house cusps. Hence the instincts represented by intercepted signs do not play into the matrix of catalytic points as represented by house cusps. (See above.) Inasmuch as house cusps serve to activate or catalyze experience, the interception of signs implies that the instinctive powers indicated by those signs do not come into play in the same manner in which other signs do; and so these instincts are liable to be not as well integrated into character and experience as the instinctive powers indicated by the other signs. By the same reasoning, when planets appear in intercepted signs, the motivations they represent may not be as fully integrated into the individual's matrix of experience as are the motivations represented by the other planets. Planets located in intercepted signs suggest a subtle element of disconnection between consciousness and the environment, wherein experience of the environment may not be fully assimilated.

4. THE ASPECTS

The aspects (angular connections) formed between planets at birth signify psychological dynamics by which the different parts of ourselves (as indicated by the planets in question) interact with one another. The intrapsychic dynamics indicated by aspects are stronger when aspects are more exact, and weaker when the angular relationships are less exact. In general, the dynamics indicated by aspects are operative when the planets are within about 8° for conjunctions and oppositions, within 5°-6° of exactitude for trines and squares, within about 2° for more minor aspects as semi-squares and quincunxes, and within only a single degree or so for the most minor aspects (noviles, quintiles, septiles). A degree or two may be added to these orbs when the sun or moon is involved.

CONJUNCTION (0°, ☌): When two or more planets are conjunct (aligned with one another) at birth, the motivations they represent become fused with one another, creating a larger and more complex motivational unit or "part" of self. The fusing of these motivations generates a kind of psychological fissioning, a spontaneous psychic combustion that contributes to impulsiveness, creativity, spontaneity, intensity, forcefulness and irrepressibility. Conjunctions indicate the tendency to unreflecting action—the tendency to speak and leap before you think and look. Yet the combustive intensity engendered by conjunctions can be *internalized* as well as externalized. In this mode of development, individuals experience life internally with a high degree of intensity, yet may appear outwardly quiescent. Hence while some people born with conjunctions prominent in their charts have a remarkably forceful presence, and an unmistakably strong manner of imposing self on the situation, others can seem to be impassive, through with a lot going on inside. A balance of both modes of development and expression is generally desirable.

OPPOSITION (180°, ☍): When planets are opposed to one another at birth, the motivations in question form a polarity with one another: an internal relationship of opposing, but potentially complementary, parts of ourselves. These polarities create channels for the powerful expression of both motivations; but the dynamics of opposition are also inherently unstable. Typically, oppositions serve to generate a back-and-forth, push-and-pull dynamic. Shifts in balance between poles may occur in widely varying rhythms: by the moment, from day to day, from one week to the next, from one month to another, or by whole periods in life. The psychological dynamics of the opposition are usually experienced in relation to others and the external world, as if one pole of the opposition was outside ourselves. Identifying with one pole at a time, the opposite pole is often experienced in terms of people with whom we have conflicts, and in terms of "opposing forces" in general. In effect, we are compelled to experience and confront what has not been owned within ourselves in the form of some other person or external circumstances. Oppositions also contribute to unstable swings of temperament.

These aspects challenge us to integrate the parts of self represented, to bring them into balance, and to appreciate the complementary and symbiotic roles they play in ourselves and in our lives. As the opposing parts of self are balanced and blended, they promote the expression not only of power but *breadth of awareness.*

The opposition works as a central axis in personality around which other aspects of self tend to become oriented.

TRINE (120°, △): When planets form (equilateral) triangular relations one to another with respect to the Earth at birth, the motivations represented tend to interact in dynamically fluid and easily coordinated ways. Trine aspects engender a sense of ease and effortless flow in expression, almost like a downhill ride. This sense of ease, however, can itself be a pitfall, as reliance on such dynamics can promote the tendency to go with the flow too much, to always take the easiest way through, to take the path of least resistance too often.

On the other hand, trine aspects indicate gifts to be cultivated. In promoting full and effortless expression of diverse aspects of self, these aspects translate into latent *talents and abilities* that may be progressively developed and expressed. The planets which form the trine indicate the type of gifts engendered. For example a trine between Mercury and Uranus indicates latent gifts for such things as communications, reporting, mental processing of data and fast thinking.

SQUARE: (90°, □): The square angle signifies the development of *dynamic tension.* Planets in square aspect to one another at birth generate tensions that typically become manifest in terms of conflicts of both internal and external nature. To the extent that they remain unresolved, the tensions engendered by square aspects may manifest psychosomatically.

The square angle represents an ongoing crisis of attitude. The square is an angle of construction, and the psychological tensions generated by squares demand resolution in terms of developing *constructive attitudes.* The presence of square aspects at birth challenges us to develop constructive means of channeling internal tensions. And the tensions engendered by squares form the impetus to resolve the very conflicts they create. Likewise, while square aspects indicate attraction to conflict, they also indicate the potential for developing positive attitudes toward resolving conflict. Square aspects demand development of *working attitudes* toward tasks and problems. In the development of such attitudes, squares indicate the potential for *strength of character,* and the practice of "constructive engagement."

SEXTILE (60°, ✳): Like cogs of meshing gears, the motivations represented by planets forming 60° angles at birth mesh with one another in smooth, even fashion. Sextiles in the birth chart indicate motivations that are naturally "in synch" with one another, and so they contribute to a well integrated personality. Sextiles generate a good coordination of the motivations in question, and promote fine expression of the combination of motivational forces. Similar to trines, sextiles indicate talents and abilities that may be progressively developed.

SEMISQUARE (45°, ∠) and SESQUIQUADRATE (135°, ⟐): Both these aspects involve half-squares, and much as square aspects denote the need to develop constructive attitudes, the semisquare and the sesquiquadrate both indicate the potential to respond in terms of constructive *actions.* These aspects indicate dynamics that tend to manifest in terms of crises of action and response. Both engender tensions that support *overreaction.* Hence these aspects indicate the challenge to learn to respond to acute situations constructively, without overreacting—without becoming upset. These aspects incline to types of temperament that can benefit greatly from the development of calm and consideration in the face of life's bumps and turbulence.

QUINCUNX (150°): The 150° angle usually connects planets that are in signs of dissimilar "mode" (a planet in a cardinal sign for example will almost always form a quincunx with a planet in either a fixed or mutable sign), as well as dissimilar element. Quincunx angles challenge the individual to integrate essentially *disparate* and dissimilar parts or facets of self, and likewise to assimilate dissimilar dimensions of experience. The process of integrating disparate parts of self typically requires slow, sustained effort over a long period of time. In challenging us to bring together the expression of disparate aspects of self, quincunx aspects encourage the development of deep and genuine *originality*. Quincunx dynamics involve subtle tensions, and until the dissimilar potentials indicated by the two planetary place-ments are substantially integrated and synthesized, development may be marked by difficulties in making basic adjustments to life, in being "out of synch" or "out of phase" with outer circum-stances. The dynamics of this aspect serve to attract unusual and interesting, if also problematic, forms of experience.

QUINTILES (72°, 144°): Quintile angles pertain to the division of the zodiac by 5, and akin to the 5th sign Leo, quintiles indicate dynamics that contribute to *creative expression* of the motiva-tions involved. Quintiles indicate a potential flair for creativity in expressing a particular combination of motivations. This aspect also appears to promote attitudes of being a *free spirit*.

NOVILES (40°, 80°, 160°): Novile angles (all multiples of 40°) relate to the Cancerian principle in that they encourage attitudes of *nurturing growth*. When noviles are prominent, such attitudes tend to develop in connection with experiences of needing an exceptionally long period of gestation to reach developmental plateaus, plateaus that others reach much more quickly and easily. These aspects seem to engender delays and difficulties in development that can eventually translate into deep appreciation for similar trials of growth and development as experienced by others. Thus noviles indicate the potential to develop attitudes of helping others who are struggling to get through earlier stages of development.

SEMISEXTILE (30°, ⩒): The semisextile is an acute angle, and it effects acute modes of response. Semisextiles promote the generation of *reactive* and quick, intuitive types of response, responses that can be problematic in their lack of forethought. Semisextiles challenge us to anticipate our own reactions, so that we know when it is appropriate—and inappropriate—to cut loose impulses to react. These influences appear to contribute to abilities in movement, music and dance.

SEPTILES (multiples of 51° 25′): Septiles pertain to the divi-sion of the zodiac by 7. While there is disagreement as to the meaning of the septiles, it appears that as with the number 7 in numerology, septiles indicate an emphasized role of luck or fate in one's life. Septiles may indicate the presence of an evolutionary dynamic in which the individual, seemingly by fate, finds that his more personal goals or trajectories do not work out in the smaller scheme of things. Instead, the individual finds himself thrust into a wider orbit in life, and is compelled to open to dimensions of life far beyond what was originally recognized.

There is some evidence to suggest that septiles contribute to qualities of subtle but profound inspirational genius.

UNASPECTED PLANETS: Planets that do not form any angles to other planets are figuratively as well as literally unintegrated with the others. Motivations represented by unaspected planets sometimes translate into experiences of isolation in childhood. Similarly, unaspected planets tend to be expressed in isolated— but also special—contexts in adult life. Unaspected planets indicate special "spheres" of experience that may be uniquely emphasized.

Forming relationships with people who were born with planets conjuncting one's own unaspected planets serves to integrate the parts of self symbolized by unaspected planets.

☋ 5. THE NODES OF THE MOON ☊

The two nodes of the moon refer to the opposing points at which the orbit of the Earth around the sun intersects the orbit of the moon around the Earth. The psychological dynamics of the moon's nodes are complementary, and very much connected to one another.

Metaphorically, the nodes of the moon represent valves for the intake and release of energy. According to placement by sign and house, the North Node of the moon (☊) indicates the direction that is most geared to the *intake of new energy,* and where there is maximum potential for new growth. The North Node indicates the aspect of self and direction in life that most needs and will most benefit from opening to new energies. Myrna Lofthus writes: "In past lives, we have neglected the affairs of the North Node House and now the matter is of extreme importance."[91] The North Node placement indicates the instincts and area of life through which the self can become newly energized on an ongoing basis.

Inasmuch as the North Node holds such generally positive indications, it might be assumed that conjunctions to the North Node at birth amount to an unalloyed good. As with everything else in astrology, however, these conjunctions can manifest in both favorable and unfavorable ways. On one hand, conjunctions to the North Node serve to channel powerful energies. On this account people born with these conjunctions can become "power magnates," possessed of unusual, strong and even uncanny powers.* On the other hand these conjunctions indicate a proneness to being overwhelmed by exotic and sometimes potentially dangerous exterior energies and powers. Conjunctions to the North Node represent the challenge to open to strong powers within oneself, and to channel new powers without personal attachment to such powers.

The South Node of the moon (☋) indicates that place in ourselves that is geared to the release of "old energy." As signified by its sign and house placements, the South Node indicates where old habit patterns and modes of response need to be released. Apparently karmic in nature—i.e. carried over from past lives—these patterns may be deceptively comfortable, tempting and attractive to replay. Yet the South Node is sometimes called the "drain" of the chart, suggesting the potential for dissipating energies by holding on to patterns of behavior and attitude that have effectively become effete, worn out. The South Node indicates the place in one's life where reliance on, and regression to, old forms of response will most likely have negative results, *except* as such activity results from direct connection to new energies and new areas of experience as indicated by the North Node. ("The seeds we grew and cultivated in the North Node house can be harvested ... and shared ... through the South Node house affairs." —Myrna Lofthus[92])

By sign and house, then, the South Node represents the natural directions for releasing the old. Conjunctions of planets to the South Node of the moon, meanwhile, signify what I have identified in terms of the *karma of loss*.[93] From a reincarnational perspective, these conjunctions indicate patterns of loss carried

---

* People born with the sun conjunct the North Node include J.P. Morgan, Donald Trump, Karl Marx, Jesse Helms, Joseph Stalin, Pablo Picasso, Hank Aaron and Jack Kevorkian.

over from previous lifetimes. The implication is that in recent lifetimes, the individual experienced not only major but premature experiences of loss. These experiences include loss of one's own life, loss of loved ones, and losses of livelihood, home and homeland. Emanating from such sources, people born with these conjunctions tend to attract experiences of loss early in (this) life, and may go on attracting experiences of loss until the root experiences (of this lifetime at least) are resolved. Resolution classically involves becoming conscious of and articulating experiences of loss so as to release related fear and grief. Until such experiences are resolved, these conjunctions indicate a proneness to try to hold on to others and/or to things, or to try to get from others what is not there to give. South Node conjunctions indicate the challenge to *let go,* to hold out one's palms openly so that we can open to what is to be truly and freely given to us.

Conjunctions to the South Node also suggest the presence of unusual gifts, perhaps carried over from previous lifetimes, that may be rather effortlessly developed, gifts that are given to us to give. These conjunctions represent the challenge to learn to give without attachment.

6. A NOTE ON THE COLORS

The colors listed in association with each of the zodiac signs in Chapter 9 may be considered the visual energetic equivalent of the vital energies represented by the signs. The scheme of color correspondence presented in Chapter 9 is chromatic and relates to the similarly chromatic nature of zodiacal energies/ instincts. In this scheme, the first color of the visible spectrum, red, correlates to the first sign of the zodiac, Aries. This pattern proceeds in steps of primary–tertiary–secondary–tertiary; primary–tertiary–secondary, etc. through the rainbow spectrum. It ends with the last color of the visible spectrum, violet, being associated with the last sign of the zodiac, Pisces. By this system of correspondence, the three fire signs correlate with the three primary colors, the three air signs correlate with the three secondary colors, and the earth and water signs with the six tertiary colors. The resulting correlations—Aries with red, Leo with yellow, Scorpio with blue-green (turquoise), Pisces with violet, etc., are appropriate and meaningful in the context of the respective astrological principles.

RADICALLY RETHINKING RULERSHIPS

Few systems are more basic to astrology than planet-sign rulerships. But nowhere in the field are there more signs that the construction of this system has been—it should be no shock to people in the field to say—fudged.

The discovery of the outermost planets mandated a total reassessment of the ancient system of dual rulerships. What actually happened, however, was considerably more haphazard. In the old system, the five known planets each ruled two signs. Yet the newer systems sometimes have *two planets ruling one sign,* but still—also—have certain planets ruling two signs each. These "systems" of correlation are not particularly logical, nor are they intellectually satisfying. Numerous astrologers have cast the issue of rulerships in terms of questions that have no definitive answers. Some few astrologers have offered their own answers.

Evident in the original system is a pattern that begins with Mercury's rulership of Virgo, connects Venus to Libra, Mars to Scorpio, Jupiter to Sagittarius and Saturn to Capricorn. All the newer system continue this progression with Uranus ruling Aquarius and Neptune ruling Pisces. How, then, did Pluto come out as the primary ruler of Scorpio? Taken to its conclusion, this progression would bring Pluto to rule not Scorpio but Aries, as is delineated in Chapter 8.

The illogic of modern tradition coincides with a lack of coherence in basic symbolic meanings. Take for example Mars and its generally favored rulership of Aries. As far as Mars is concerned, it is no accident that virtually every interpretation centers on fundamental capacities of sex and desire. Mars is universally interpreted in terms that include "the desire nature," "sexual desire," "passion," "physical desire," "masculinity," "masculine sexuality," "physical love," "*eros*," "the desire principle," "the seat of desire" and similar terms.

No astrologer challenges the validity of such attributions. The real question is: Are these motivations fundamental to *Aries*? Rarely, it seems, has real thought been devoted to this question. For at best, to interpret Aries in terms of such emotional and sexually-oriented capacities as are listed above would be to stretch the dimensions of Aries in a strange direction. In fact it would be hard to find any description of the nature of Aries that embraces anything close to this constellation of capacities. It is true that Aries characters are occasionally described as passionate; but they are characterized more clearly in terms of being, as Rob Hand puts it, "asocial or even antisocial."[94] These traits are hardly hallmarks of love, *eros* and the desire nature.

When we turn to Scorpio, by comparison, the picture is dramatically different. Straight away, what are the keywords of Scorpio but "I Desire," and what parts of the body does Scorpio rule but the sexual organs? *To separate the intrinsic nature of Scorpio from sexuality, eros, and the desire nature is to defy the most basic symbolic indications of the sign.*

When we look at other basic potentials attributed to Mars, most of them relate to Scorpio principles at least as well as to Aries. Consider other classic Martian motivations: aggression, self-preservation, action, fight, combat, competition, survival, strength, anger, virility and self-assertion. As noted in Chapter 9, the scorpion is a classic symbol of the instincts for these very capacities of survival. While astrologers tend to characterize Scorpios in terms of a number of esoteric motivations, the symbolism of the scorpion could not be more clear in indicating that the fundamental principle underlying Scorpio is not only more mundane but more recognizable, one that centers on motivations of sex, self-preservation and survival.

Regarding Pluto, it does well to recall that Pluto was discovered concurrent with the entrance of atomic energy into human consciousness and experience. The fact of this concurrence is well recognized in astrology, but its significance seems not to be well appreciated. Atomic energy focuses on the atomic unit—the unitary, the indivisible, the power of *one*. It was as *both* Pluto and atomic energy came into collective consciousness that, as noted in Principle 1, no longer did traditional bonds of community, nation, tribe or even family hold sway over the individual. For the first time in history, the individual became the *atomic, indivisible,* autonomous unit in society. This phenomenon of the Atomic Age seems clearly to cleave to the symbolism of the Number One principle. Nuclear power is, further, a phenomenon of *fire,* and as much as the symbolism of electricity conforms to the nature of Aquarius, the explosive, fissioning and fiery nature of nuclear power—and Pluto—conforms elegantly to the nature of Aries as a fire sign.

As with Mars and Aries, internal contradictions in the traditional rulership of Taurus by Venus have long been accepted simply because the rulership is traditional. Rob Hand has taken to task some key Venus-Taurus contradictions. As part of a larger discussion in *Horoscope Symbols* regarding how Venus originally became identified with Taurus, Hand asserts:

> It seems at first as if we have no planet with a clearly Taurean symbolism, and yet we do: the one planet whose symbolism ... fits perfectly with that of Taurus ... is the Earth. Taurus is the most perfectly earthy of the earth signs. Everything we think of as pertaining to Earth goddesses, everything that relates to adjectives like "earthy," pertains to Taurus. The Earth has much in common with Venus, but it could never be the significator of romantic love, which is too unreal, not sufficiently sensible, and too removed from the affairs of the daily world to be relevant to an Earth [or Taurean] person.[95]

The traditional association of Venus with Taurus also requires other unnatural stretches of the symbolic imagination. Consider for example the intrinsically social nature of Venus. As the feminine complement to Mars, the symbolism of Venus is charged with values of social relationship: affection, social harmony, flirtation, appeal, beauty, social warmth. All these values can clearly be applied to the nature of Librans, while few can be easily associated with the Taurean nature. While Aphrodite, Venus' predecessor, combined Taurean and Libran values (see Principle 2 of Chapter 9), the symbolism of Venus has largely dropped Aphrodite's embodiment of the Earth and of related organic forces of nature. Conversely the nature of Taurus, charged with values of persistence, productivity, industry, pragmatism, stability, the land, habit and earthiness, does not ring of Venus. Instead, arguably, Venus has remained falsely associated with a few Taurean values such as possession and luxury out of the need for consonance between the two as based on the traditional rulership.

With regard to Gemini, the Earth is not the only planet—or at least the only planetary orbit—to have been excluded from rulership systems. As noted in Principle 3, the Asteroid Belt occupies an orbital ring that falls squarely (elliptically?) into the larger astronomical pattern of planetary orbits. Equally, astrologers have taken increasing notice of the most prominent individual asteroids, to the point where now consideration of the goddess asteroids—Ceres, Pallas, Juno, and Vesta—are collectively taken virtually on par with the rest of the planets.

The asteroids comprise the perfect candidate(s) for correlation with Gemini. Just as the asteroids literally embody multiplicity, the scattered aspect of the Gemini nature goes hand in hand with the concepts of multiplicity and diversity: a bit of this and a bit of that and a bit of the other.

In analyzing fundamental correlations between signs and planets, it seems far more than a meaningless coincidence that our solar system has ten known planetary orbits, which combined with our sun and moon, add up to the magic number of 12. Hence, every one of the planetary orbits would seem to merit a natural correlation with a zodiacal sign.

REFERENCES

1. From Jung's commentary in *The Secret of the Golden Flower* (Wilhelm-Baynes trans.) NY: Harcourt Brace Jovanovich; 1962. p. 142.

2. Ronald W. Clark, *Einstein: The Life and Times.* NY: Avon Books, 1971. p. 243.

3. C.G. Jung et al., *Man and His Symbols.* NY: Dell; 1973. p. 43.

4. John Bowlby, *Attachment and Loss.* NY: Basic Books; 1969. p. 37.

5. Jerome Kagan, *Galen's Prophecy.* NY: Basic Books; 1994. p. 273.

6. Joseph Campbell, *Myths To Live By.* NY: Bantam Books; 1972. p. 13.

7. Alan Oken, *Alan Oken's Complete Astrology.* NY: Bantam Books; 1980. p. 123.

8. C.G. Jung, *Synchronicity: An Acausal Connective Principle.* Princeton: Princeton University Press; 1969, 1973.

9. C.G. Jung, *On the Nature of the Psyche* (R.F.C. Hull, trans.). Princeton: Princeton University Press; 1969. p. 111.

10. C.G. Jung, *On the Nature of the Psyche.* p. 111.

11. C.G. Jung, *On the Nature of the Psyche.* p. 115.

12. C.G. Jung, *Man and His Symbols.* NY: Dell; 1968. p. 58.

13. C.G. Jung, *Man and His Symbols.* p. 59.

14. From "On Synchronicity" in *The Portable Jung,* Joseph Campbell ed. NY: Penguin Books; 1977. p. 514.

15. C.G. Jung, *On The Nature of the Psyche,* p. 105.

16. Liz Greene, *The Astrology of Fate.* York Beach, Maine: Samuel Weiser Inc.; 1984. p. 202.

17. Harry Crews, *A Childhood: The Biography of a Place.* NY: Harper & Row; 1978. p. 4.

18. Charlotte Bronte, *Jane Eyre.* NY: W.W. Norton & Co.; 1971. pp. 8, 23.

19. Peter Maas, "A Woman of Valor." *Parade Magazine*; May 29, 1983. p. 6. The woman referred to is Marie Ragghianti.

20. R.C. Bolles, *Theory of Motivation*, 2nd Ed. NY: Harper & Row; 1975. p. 100.

21. John Bowlby, *Attachment and Loss*; Vol. 1: *Attachment*. NY: Basic Books; 1969. p. 45.

22. Gregory & Sutch eds., *Sociobiology and Human Nature;* San Francisco: Jossey-Bass; 1978. p. 5.

23. Gregory & Sutch eds., *Sociobiology and Human Nature*. p. 24.

24. Robert Wright, *The Moral Animal*. NY: Pantheon; 1994. pp. 365-367.

25. Associated Press; January 3, 1996.

26. "Maybe It's Not a Gene Behind a Person's Thrill-Seeking Ways." *The New York Times;* Nov. 1, 1996. p. 22.

27. Winifred Gallagher, "How We Become What We Are." *The Atlantic Monthly* Vol. 274, No. 3. September, 1994. pp. 49-50.

28. Peter H. Raven and George B. Johnson, *Biology*. St. Louis: Times Mirror/Moseby College Publishing; 1989. pp. 436-437.

29. Associated Press; April 18, 1984.

30. Stephen Forrest, To Prove Astrology; Part II in *Welcome to Planet Earth Magazine*. Vol. 6, No. 10 Aries 1987. pp. 12, 18.

31. Michel Gauquelin, *Birthtimes*. NY: Hill and Wang; 1983. p. 12.

32. Michel Gauquelin, *Birthtimes*. p. 131.

33. Michel Gauquelin, *Birthtimes*. p. 12.

34. Morton Hunt, *The Story of Psychology*. NY: Doubleday; 1993. p. 328.

35. Michel Gauquelin, *Birthtimes*. pp. 122-125.

36. Michel Gauquelin, *Cosmic Influences On Human Behavior*. London: Garnstone Press. 1973. p. 254.

37. Richard A. Crowe, "Astrology and the Scientific Method." *Psychological Reports*. Vol. 67 Aug. 1990. pp. 163-191.

38. Michel Gauquelin, *Birthtimes*. p. 11.

39. Barbara Brennan, *Hands of Light*. NY: Bantam Books; 1988. p. 25.

40. cf. Dr. Valerie Hunt, *Infinite Mind: The Science of Human Energy Fields*. Malibu, CA: Malibu Pub. Co.; 1989.

41. See Harry Oldfield and Roger Coghill's *The Dark Side of the Brain*. Element Books. The implications of Oldfield's theories regarding disease are fascinating.

42. Elaine Marieb, *Essentials of Anatomy & Physiology* 3rd Ed. Redwood City, CA: Benjamin Cummings Pub.; 1991. pp. 206-207.

43. See Peter Malsin, "Shut Out At the Ivory Tower: An Astrologer's Confrontation With Carl Sagan." *The Mountain Astrologer* Vol. 9, No. 8, Aug/Sep 1996. pp. 92-93. Article includes complete transcript of dialogue.

44. Don Cameron Allen, *The Star-Crossed Renaissance.* Durham, NC: Duke University Press; 1941. p. viii.

45. Patrick Curry, "Saving Astrology in Restoration England." *Astrology, Science and Society.* Patrick Curry, ed. Suffolk: Boydell (Press); 1987. p. 245.

46. Patrick Curry, "Saving Astrology in Restoration England." *Astrology, Science and Society.* p. 248.

47. Mark Graubard, "Astrology's Demise and its Bearing on the Death and Demise of Beliefs. *Osiris* No. 13, 1958; Bruges, Belgium. p. 232-234.

48. Carola Baumgardt, *Johannes Kepler: Life and Letters.* NY: Philosophical Library; 1951. p. 99.

49. Mark Graubard, "Astrology's Demise and its Bearing on the Death and Demise of Beliefs. *Osiris* No. 13, 1958; Bruges, Belgium; p. 232-233.

50. Quoted in Louis MacNeice, *Astrology.* NY: Doubleday; 1964. p. 156.

51. Mark Graubard, "Astrology's Demise and its Bearing on the Death and Demise of Beliefs. *Osiris* No. 13, 1958; Bruges, Belgium; p. 232.

52. S.J. Tester, *A History of Western Astrology.* NY: Ballantine Books; 1987. p. 220.

53. Shawn Carlson, "A Double-Blind Test of Astrology." *Nature.* Vol. 318, No. 5. December, 1985. pp. 419-425.

54. Angenent & DeMan, "The Validity of Astrological Statements." *Psychological Reports.* Vol. 62. April, 1988. p. 650.

55. Robert Hand, *Planets In Transit.* West Chester, PA; Schiffer Pub.; 1976. p. 307.

56. *Webster's New World Dictionary.* Cleveland, 1974. p. 587.

57. Joseph R. Royce ed., *Psychology and the Symbol.* New York: Random House; 1965. p. 54.

58. Edith Hamilton, *Mythology.* NY: Mentor Books; 1942. p. 33.

59. Edith Hamilton, *Mythology.* p. 42.

60. Liz Greene, *The Astrology of Fate.* York Beach, ME: Samuel Weiser; 1986. p. 208.

61. Anne Morrow Lindbergh, *A Gift From the Sea*. NY: Random House; 1991. p. 104.

62. *The Mountain Astrologer,* Vol. 9, No. 1, Dec. 1995. p. 29.

63. Richard Tarnas, "Uranus and Prometheus." *Geocosmic Research Monographs*. San Francisco No. 2; 1981. pp. 2-3.

64. Thomas Bullfinch, *Bullfinch's Mythology*. NY: Crown Pub.; 1979. p. 12.

65. Ronald W. Clark, *Einstein: The Life and Times*. NY: Avon Books; 1971. p. 37.

66. C.G. Jung, *On the Nature of the Psyche*. p. 93.

67. *Psychology Today*. May 1982. Vol. 16 No. 5.

68. Ruth L. Munroe, *Schools of Psychoanalytic Thought*. NY: Holt, Rinehart and Winston; 1955. p. vi.

69. T. Strongman, *The Psychology of Emotion*. Chichester, England: John Wiley & Sons; 1978. pp. 1-2.

70. Carroll Izard, "Basic Emotions, Relations Among Emotions, and Emotion-Cognition Relations." *Psychological Review*. July, 1992; Vol. 99, No. 3. p. 565.

71. Richard A. Shweder, "'You're Not Sick, You're Just in Love': Emotion as an Interpretive System." *The Nature of Emotion*. NY: Oxford University Press; 1995. p. 37.

72. Richard A. Shweder, "'You're Not Sick, You're Just in Love': Emotion as an Interpretive System." *The Nature of Emotion*. p. 43.

73. H.H. Goldsmith, "Parsing the Emotional Domain from a Developmental Perspective." *The Nature of Emotion*. p. 68.

74. *Journal of Abnormal Psychology*. 1978, Vol. 87, No. 2. pp. 256-271.

75. Abraham Maslow, *Toward a Psychology of Being*. NY: D. Van Nostrand Co.; 1968. p. 191.

76. Carl Jung, *Memories, Dreams, Reflections*. Aniela Jaffe ed. NY: Vintage Books; 1963. p. 340.

77. Marcia Moore and Mark Douglas, *Astrology, The Divine Science*. York Harbor, ME: Arcane Pub.; 1971. p. 132.

78. Paramahansa Yogananda, *Autobiography of a Yogi*. LA: Self-Realization Fellowship; 1974. p. 189.

79. Elaine Pagels, *The Gnostic Gospels*. NY: Vintage Books; 1981, p. xix.

80. Quoted in Stephen Arroyo, *Astrology, Karma, and Transformation*. Davis, CA: CRCS Pub.; 1978. p. 8.

81. Frances Sakoian and Louis Acker, *The Astrologer's Handbook.* NY: Harper & Row, 1973. p. 186.

82. Myrna Lofthus, *A Spiritual Approach to Astrology.* Reno, NV: CRCS Pub.; p. 145.

83. Debbi Kempton-Smith, *Secrets From a Stargazer's Notebook,* NY Bantam Books; 1982. p. 227.

84. *The Mountain Astrologer.* Vol. 8, No. 9, November 1995. p. 16.

85. Quoted in Michael R. Meyer, *A Handbook for the Humanistic Astrologer.* Garden City, NY: Anchor Press; 1974. p. 13.

86. M.J. Maransky, "The Hell-Bent-for-Leather Syndrome." *Considerations.* Mt. Kisco, NY: Vol. VII, No. 4. 1992. p. 39.

87. Bil Tierney, *Dynamics of Aspect Analysis.* CRCS Pub.; 1983. p. 245.

88. Debbi Kempton-Smith, *Secrets From a Stargazer's Notebook.* p. 96.

89. Source: Michael Meyer, *A Handbook for the Humanistic Astrologer.*

90. Franklin Le Van Baumer, *Main Currents In Western Thought.* New Haven: Yale University Press; 1978. pp. 249-250.

91. Myrna Lofthus, *A Spiritual Approach to Astrology.* p. 199.

92. Myrna Lofthus, *A Spiritual Approach to Astrology.* p. 199.

93. See Peter Malsin, "South Node Conjunctions and the Karma of Loss." *The Mountain Astrologer* Vol. 8. No. 4. April/May 1995. pp. 33-34.

94. Robert Hand, *Horoscope Symbols.* West Chester, PA: Whitford Press; 1981. p. 211.

95. Robert Hand, *Horoscope Symbols.* p. 214.

ABOUT THE AUTHOR

Peter Malsin lives in Meriden, New Hampshire with his wife and two children. He enjoys sports and people as children's coach, player, spectator and astrologer.

In his astrological practice, Mr. Malsin highlights counseling as well as consulting. He may be reached at Meridian Astrology, 24 Lower Shaker Village, Enfield, NH 03748, U.S.A. His e-mail address is solarize@Connriver.net.

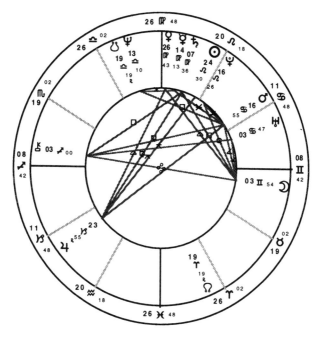

FIGURE 7
PETER MALSIN
AUGUST 17, 1949. 3:01 PM EDT NEW YORK CITY, NY